Evangelical Disenchantment

Evangelical Disenchantment

Nine Portraits of Faith and Doubt

David Hempton

Yale University Press/New Haven and London

Published with assistance from the Louis Stern Memorial Fund.

Designed by Mary Valencia
Set in Adobe Caslon type by Integrated Publishing Solutions,
Grand Rapids, Michigan
Printed in the United States of America by Vail-Ballou Press,
Binghamton, N.Y.

Library of Congress Cataloging-in-Publication Data
Hempton, David.
Evangelical disenchantment : nine portraits of faith and doubt /
David Hempton.
p. cm.
Includes bibliographical references and index.
ISBN 978-0-300-14067-5 (hardcover : alk. paper)
1. Religious biography.   2. Spiritual biography.   3. Evangelicalism.
I. Title.
BL72.H46 2008
270.8092'2—dc22
[B]
2008019003

A catalogue record for this book is available from the British Library.

This paper meets the requirements of ANSI/NISO Z39.48-1992 (Perma-
nence of Paper).
It contains 30 percent postconsumer waste (PCW) and is certified by the
Forest Stewardship Council (FSC).

10   9   8   7   6   5   4   3   2   1

For Louanne

Contents

Preface

This book is about the faith journeys of nine creative artists, social reformers, and public intellectuals who once were associated with the evangelical tradition, but who later repudiated that tradition. How they became enchanted and then disenchanted with evangelical religion not only helped shape who they were as creative individuals, but also is deeply revealing of the strengths and weaknesses of one of the fastest growing religious traditions in the modern world. These portraits include: George Eliot, one of the English-speaking world's greatest novelists; Francis Newman, the distinguished Victorian intellectual (brother of John Henry Newman), who was also an early Protestant missionary to Baghdad; Theodore Dwight Weld, the firebrand antislavery orator; the pioneering feminist social reformers Sarah Grimké, Elizabeth Cady Stanton, and Frances Willard; the great Dutch painter Vincent van Gogh; Edmund Gosse, whose *Father and Son* is a classic and controversial description of an evangelical childhood; and James Baldwin, the distinguished African American writer and commentator on the state of race relations in the United States. The purpose of the book is not to offer censorious moral judgments on their journeys of faith and doubt, but rather to try to understand the factors at work in the shaping of their religion, and how their negotiations of faith informed their private and public lives. As much as possible my intention has been to allow each of them to speak for themselves through their letters, essays, speeches, novels, apologias, and paintings. All of the figures represented here were great public communicators, but they also had private lives often characterized by deep uncertainties. Their faith portraits are at once revealing and profoundly moving. They are affairs of the heart as much as of the head. Though often clouded by doubt and disenchantment, their lives, in however strange and unpredictable ways, are also inspirational.

In finding materials for these portraits I have incurred many debts, especially to colleagues and librarians at Boston University and Harvard University, where much of my research was prosecuted. I am especially grateful to my colleagues Dana Robert, Jon Roberts, Ann Braude, Bob Orsi, David Hall, James Reed, Frank Clooney, Ron Thiemann, Anne Monius, François Bovon, and Michael Puett, who supplied any number of suggestions about religious disenchantment, saved me from some errors, and sustained an intellectual culture of unusual stimulation and support. I am grateful also to the graduate students in the Division of Religion and Theological Studies at Boston University and to the members of the North American Religion Colloquium at Harvard for tolerating my interest in evangelical disenchantment while they were doing more important things. The same goes for the hardy band of students at Harvard who signed up for an 8.00 am class on evangelical conversion and disenchantment narratives. It is, alas, true that for the first half hour of the class only caffeine kept us awake, but after that ideas were created and refined in the most delightful way. As always I am grateful to my friends John Walsh, Reg Ward, Mark Noll, David Livingstone, Bruce Hindmarsh, and Jennifer Fitzgerald for being willing to talk about issues relating to the evangelical tradition and for sharing their considerable expertise. The same goes for the anonymous reviewers of Yale University Press, who saved me from much ignorance and not a few embarrassments. All remaining errors, infelicities, and limitations are my responsibility alone.

It is well to state at the outset what I say at more length in the first chapter, that, having tried as hard as anyone over many years to explain the remarkable success of popular evangelicalism in the eighteenth and nineteenth centuries, what follows is meant to be not a change of tack, but only a change of approach. To look at disenchantment within religious traditions is, after all, to presuppose enchantment. It seems to me that both approaches to the evangelical tradition, or more accurately, to manifold evangelical traditions, are useful and revealing fields of enquiry that are worth pursuing for their own sake.

Finally, my wife, Louanne, and children Stephen and Jonathan, for good reasons, have had their fill of disenchantment, and would look to the future with more optimism if only they did not fear that even less riveting projects might be on their way. They have done a remarkable job of showing interest whenever possible, and feigning it when not. What more can you ask of any family?

Evangelical Disenchantment

1 Introduction
Evangelicalism and Disenchantment

I never could understand the light manner in which people will discuss the gravest questions, such as God, and the immortality of the soul. They gossip about them over tea, write and read review articles about them, and seem to consider affirmation or negation of no more practical importance than the conformation of a beetle. With me the struggle to retain as much of my creed was tremendous. The dissolution of Jesus into mythologic vapour was nothing less than the death of a friend dearer to me than any other friend whom I knew.
—William Hale White, *The Autobiography of Mark Rutherford* (1881)

The idea for this book first occurred to me some thirty years ago when, as a research student in the University of St. Andrews, I spent the time between the completion of my Ph.D. dissertation and my oral defense by engaging in research for a journal article on the so-called crisis of evangelicalism in the 1820s and '30s. The article eventually appeared as "Evangelicalism and Eschatology" in the *Journal of Ecclesiastical History* (1979), but more important than my rather pedestrian article was a riveting anonymous essay I read in the *Westminster Review* for 1855. What was striking about the essay was how beautifully it was written and how clever were its insights into the state of early Victorian evangelicalism. It was clearly written by someone of unusual brilliance, and I soon found out that it was by George Eliot, who also happened to be the author of *Middlemarch*, which was then, and remains to this day, my favorite novel.

As is the way in scholarship, my research soon took a different turn, but the essay on evangelicalism in the *Westminster Review* continued to intrigue me, so much so that I collected everything I could find written by Dr. Cumming, the evangelical Presbyterian minister who was the object of the essay's attack. It was clear from a first read that Eliot's acerbic treatment of Cumming was motivated by more than mere passing interest. The prose leaps from the page, reflecting someone with an unusually personal engagement with the issues at stake. In fact it was written by Eliot as an ex-evangelical about the aspects of the evangelical tradition she came most to dislike. More than a commentary on Dr. Cumming, the metropolitan preacher, Eliot's essay is really a religious disenchantment narrative reflecting her own journey of faith.

In the years that followed my reading of Eliot's essay I became more interested both in what motivated people of all classes, colors, and genders to embrace evangelical Protestantism, and also in what caused some of them subsequently to repudiate that religious tradition. This book stems from that interest. It is not intended to be a subversive book of a great and multifaceted religious tradition or its devotees; nor is it meant to imply that disenchantment was anything other than a minority pursuit within the evangelical tradition, though that minority is probably more substantial than some might think. The great majority of evangelicals, past and present, have lived and died contentedly within their faith tradition. But many did not. In a book called *Leaving the Fold*, published in 1995, Edward T. Babinski produced a litany of testimonies by former fundamentalists who later became moderate evangelicals, liberal Christians, agnostics, or atheists.[1] Among those who remained as Christians of some stripe were the Harvard Divinity School professor and writer Harvey Cox, the distinguished religious journalist Tom Harpur, and the historian of Christian origins Dennis Ronald McDonald. Among those who became agnostics or atheists were Babinski himself, Charles Templeton, a one-time revivalist associate of Billy Graham, and the free thought activist Dan Barker. Although Babinski cites some historical figures in his book of testimony, including the influential nineteenth-century public intellectual Robert G. Ingersoll, his concern is more with contemporary figures and also with promoting the agenda of "leaving the fold" of fundamentalism. My intentions are rather different.

This book is about a collection of energetic and talented historical figures who once had close encounters with various species of evangelical Christianity, but who did not remain in that tradition. What attracted them to evangelicalism and what later caused disenchantment are intriguing questions that reveal much, not only about their own aspirations and limitations, but also about the strengths and weaknesses of the evangelical tradition. Perhaps there is no better way of understanding the essence of any religious tradition than by looking at the lives of those who once loved and later repudiated it. Put another way, it has been said that nothing reveals as much about the inner workings of institutions as their complaint departments. Evangelical disenchantment narratives are in reality referrals to the complaint department of the evangelical tradition. What motivated them, how they were handled, and what their outcomes were all tell a story about the nature and values of that tradition. In that sense this book is as much about the evangelical tradition and its struggles over important issues as it is about the biographies around which the book is organized.

I hope the following pages will be of interest to the countless millions who remain spiritually engaged in the evangelical tradition, to those who have left it, whether actively disenchanted or merely apathetic, and to still others who have wanted to know more about it but who have not found conventional historical treatments to be of their liking. Biography, or in this case multiple minibiographies organized around a single theme, is often a more accessible window into religious faith than are other kinds of historical analysis. As a social historian who has devoted much of my career to understanding and accounting for the popular appeal of evangelical movements to countless millions of people, I offer the following narratives as complementary, not alternative, materials for understanding the inner workings of a tradition that is now a rapidly expanding global phenomenon. Moreover, by concentrating on evangelical disenchantment it is not my intention to deny that most evangelicals remained enchanted with their religious faith or, as Timothy Larsen recently has shown, that a vigorous tradition of reconversion to orthodox Christianity existed among cohorts of Victorian secularists.[2] As a new generation of scholars disenchanted with old secularization theories is beginning to find out, in the ebbing and flowing of religious faith not all the water has flowed in the same direction. In that sense, this book makes no grand representative claims beyond the intrinsic interest of the stories themselves and what they reveal about the strengths and weaknesses of the evangelical tradition.

It also has become clear to me that disenchantment is almost inevitably a part of *any* religious tradition, Christian or otherwise, as noble ideals of sacrifice, zeal, and commitment meet the everyday realities of complexity, frustration, and disappointment. Another book could be written, for example, about those who became frustrated with the apparent accommodationism of more liberal brands of Christianity, which sometimes leaves its adherents with the perception that there is no longer left any solid ground upon which to stand. It may be, however, that disenchantment is a particularly marked characteristic of evangelicalism because so many are swept into the tradition at a relatively young age, and because the claims and aspirations are so lofty while the liturgical management of failure and dissatisfaction is so weak. Roman Catholicism, for example, has its symbols, rituals, and confessionals, and differential levels of religious commitment, whereas evangelical Protestants are often thrown back on the infallible word and the local church, which may in fact be as much part of the problem as the solution for those tasting the bitter fruits of disenchantment.

The Evangelical Tradition

From its inauspicious beginnings among the religious revivals that swept the North Atlantic, Anglo-American world in the early eighteenth century, evangelical Protestantism, broadly conceived, has become one of the most popular faith traditions in modern history. Given the difficulties of offering a precise definition, and the fact that it is a multidenominational tradition with many different styles and characteristics, it is difficult to offer a fully accurate assessment of its current numbers. Conservative estimates place the figure at around fifty million evangelicals in the United States and close to half a billion worldwide, but more expansive estimates suggest that the number approaches one hundred million in the United States and, if Pentecostals are included, as many as eight hundred million worldwide.[3] The disparity in these figures shows how difficult it is to agree on definitions of evangelicalism, or to estimate the extent of its transmission, but even the conservative figures point to a remarkable worldwide expansion. Since most of this growth has been sponsored, not by armed states and military conquest, but by the voluntary activities of the evangelical faithful, it is evident that evangelicalism has been a remarkably successful conversionist movement, perhaps one of the most successful in the history of civilization. Although evangelicalism has benefited from large scale population movements, and from being associated with two expanding empires of commerce and civilization, the British and the American, its growth, on the whole, was largely self-produced and self-directed. Its expansion has benefited from, but was not caused by, favorable circumstances. Changes in global culture, associated with the rise of market economies and democratic structures, facilitated the growth of evangelicalism in the modern era. However, although evangelicalism's populist and democratic style was a good fit for the population migrations and economic transformations associated with modernity, its growth was produced primarily by the dedicated women and men who disseminated the evangelical message.[4]

Determining the content of that message, even in a particular place at a particular time, is a difficult matter, since evangelicalism has always been a broad church of theological traditions, social classes, religious denominations, and voluntary organizations. Definitions have nevertheless been attempted. It has become a commonplace for commentators to cite the historian David Bebbington's fourfold definition of evangelicalism as conversionist, biblicist, crucicentric, and activist.[5] According to this scheme evangelicals have been those who have emphasized a conscious religious conversion over inherited beliefs, the Bible as an authoritative sacred text in determining all matters of faith and conduct, Christ's death on the cross as the centerpiece of evangelical theologies of atonement and redemption, and disciplined action as a way of redeeming people and their cultures. In each of these categories evangelicals have often disagreed about precise formulations of their beliefs and practices, but most evangelicals, past and present, would locate their faith tradition somewhere within the bounds of this quadrilateral. A rather different approach to defining evangelicalism, however, can be found in the recent work by the distinguished historian of early evangelicalism W. R. Ward. He suggests that early evangelicals, deriving from the intellectual culture of the Enlightenment, were broadly united in their embrace of a hexagon of religious ideas: experiential conversion, mysticism, small-group religion, vitalist conceptions of nature, a deferred eschatology, and opposition to theological systems.[6] He also shows how profoundly nineteenth-century evangelicals departed from the tradition they claimed to inherit. Biblical inerrancy, premillennial dispensationalism, propositional systems of all kinds, and bureaucratic denominationalism all eroded what was once an engaging intellectual culture. An infallible text read with wooden literalism, an instant millennium, an absence of mystery, a lack of interest in nature, priestly personality cults, and modernist soteriological systems are not what the early evangelicals had in mind. Ward's approach has a particular resonance for what follows in this book, because it could be argued that some kinds of evangelical disenchantment were caused more by what the evangelical tradition had become by the second half of the nineteenth century than by the principles of its seventeenth- and eighteenth-century founders and shapers.

Writing more specifically about the United States, George Marsden has defined evangelicals as those who believe in the final authority of Scripture, the historical reality of God's saving work as recorded in Scripture, salvation to eternal life based on the redemptive work of Christ, the centrality of evangelism and missions, and the importance of a spiritually transformed life. These propositions are very close to Bebbington's quadrilateral. But the evangelical tradition is not easily contained within a tidy geometrical structure, or a convenient statement of propositions. Some interpreters have emphasized the importance of religious experience and assurance of salvation. Others have drawn attention to the importance of an evangelical style—populist and pugnacious—as being almost as important as its core beliefs and practices. Still others have drawn attention to the way evangelicalism has both adapted to, and been shaped by, its surrounding culture and has therefore changed substantially over time and location. Sometimes perceived pressure from the surrounding culture has led sections of evangelicalism to morph into fundamentalism, which Marsden describes as an angrier, more militant, more conservative, more anti-intellectual, and more antiliberal species of evangelicalism. But whatever the disagreements on points of emphasis, there is no doubt that evangelicalism has been in the past, and remains in the present, an influential shaper of religious cultures, first in the North Atlantic region, and then throughout the world.[7]

Although evangelicalism was once a despised and little studied tradition, there is now no shortage of good scholarship on how, why, and where it expanded since the early 1700s. There is equally no shortage of biographies of leading evangelicals, even if women and people of color remain significantly underrepresented.[8] There is also a luxuriant literature, from the eighteenth century to the present, of how evangelicalism has been excoriated by its opponents. Evangelicals have been lambasted for, among other things, weakmindedness, naked enthusiasm, telescopic philanthropy, pervasive hypocrisy, financial fraudulence, sexual lasciviousness, anti-Catholic bigotry, and psychological manipulation.[9] What is surprisingly lacking in the literature, however, and what this book hopes to address, is the question of how evangelicalism was viewed by those who once found it appealing, but who for a variety of reasons left its fold for greener pastures. Francis Newman stated that such a perspective was especially important because erstwhile evangelicals, having experienced the tradition as both insiders and outsiders, were in the best position to evaluate its strengths and weaknesses. In some respects that is a highly contentious claim, since the disenchanted are rarely dispassionate or disinterested observers.

As with all powerful religious traditions, evangelicalism has had its fair share of conscientious objectors and wounded lovers.[10] What is surprising is not the truth of that statement, but the lack of research on its implications. One explanation is that because evangelicalism is not a formal religious denomination or a national religious tradition, its followers have been able to slide in and out of allegiance without requiring excommunication or formal disinheritance. Another reason is that evangelicals themselves have paid little attention to their disenchanted. Not only has it been an activist tradition without much time or inclination for rumination and self-criticism, but also the assumption generally has been that those who fell by the wayside were either theologically heterodox or morally reprehensible, or both, and hence not deserving of much consideration, except as warnings to the faithful. The idea that disenchantment from a religious tradition is an interesting field of enquiry in its own right, as well as an unusual and potentially revealing vantage point from which to view that tradition, is what motivates this book.

Principles of Selection

It is scarcely surprising that a religious tradition that attracted the loyalty of millions of people worldwide should have failed to sustain the faith of some of its own converts or capture the imagination of some of its own children. Many of its most famous leaders have experienced the shock and grief caused by the alienation from the tradition of their own children. Charles Wesley, the greatest poet and hymn writer of the evangelical revival, penned some of his most melancholic verses in response to his son Samuel's conversion to Roman Catholicism.[11] Even the first great generation of English evangelicals associated with the Clapham Sect seemed unable to produce family dynasties of evangelical longevity. "There is some pathos," writes Ford K. Brown, "in the departure from the Protestant Reformation ranks of so many of the sons of the leaders—in the Protestant evangelical families or among those sons and daughters of the evangelicals who were brought up to write their names in England's records, almost all. They were brought up with Christian love and confidence that they would take their place in the front line."[12]

Yet the list of casualties is too impressive to be merely accidental: "In their university days, or before, or after, the children of the Clapham inner circle and the evangelical directorate elsewhere, and the children of the lesser known or unknown evangelical families who were also to become eminent

Victorians, depart steadily for High Church, Roman Catholic Church, or no church: Macaulay and De Quincey, the sons of Babington and Gisborne and Stephen, the four sons of Wilberforce, the three daughters of Patrick Brontë, Marian Evans who called herself George Eliot, John Henry Newman, the son or sons of Charles Grant, Lord Teignmouth, Buxton, Lady Emily Pusey, Benjamin Harrison, Sir James Graham, John Gladstone, Sir Robert Peel and William Manning."[13] Brown's explanation for this great familial exodus is that the upper-crust leaders of the evangelicalism of the Clapham Sect, as befitted their social position, valued elegance, cultivation, and style as cohabitable companions with virtue, piety, and holiness. The evangelical generation that followed theirs, however, was dominated by the rising ranks of earlier populists who had an altogether different style. Having neither aristocratic panache nor populist honesty, the new generation of evangelical leaders, according to Brown, was altogether less appealing to the well-educated children of the Clapham Sect: "As means come more and more to be taken for ends, leaders become less important, followers more; genuine beliefs harden into doctrinaire convictions and once heartfelt truths become shibboleths. Great moral societies grow into huge moral bureaux, good parish priests become platform preachers, organizers and religious executives in 'the bustle of the religious world,'" and "breeding, education, and good manners" become less valued commodities.[14]

As evangelicalism lost its style, the stylish lost their evangelicalism. Consider for example the career of the great Victorian art and social critic John Ruskin, who also abandoned the evangelicalism of his youth. Ruskin was raised in a fervently evangelical home on a diet of the King James Bible and the Scottish paraphrases of the Psalms. An inner civil war between the Puritanism of his religious sensibilities and the sensual appeal of much of the art he admired contributed to some psychologically tortuous views of his sexuality and body. Ruskin's marriage to Euphemia Chalmers Gray, for example, was never consummated and was subsequently annulled amid a glare of unfriendly publicity.[15] Ruskin's disenchantment with evangelicalism is self-dated to his visit to Turin in 1858, when he contrasts his experience of viewing Veronese's luscious painting *The Presentation of the Queen of Sheba to Solomon* with his visit to a dispiriting Waldensian church. His description of the little congregation of predominantly gray-haired women served by an unprepossessing preacher positively reeks of narrowness and sterility. Ruskin writes that the preacher "after leading them through the languid forms of prayer which are all that in truth are possible to people whose present life is dull and its terrestrial future unchangeable, put his utmost zeal into a consolatory discourse on the wickedness of the wide world, more especially of the plains of Piedmont and city of Turin."[16] Ruskin concludes his comparison of this desultory worship service with his sight of Veronese's painting glowing in full afternoon light with the comment that his "meditation in the gallery of Turin only concluded the courses of thought which had been leading me to such end through many years. There was no sudden conversion possible to me, either by preacher, picture, or dulcimer. But, that day, my evangelical beliefs were put away, to be debated of no more." Although it is clear from Ruskin's letters that he was right to claim that he had been having doubts about his faith for years before his experience in Turin, Ruskin's statement that he ended all engagement with evangelicalism in 1858 is not strictly true. Therefore his description of himself as a "conclusively un-converted man" is at least in part a deliberate and parallel reversal of the evangelical conversion narrative. If conversion was regarded by most evangelicals as an instantaneous event, so, according to Ruskin, could be its opposite.

In a letter to his father near the end of his momentous visit to Turin Ruskin attributed the evils of the world to two things, both of which could be regarded as characteristics of the evangelical tradition he abandoned: "1. Teaching religious doctrines and creeds instead of simple love of God & practical love of our neighbour. This is a terrific mistake—I fancy the fundamental mistake of humanity. 2. Want of proper cultivation of the beauty of the body and the fineness of its senses—a modern mistake chiefly."[17] Unsurprisingly, therefore, Ruskin's disenchantment with evangelicalism was accompanied, and partly caused by, equally profound changes in his views about nature, art, and the history of architecture and painting. As Ruskin's religious opinions changed, as with van Gogh, so too did his growing appreciation of art, form, color, and nature.

This leakage from evangelicalism of leadership, talent, and quality is not a purely English phenomenon. Allowing for the obvious differences in class structure and social mores, something similar happened in the United States in the nineteenth century.[18] Evelyn Kirkley has shown how many of the leaders of the American free thought movement, such as Moses Harmon and Samuel Porter Putnam, were converts to Christianity and ministers of churches before preaching the freethinking gospel. Harmon, who left the Methodist ministry over the proslavery stance of southern Methodists, later wrote that whoever "tries to hold himself to a creed or 'confession of faith,' stultifies his own reason, bars his future growth, denies and dishonors manhood, if he does not commit intellectual or moral suicide." Putnam, who was an ordained Congregational minister, left the church because he considered it a bad institution "opposed to liberty, progress, and the highest morality. It was the influence of modern science and life that compelled the change."[19] The life of America's most famous sex researcher, Alfred C. Kinsey, the man Billy Graham accused of doing more than any other American to undermine Christian morality, followed a similar trajectory. Kinsey was raised in a fervently evangelical Methodist home, the son of an autocratic father, and was a committed member of the YMCA during his college years at Bowdoin. Although there are some signs of a growing scientific materialism in his Bowdoin years, it was while he was a graduate student at Harvard that Kinsey's Christian faith seems to have ebbed away. According to his biographer, Kinsey emerged from Harvard a changed man; "somewhere along the way, the young Christian gentleman had started losing ground to the hard-nosed young scientist who demanded proof for everything."[20] Unfortunately Kinsey has left no records of the change in his religious convictions, and one can only speculate on the respective roles played by his difficult family background, suffused as it was in a harsher form of evangelicalism, his struggles with sexuality and sexual identity, and his growing appreciation of art and science.

Although the slowdown or absence of generational transmission within a religious tradition is one sure predictor of its incipient decline, evangelicalism throughout its history has generally imported more people from the bottom than it has exported from the top. Nevertheless, over the past three centuries there have been tens of thousands of ex-evangelicals who have slipped noisily or silently out of the tradition.[21] Most of these were short stay tenants who were converted at emotional revival meetings and forsook evangelicalism before they had ever properly embraced it. One such was Herbert Asbury, the great-great nephew of American Methodism's most famous leader, Francis Asbury, and the author of *The Gangs of New York*, who has left a bitter account of his "conversion" at a Methodist revival in his hometown of Farmington, Missouri, at the beginning of the twentieth century. Asbury was a cynical skeptic before his "conversion experience" and a more pronounced one after, but he has left a vivid account of the revival meeting at which he was press-ganged into the community of the faithful. "The thunderous cadences of 'Nearer, My God to Thee,' pealed from the organ, and I couldn't stand it. I was being torn to pieces emotionally, and I staggered and stumbled down the aisle, sobbing, hardly able to stand. They thought it was religion, and the Brothers and Sisters who were pushing and shoving me shouted ecstatically that God had me; it was obvious I was suffering, and suffering has always been accepted as a true sign of holiness. But it was not God and it was not religion. It was the music."[22]

Asbury's encounter with the psychological battering ram of evangelical revivalism is vividly recounted and vigorously repudiated, and is far from unique. The history of popular evangelicalism is replete with Elmer Gantry stories of emotional revival meetings and the pressures that were brought to bear on the unawakened.[23] The purpose of this book, however, is not to revisit those stories, interesting though they are, but to look at an altogether different cohort. The people represented here are figures of some eminence who embraced evangelicalism for a season before repudiating it. I have selected people who have left sufficient written evidence of their entrance and exit from evangelicalism to show the power of the tradition they embraced, how it affected their lives, and the reasons why they left it. I have also selected individuals who point up a much bigger issue within the evangelical tradition and how it has related to issues of morality, mission (and comparative religion), political reform, secularism, feminism, childhood, race, and creativity. The aim has been to keep conjecture to a minimum and, as far as possible, to allow the writers, artists, and activists to tell their own stories, or at least to have their distinctive voices heard and interpreted. But interpreters of other people's religious trajectories are faced with a difficult, if not an impossible, task. The reasons supplied by individuals for believing or not believing in a particular faith tradition are not always to be trusted, not because of deliberate deception, but because their self-understanding is often restricted by upbringing, culture, relationships, hidden influences, circumstances, and public taste. Even exhaustively researched, full-scale biographies are merely representations of lives, seen through the eyes of another, not the lives themselves. How much more circumscribed, then, are the following rather brief biographical portraits, which concentrate chiefly on the subject's encounter with a particular species of evangelical Protestantism.

Aside from choosing figures who have left compelling evidence of their faith journeys, I have tried to select people whose stories are engaging, who write (or paint) with insight and aplomb, and who represent much larger and complex issues in the historic relationship between evangelicalism and culture. I have selected individuals whose faith transactions, creative output, and public exposure fall between the early nineteenth and the late twentieth centuries, though the preponderance falls in the second half of the nineteenth and the early twentieth century. By then evangelicalism had passed through a century of prodigious growth in the British Isles and North America and had achieved a sufficiently established position in the cultural landscape to be ripe for serious counterattacks from within and without. Who, then, became disenchanted and what caused their disenchantment?

The Disenchanted

It is sometimes assumed that at the heart and center of the long conflict between evangelicalism and culture lay new scientific claims about a long earth history and the theory of evolution by natural selection. The so-called war between the competing claims of Christianity and Science has attracted a great deal of attention, but specialists in the field generally agree that the military metaphor of war is overblown and that a great number of eminent scientists remained orthodox Christians. Moreover, many evangelicals, past and present, have been able to work out some kind of harmony between their faith convictions and their scientific understanding. It is therefore possible to identify large numbers of scientists who were also evangelical Christians, and large numbers of evangelical Christians who adapted their views of the natural order to take into account new scientific ideas.[24] With so much good work already written on this subject, I decided not to choose scientists as disenchanted evangelicals. More than just a tactical decision, it also reflects my view that as a percentage of their respective secular cohorts there were far fewer creative artists of real distinction (writers, novelists, poets, and painters) than there were scientists who were evangelical Christians. For all the well-known and oft debated problems associated with reconciling faith and science, the ability to reconcile artistic creativity with Christian orthodoxy has proved to be a much bigger stumbling block for the evangelical tradition. Part of the reason for that lies in the long-standing evangelical distrust of the evils of fiction, theater, and the visual arts, or indeed anything to do with those strictly imaginative pursuits that emphasize passion over piety.[25] That historical pattern is now changing quite rapidly within modern evangelicalism.

In addition to the tension between artistic creativity and evangelical religion, many distinguished figures who moved away from evangelicalism, such as William Ewart Gladstone and Mark Pattison, drew attention also to the intellectual limitations of the evangelical tradition. Pattison, who was brought up in a strict evangelical home, stated that evangelicalism "insisted on a 'vital Christianity,' as against the Christianity of books. Its instinct was from the first against intelligence. No text found more favour with it than 'Not many wise, not many learned.'"[26] A tradition built on the absolute authority of the Bible and, as time went on, on propositional statements of faith has apparently left little creative space for intellectual pursuits or the unfettered imagination. Hence, many of the figures selected in this study are either creative artists or independent thinkers and public intellectuals who increasingly chafed at the restrictive dogmatism of the evangelical tradition.

George Eliot was chosen to lead off the parade largely because she wrote one of the most savagely polemical essays ever written against evangelical teaching and also, confusingly, one of the most winning portraits of an evangelical character in all of literature.[27] Eliot was also a polymath, one of the most widely read and deeply learned women of the nineteenth century. Her diaries, letters, and critical essays, quite apart from her brilliance as a novelist, mark her as an intellectual of real distinction. She not only pioneered the translation of German Higher Criticism of the Bible into English, but was also aware of intellectual trends in history, philosophy, and the sciences. It is difficult to think of another figure who was as aware as Eliot of the sheer range of attacks on traditional evangelical orthodoxy, especially on the reliability of the Bible as a sacred text. There is also no one who so deeply appreciated the strengths and weaknesses of the evangelical temperament as Eliot, or who was able to invent fictional characters who so compellingly represented those strengths and weaknesses, sometimes in the same personality. Her rejection of evangelicalism was partly an intellectual transaction, partly a protest against evangelical morality, and partly an expression of her position as an unmarried woman flouting the marital conventions of Victorian England.

Francis Newman, the brother of the more famous John Henry Newman, was a contemporary of George Eliot. Although not close associates or friends, they met and read one another's work. Newman, one of the brightest Oxford undergraduates of his generation, later became a university teacher, writer, and public intellectual. His career is particularly interesting because of his early encounter with John Nelson Darby, the father-founder of the theological tradition of dispensationalism, which has exercised such a profound influence on American evangelicals/fundamentalists and their perceptions of events in the Middle East. Newman was also one of the earliest evangelicals to grapple seriously with Islam and therefore with the whole issue of Christian uniqueness and comparative religion. His journey as an evangelical missionary to and from Baghdad, both geographically and intellectually, is one of the most intriguing episodes in the history of evangelicalism. Newman's career is also illuminating for what it reveals about styles of discourse within evangelicalism as the full extent of his heterodoxy became clear to his family, friends, and mentors. Newman's temperament and fierce desire to get at the "truth" did not permit him to withdraw silently from the evangelical tradition. His rejection of the tradition was noisy, controversial, and attention grabbing. It was also born out of the disappointment of a grand youthful idealism that dared hope for the conversion of the world and the improvement of humankind. He was not the first Westerner, and most certainly not the last, to have those hopes dashed amid the religious and cultural realities of Palestine and Persia.

In the same decade that Francis Newman was coming under the influence of the romantic figure of John Nelson Darby, an Anglican clergyman with a roving mission to the Irish poor in the Wicklow Mountains, Theodore Dwight Weld, was inspired by a yet more influential figure in the evangelical tradition on the other side of the Atlantic, Charles Grandison Finney. Weld owed his evangelical conversion to Finney and soon identified black slavery and the racist assumptions upon which it was built as the principal defining issues of nineteenth-century America. Unlike Finney, his faith mentor, Weld first came to the conclusion that evangelical conversions alone could not eradicate the evil of slavery, and later came to accept that no amount of moral reformism could end an institution so deeply embedded in the economic and social structures of American life. Weld's faith in the evangelical remedies of conversionism and activism declined in proportion to the growth of his conviction that only a terrible conflagration could end an evil in which so many were personally invested. But Weld's disenchantment with evangelicalism, as with the others in this study, was no simple matter. Personal disappointments, marital influences, family problems, disillusionment with the moral frailties of the evangelical tradition, and wider cultural changes that he barely understood all played their part in his inexorable drift toward more liberal versions of the Christian tradition. Indeed so complex were the operational factors in Weld's particular faith journey, many of which were too personal to write about, even in private letters, that some degree of agnosticism is appropriate in the interpretation of his religious life.

As with Weld, Elizabeth Cady Stanton was also converted to evangelicalism in the context of Finney's revivals in New York State. Although her conversion was short-lived, Stanton, along with many other nineteenth-century feminists, including Sarah Moore Grimké, Lucy Stone, and Frances Willard, had to negotiate the varied residues of their evangelical faith with their aspirations as feminists and social reformers.[28] Although Stanton's skepticism and rejection of all forms of Christian authority paved the way for her crusading zeal on behalf of oppressed women, she could not afford to ignore the influence of evangelicalism on the women she hoped to liberate. Not only were women a substantial majority in the evangelicalism that Stanton believed oppressed women, but also evangelical women formed the majority of those enlisted in movements of social reform. Here was a paradox that Stanton found hard to resolve, not least because she regarded the myths propagated by religion as major contributors to male domination. It was partly to resolve these ambiguities that Stanton made *The Woman's Bible* the subject of her last great project. The very Scriptures evangelical women held dear, and to which many attributed their superior status to women of other world religious traditions, were, according to Stanton, inherently and irredeemably patriarchal.[29] Stanton, Sarah Grimké, and Frances Willard all experienced conventional evangelical conversions, but their subsequent faith journeys were very different. Willard, like Stanton, came to see that male biblical hermeneutics were disastrous for women, but her continuing affection for the Midwestern Methodism of her youth put a brake on her skepticism. While Willard challenged male interpretations of the Bible, Stanton thought the Bible itself was the real stumbling block to female emancipation.

It is hard to think of a greater contrast between Willard, America's most famous temperance crusader, and the subject of the subsequent chapter, the very intemperate Vincent van Gogh. Yet both were evangelical believers (van Gogh only for a short time), both struggled with inner demons, both fetched up in Paris for short sojourns within a few years of one another in the late 1860s and early '70s, and both had a tough time with the male leaders of churches and evangelical organizations. But van Gogh's life was infinitely more complex, marked as it was with serious bouts of mental illness and tortured relationships with family, women, and fellow painters. Van Gogh's flirtation with evangelicalism was characteristically intense and unstable. To his own mental instability were the added pressures of coming of age in a period of remarkable social, economic, and intellectual change in Western Europe. Van Gogh moved around fast-growing European cities in the age of great cities, fell afoul of the commercial machinations of the art market, which both employed him and spat him out, and participated as a reader and an artist in a period of almost unprecedented intellectual instability. With all the considerable ardor of which he was capable, van Gogh was attracted first to Christ's love, then to Christ's followers, and then to Christ's poor, but soon found the whole ecclesiastical superstructure of seminaries, theological education, and mission boards to be deeply depressing. Despite, and partly because of, the intensity of his evangelical phase when he devoured the Bible and sought out opportunities for heroic Christian service, van Gogh was a poor candidate for any creed that emphasized deference to authority, literalness of interpretation, and acceptance of respectable social mores. Evangelical disenchantment and van Gogh were almost bound to find one another.

Although born four years before van Gogh, Edmund Gosse, who among other things was an eminent art critic, comfortably outlived him, producing his most famous work, *Father and Son,* in 1907. It is an autobiographical account of his childhood. He was raised as an only child by his father, Philip Henry Gosse, a distinguished naturalist and contemporary of Charles Darwin, and his mother, Emily Bowes, a prolific evangelical tract writer. Gosse's parents were members of an austere evangelical sect called the Plymouth Brethren (John Nelson Darby was one of its founders), and his upbringing was designed to help him flee from the world and make secure his eternal destiny. While it would be a mistake to regard Edmund Gosse's tightly controlled upbringing as typical of evangelical families and patterns of child rearing in the nineteenth and twentieth centuries, it is suggestive—in its highly colored way—of tendencies that were more widespread in evangelical culture. The desire to protect the children of the godly from the ravages of secularism and immorality is a repeated refrain in the evangelical tradition, from John Wesley's rules for the education of children to the modern popularity of evangelical schools and homeschooling. The passing of the baton of evangelical faith from parents to children is one of the most highly prized aspirations of the tradition. Rarely has it been pursued with such single-minded devotion as in the Gosse household, even after, or perhaps especially after, the premature death of Gosse's mother. Whether entirely accurate or not (a point more fully discussed later in the text), Gosse's *Father and Son* is perhaps the most powerful evocation of an evangelical childhood ever penned. It is also a liberation struggle, as Edmund negotiated the space he needed to realize "a human being's privilege to fashion his inner life for himself." What rescues Gosse's *Father and Son* from being merely an embittered rant against fundamentalist excess is the obvious affection he had for his father and the fact that, whatever his other weaknesses, Philip Gosse was no hypocrite. What he believed, he believed intensely and consistently. Indeed that was what made Edmund's liberation struggle so painful.

A different kind of liberation struggle (also partly against a fervently Christian father), but with some of the same intellectual components, is represented in the life of James Baldwin. Baldwin, unlike the other figures represented in this book, was not born into a relatively comfortable bourgeois household but rather was the eldest of nine children born in Harlem on the eve of the Great Depression. He absorbed, then chose, then preached for, and then rejected a holiness Pentecostal variety of black evangelicalism that has contributed much to the shaping of black religion in the United States. Evangelicalism has been to black religion what jazz and blues have been to black music; it has largely determined the religious style, rhythm, identity, and expression of an oppressed people. Baldwin was a complex, interstitial figure—puny, bisexual, and an American writer in European exile—which enables him to look at black evangelicalism through unusual lenses. He could not, and did not wish to, deny the importance of evangelicalism in shaping American black identity, but he also hated its manifold petty hypocrisies, its collaborationist instincts, and its propensity to avoid the tough issues in facing up to the realities of the black experience in America. If Gosse left the Plymouth Brethren to fashion his own inner life and to write free from the shackles of evangelical dogmatism, Baldwin left the black church to become "an honest man" and as a writer to explore the black experience without the "safety" of evangelical social ethics as his guide. The desire for intellectual and moral liberation among the creative misfits of the evangelical tradition is one of the underpinning themes of this book.

The biographical portraits that follow are not meant to be comprehensive essays on their characters' intellectual and artistic development; rather, they concentrate on their enchantment and disenchantment with evangelicalism. They also seek to say something about how evangelicalism shaped their thoughts and habits, even after formal disenchantment was expressed. Disenchantment did not usually result in a complete abandonment of their religious faith and an embrace of atheism. More common was a renegotiation of their religious sensibilities. Sometimes it is not entirely clear what they ended up believing and practicing, for one of the benefits of repudiating evangelicalism was not seeing the need to produce a clear statement of faith or to defend a codification of dogmatic principles. But it would be a mistake to conclude that the subjects examined here ended up as defenders and purveyors of an insipid moral relativism and behavioral libertinism. Although Eliot, van Gogh, and Baldwin were capable of outraging religious and social conventions, they were anything but casual in their advocacy of honesty, truth, and love. Whether moral earnestness was the cause or the consequence of their attachment to evangelicalism (persuasive evidence could be presented for both), their encounters with evangelicalism intensified it to such a degree that it remained with them for the rest of their lives.

The book that follows is designed to be a work of history, not a comment on the current state of evangelicalism in any particular part of the world. It is nevertheless the case that the themes addressed in this study continue to be of relevance to the present generation of evangelicals or to those who abandoned the tradition for reasons not too dissimilar to those of their predecessors. For example, the dispensational fundamentalism pioneered by the Plymouth

Brethren, which so afflicted the young Edmund Gosse, also characterized the education of Christine Rosen, whose *My Fundamentalist Education* was a recent best seller. Rosen's account of her education, although of a much less traumatic kind than Gosse's, nevertheless similarly combines an ability to evoke the absurdities of some fundamentalist emphases with an admiration for many of its core values. Although writing from an avowedly secular perspective, Rosen acknowledges that her fundamentalist education nurtured in her a respect for her fellow human beings, taught her the dangers of pride, gave her a love for the Bible, and developed in her a lifelong devotion to language and music. Nevertheless, as her life unfolded Rosen found herself turning more to scholarship than to the Bible for answers to her deepest questions. She wanted to be more engaged in the world, not less, and to understand and appreciate culture, not avoid it or fight against it.[30] Rather like Edmund Gosse a century and a half earlier, she chose the individual's right to forge her own inner and outer life free from the dogmatic constraints of fundamentalism.

A less lighthearted trajectory, perhaps more in keeping with the earnest intellectual tradition represented in this book, is the self-described faith journey of Evelyn Kirkley, author of *Rational Mothers and Infidel Gentlemen*. Raised as an evangelical Southern Baptist, Kirkley had her faith nourished by campus evangelical groups before finding a home as a feminist evangelical working for social justice and human rights. A combination of theological education—which raised more questions than answers—the fundamentalist takeover of the Southern Baptist Convention in the early 1980s, the rise of what came to be known as the Religious Right, and other more personal factors persuaded her to abandon the evangelicalism of her youth and write about the rise of free thought in America.[31] There are thousands of such stories, past and present, that lie buried in unvisited tombs. What follows are the stories of nine of the most eminent members of this buried tradition. Aside from their intrinsic interest as the faith journeys of a distinguished group of creative artists and public intellectuals, their stories hopefully will provoke reflection both in those who proudly remain evangelicals and in those who have become disenchanted with a tradition they once embraced. How a tradition treats its casualties, past and present, is, after all, as revealing of its values as its more public success stories.

2 George Eliot—Dr. Cumming's Fundamentalism
Evangelicalism and Morality

For the growing good of the world is partly dependent on unhistoric acts; and
that things are not so ill with you and me as they might have been is half owing
to the numbers who lived faithfully a hidden life, and rest in unvisited tombs.
—George Eliot, *Middlemarch* (1872)

Consider the following two accounts of evangelicalism, one written anonymously and the other under a pseudonym, but both in fact written by the same
person. They were published within a few years of one another in the later
1850s, which is conveniently about the halfway mark between the rise of
evangelicalism among the displaced and persecuted Protestants of central
Europe in the late seventeenth century and its remarkable global expansion
in our own time. The author of both accounts is the English novelist Mary
Ann Evans, alias George Eliot. The first is a blistering critique of a metropolitan Calvinist preacher called Dr. Cumming, minister of the national
Scottish Church in London's Covent Garden, and the second is taken from
Eliot's first full-length novel, *Adam Bede*. Eliot's searing attack on Dr. Cum-
ming was first published in the pages of a liberal periodical, the *Westminster
Review*, in 1855:

Mary Ann Evans (pen name George Eliot) as a young woman. Engraving (© Bettmann/CORBIS)

Given a man with moderate intellect, a moral standard not higher than the average, some rhetorical affluence and great glibness of speech, what is the career in which, without the aid of birth or money, he may most easily attain power and reputation in English Society? Where is that Goshen of mediocrity in which a smattering of science and learning will pass for profound instruction, where platitudes will be accepted as wisdom, bigoted narrowness as holy zeal, unctuous egoism as God-given piety? Let such a man become an evangelical preacher; he will then find it possible to reconcile small ability with great ambition, superficial knowledge with the prestige of erudition, a middling morale with a high reputation for sanctity. Let him shun practical extremes and be ultra only in what is purely theoretic: let him be stringent on predestination, but latitudinarian on fasting; unflinching in insisting on the eternity of punishment, but diffident of curtailing the substantial comforts of time; ardent and imaginative on the premillennial advent of Christ, but cold and cautious towards every other infringement of the *status quo*. Let him fish for souls not with the bait of inconvenient singularity, but with the drag-net of comfortable conformity. Let him be hard and literal in his interpretation only when he wants to hurl texts at the heads of unbelievers and adversaries, but when the letter of the Scriptures presses too closely on the genteel Christianity of the nineteenth century, let him use his spiritualizing alembic and disperse it into impalpable ether. Let him preach less of Christ than of Antichrist; let him be less definite in showing what sin is than in showing who is the Man of Sin, less expansive on the blessedness of faith than on the accursedness of infidelity.[1]

The second account of evangelicalism written by Eliot requires a little more scene setting. Her novel *Adam Bede* takes place in a small English village at the end of the eighteenth century. The novel opens with some good-natured, but pointed, banter about religious faith among a group of rough carpenters in a village workshop. One of these village artisans is a Methodist who advertises to the others the impending visit of a Methodist preacher who, as it happens, turns out to be a young woman. Variously referred to as a prophetess, a "Methodiss," and a preacher woman, Dinah Morris is a character who was based on Eliot's aunt and who came to preach an outdoor sermon on a picturesque village green serenely bathed in evening sunlight. Eliot, who wants the reader to be in no doubt about Dinah's superior character, describes her demeanor as serene and completely without self-consciousness, much to the surprise of one skeptical observer who previously knew of only two types of Methodist, the ecstatic and the bilious. Dinah chooses as her sermon text the words attributed to Jesus in Matthew's gospel, "The Spirit of the Lord is upon me, because he hath anointed me to preach the gospel to the poor."[2] Dinah tells the assembled crowd that she first heard these words not from the lips of Jesus in a dream, as some Methodists claimed, but from the mouth of an old white-haired saint when she was only a little girl. As the novel is set back in the 1790s, this reference is to John Wesley, the founder of Methodism, who was also a countercultural facilitator of lay and female preaching. Dinah's opening prayer and hour-long sermon are devoted to preaching good news about a suffering and compassionate savior who came to the earth's poor with a message of love and forgiveness. She finishes, in the best traditions of Methodist field-preaching, with a stirring evangelistic appeal:

> "Dear Friends," she said at last, "brothers and sisters whom I love as those for whom my Lord has died, believe me, I know what this blessedness is; and because I know it, I want you to have it too. I am poor, like you: I have to get my living with my hands; but no lord nor lady can be so happy as me, if they haven't got the love of God in their souls. Think what it is—not to hate anything but sin; to be full of love to every creature; to be frightened at nothing; to be sure that all things will turn to good; not to mind pain, because it is our Father's will; to know that nothing—no, not if the earth was to be burnt up, or the waters come and drown us—nothing could part us from God who loves us, and who fills our souls with peace and joy, because we are sure that whatever he wills is holy, just, and good.
>
> "Dear friends, come and take this blessedness; it is offered to you; it is the good news that Jesus came to preach to the poor. It is not like the riches of this world so that the more one gets the less the rest can have. God is without end; his love is without end. . . ."

The outdoor meeting ends, as most Methodist gatherings did, with a hymn. The sun goes down to the communal harmonic sounds of the Methodist faithful whose voices rise and fall "in that strange blending of exultation and sadness which belongs to the cadence of a hymn."

Eliot then has her readers take leave of this charming village scene, but, in the best traditions of Victorian didacticism, she, the author, does not take leave of the Methodists. After serving the conventions of the Victorian novel by having Dinah turn down the marriage proposal of Seth Bede, because she is already married to the ministry of the gospel, Eliot goes on to draw a romantic distinction between the old Methodism of rough men and weary-hearted women drinking in a faith, which she calls a "rudimentary culture," and its tacky Victorian successor characterized by low-pitched gables up dingy streets, sleek grocers, sponging preachers, and hypocritical jargon. Dinah was of course a representative of Eliot's romanticized old Methodism who "believed in present miracles, in instantaneous conversions, in revelations by dreams and visions; they drew lots, and sought for Divine guidance by opening the Bible at hazard; having a literal way of interpreting the Scriptures, which is not at all sanctioned by approved commentators; and it is impossible for me to represent their diction as correct, or their instruction as liberal. Still—if I have read religious history aright—faith, hope, and charity have not always been found in a direct ratio with a sensibility to the three concords; and it is possible, thank Heaven! to have very erroneous theories and very sublime feelings."

With that comment Eliot is able simultaneously to satisfy her preference for old Methodism over the new with her enlightenment sensibilities about the absurdities of all species of religious enthusiasm. To her what mattered most was not what people believed, but who they were, and what they did. Charming eccentricity when mediated by faith, love, and charity was much more to be admired than evangelical zeal when mediated by self-interest, sanctimoniousness, and hypocrisy. What is most impressive about the life of Dinah Morris as presented in *Adam Bede* is not so much her words but her sense of empathy for, and her identification with, the earthly sufferings of the English poor. What, then, has all this to do with evangelical enchantment and disenchantment?

George Eliot was herself enchanted with evangelicalism as a teenage girl under the influence of an Irish evangelical schoolmistress, and she became disenchanted for complex reasons that included her disappointment with evangelical social ethics and her growing familiarity with the unsettling religious and theological ideas of German higher criticism. Eliot's portrayals of the heroic Dinah Morris and the hapless Dr. Cumming, allowing for the different genres and conventions within which they were written, are essentially her own enchantment and disenchantment narratives. One is about a middle-aged man, the other a young woman; one is a Calvinist spokesman for the elect, the other an Arminian advocate for all of God's poor; one is a stalwart Victorian supporter of established churches, the other a romantic young religious revolutionary preaching for the dissenters; one preaches in a metropolitan pulpit in grimy early Victorian London, the other in an amphitheater of rolling hills in William Blake's Jerusalem, "England's green and pleasant land" (1804); one prints his sermons in lilac and gold for the Sabbath reading of genteel ladies, the other preaches extempore sermons with "sincere, unpremeditated eloquence" to rough artisans and domestic servants; one uses the Bible as a blunt instrument to beat the heads of infidels, the other uses it compassionately to draw others to a loving savior; one is obsessed with prophetical speculation about the end times, the other is focused on the pressing needs of the here and now; one is well-educated and holds a doctor of divinity degree, the other has a rudimentary education but an angelic disposition; one is fiercely realistic and set in what was then the world's largest city, the other is romanticized and set in an idyllic rural past. Above all, in Eliot's aesthetic framework, the words of one produce moral mendacity and tribal self-interest of a distinctively evangelical kind, the words of the other lift people's imaginations "above the sordid details of their own narrow lives, and suffused their souls with the sense of a pitying, loving, infinite Presence, sweet as summer to the houseless needy." It scarcely needs pointing out that the skeptical George Eliot thought that both Dr. Cumming and Dinah Morris preached about things that may not be true, but their respective errors had very different pathologies and outcomes. Whatever one makes of Eliot's treatment of her two characters, one based on a real person but with a heavy interpretive gloss, the other overtly fictional and romanticized but based on a real person, there is no doubt that she put her finger on some of the most important reasons why evangelicalism has produced both enchantment and disenchantment among its adherents.

Dr. Cumming, the hapless victim of Eliot's searing attack in *Westminster Review,* was minister of the Crown Court Church in London's Covent Garden. Crown Court Church was one of the few Presbyterian churches in England claiming an affiliation to the Church of Scotland and was in a perilous state when Cumming was ordained to its ministry in September 1832.[3] Cumming's ministry in central London lasted for almost fifty years, and the Crown Court Church thrived for most of that period. Cumming, who had enjoyed a reputable academic career at Aberdeen University, was a devoted pastor, a prolific author, a fervent preacher, a formidable anti-Catholic polemicist, and a determined advocate of prophetical interpretations of the Bible, often placed in the context of a pessimistic interpretation of current events in Britain and the rest of the world. This brand of evangelical Protestantism played out well in early Victorian London. Cumming attracted to the Crown Court Church a distinguished clientele, including a number of aristocratic families with Scottish connections. While he was at the peak of his powers, Cumming's London citadel drew large crowds and Cumming became a notable feature of London's ecclesiastical life especially during the controversies surrounding the great Disruption in the Church of Scotland and the pressing of Roman Catholic claims in England. The focus of Eliot's attack on him was not so much his theological method, which she scarcely enjoyed, as it was the moral and spiritual implications of his writings, which she positively despised. According to Eliot, Cumming's mind was not of the "pietistic order," there was not the "slightest leaning towards mysticism in his Christianity," his way of salvation was forensic and schematic, not experiential and redemptive, and his view of the world, and of his opponents, was relentlessly judgmental, often savagely so. "But of really spiritual joys and sorrows," she writes, "of the life and death of Christ as a manifestation of love that constrains the soul, of sympathy with that yearning over the lost and erring which made Jesus weep over Jerusalem, and prompted the sublime prayer, 'Father, forgive them,' of the gentler fruits of the Spirit, and the peace of God which passeth understanding—of all this, we find little trace in Dr. Cumming's discourses."[4]

Comparing Cumming's Calvinistic Protestantism with the enthusiastic Methodists of whom Eliot thought better, she states that while the Methodists were made amiably gullible by their "pietistic feelings" directed toward God's glory, Cumming's reliance on the doctrine of verbal inspiration of the Bible was a mental caste with more unfortunate moral consequences: "What is for them a state of emotion submerging the intellect, is with him a formula imprisoning the intellect, depriving it of its proper function—the free search for truth." The mental habit of counting as truth only that which fits the grid of verbal inspiration, combined with an emotionally charged belief in personal salvation based upon propositions derived from Scripture, was for Eliot somewhere near the heart of Cumming's evangelical disease. "So long as a belief in propositions is regarded as indispensable to salvation, the pursuit of truth as such is not possible, any more than it is possible for a man who is swimming for his life to make meteorological observations on the storm which threatens to overwhelm him."[5]

Although Eliot devotes many pages to showing how Cumming's desire to defend scriptural truth against its manifold adversaries all too frequently descends to an "imbecility that is not even meek," her real complaint is against not Cumming's stupidity but rather the grim moral implications of his teaching. She gives three examples. The first is a deficiency of love manifested in party spirit and a kind of evangelical tribal loyalty. She accurately states that the larger proportion of what he had published was in reality a diatribe against Roman Catholics, Anglo-Catholics, and infidels of all types, including skeptics and Muslims. The Christian love that he enjoins is, according to Eliot, "the love of the *clan* [fellow evangelicals], which is the correlative of antagonism to the rest of mankind." In this way, "Dr Cumming's religion may demand a tribute of love, but it gives a charter to hatred; it may enjoin charity, but it fosters all uncharitableness."

Eliot's second example of Cumming's moral perfidy comes from the results of his obsession with prophecy. The idea that God and Satan were playing out some cosmic game in which the human actors were moved around like chess pawns in order to serve some grand providential purpose was particularly offensive to Eliot. So too was Cumming's attempted demonstration, based as it was on an evangelical interpretation of political and social events, that the second coming was imminent. Cumming's preoccupation with the premillennial Advent was, according to Eliot, merely the "transportation of political passions on to a so-called religious platform; it is the anticipation of the triumph of 'our party,' accomplished by our principal men being 'sent for' into the clouds." Here, as elsewhere, Eliot's real target is the ethical implications of Cumming's prophetical posturing. "You might as well attempt to educate a child's sense of beauty by hanging its nursery with the horrible and grotesque pictures in which the early painters represented the Last Judgment," she states, "as expect Christian graces to flourish on that prophetic interpretation which Dr. Cumming offers as the principal nutriment of his flock." In Eliot's view, far from producing "a closer walk with God," Cumming's prophetical partisanship was more likely to "nourish egoistic complacency and pretension, a hard and condemnatory spirit towards one's fellow-men, and a busy preoccupation with the minutiae of events, instead of a reverent contemplation of great facts and a wise application of great principles."[6]

Eliot's third example of the moral flaw at the heart of Cumming's theological system is his teaching on eternal punishment. It is not so much Cumming's belief in the eternal punishment of unbelievers that offends Eliot as much as it is his fierce literalistic contention for such a belief. Cumming appeared to believe in eternal punishment, not out of heavy-hearted reluctance, but out of partisan belligerence. Not for him mere resignation to "the awful mystery of eternal punishment," Eliot writes, nor even a search for refuge in the possibility of "annihilation for the impenitent," but rather a full-blooded assertion of a gruesome doctrine: "Do we object, he asks, to everlasting happiness? Then why object to everlasting misery?—reasoning which is perhaps felt to be cogent by theologians who anticipate the eternal happiness for themselves, and the everlasting misery for their neighbours." For Eliot, all comes down eventually to an argument about the character of God and the nature of humanity. While Cumming insists that God cannot be pleased except by acts done for His glory alone, thereby rendering morally useless those acts occasioned by fellow feeling for others, Eliot asserts that human beings who act out of love, sympathy, charity, affection, or devotion are contributors to the moral good of humanity in their own terms and for their own sake. To be sure the "idea of a God who not only sympathizes with all we feel and endure for our fellow-men, but who will pour new life into our too languid love" has been, according to Eliot, the glory of orthodox Christianity, especially in its emphasis on the incarnated love of God manifested in the life of Jesus. "But Dr. Cumming's God is the very opposite of all this: He is a God who, instead of sharing and aiding our human sympathies, is directly in collision with them; who, instead of strengthening the bond between man and man, by encouraging the sense that they are both alike the objects of His love and care, thrusts himself between them and forbids them to feel for each other except as they have relation to Him."[7]

George Eliot takes leave of Cumming with two wider observations. The first is that Cumming's moral disease is not just a personal problem, but rather "belongs to the dogmatic system he shares with all evangelical believers."[8] Although the baleful consequences of this dogmatic system vary from individual to individual according to the different characters of those who embrace them, the same tendency is there in all, which is partly why Eliot goes on the attack with such ferocity. Second, when all is done, Eliot makes a halfhearted attempt to be true to her own convictions by stating that her real controversy is not with Cumming the man, but with Cumming the theologian. This point would carry more weight if Eliot had not herself roundly condemned Cumming for making such a characteristic evangelical distinction in his dealings with Roman Catholics and infidels. Moreover, Eliot's criticism of Cumming's relentless emphasis on human sinfulness would have been more telling were it not obviated by her own relentless, and equally unconvincing, emphasis on human goodness.

Although George Eliot's optimistic moral meliorism probably sits less well with readers who have just endured the ravages of a grimly violent twentieth century than with the liberal readership of the *Westminster Review* in early Victorian England, there is no denying that Eliot's verbal attack on the unfortunate Dr. Cumming reads as one of the finest pieces of polemical prose in the English language, justifying George Henry Lewes's opinion that Eliot had thus demonstrated her potential to be a truly great writer. Moreover, it is difficult to read Cumming's work, the same corpus to which she had access, and not agree with most of her conclusions. Cumming's printed sermons reek of unctuous self-righteousness and are riddled with the crassest of stereotypes of Jews, Roman Catholics, English Ritualists, Muslims, and atheists. His rhetorical affluence and anecdotal style, whatever their merits in pulpit delivery, do not translate well into cold print. What, then, accounts for a figure like Cumming, and why was he such a successful author among his evangelical constituency, and possibly beyond?

What marks out his published work from the generality of printed sermons in Victorian Britain is his relentless emphasis on biblical prophecy, and his ability to relate ancient writings to contemporary events. Cumming was obsessed with the second coming of Christ and was persuaded by current events that the time was near. The European revolutions of 1848, the cholera epidemic of 1849, the growth of Roman Catholicism in the British Isles culminating in the reestablishment of the Roman Catholic hierarchy in 1850, the influence of Puseyism in the Church of England, the rise of socialism and pantheism in France, the preparations of European Jews for a return to their homeland, the growth of attacks on the authority of the Bible, and the increasing self-confidence of infidelity all persuaded Cumming that he was living in the last days.[9] In an attempt to mark out the timetable of Christ's return, Cumming matched the prophecies of the book of Daniel with key events in world history such as the appointment of Pope Boniface II as universal head of the church in 607 CE and the demise of papal powers during the French Revolution. In this way Cumming was able to fuse anti-Catholicism, disillusionment with the world order, and verbal inspiration of the Bible to produce a timetable for the wrapping up of time.

It was this combination of world-weary pessimism and eager millennial anticipation that most annoyed George Eliot. For her "the more spiritually minded class of believers, who look with greater anxiety for the kingdom of God within them than for the visible advent of Christ in 1864, will be likely to find Dr Cumming's declamatory flights and historico-prophetical exercitations as little better than 'clouts o' cauld parritch.'" Eliot's Carlylean put-down had some weight, because Cumming, displaying the exegetical elasticity that so incensed Eliot about evangelical believers in verbal inspiration, soon fast-forwarded his end time to 1867/68, the date of yet another of his best-selling millennial tracts for the times. In the introduction to his aptly named *The Sounding of the Last Trumpet or The Last Woe*, Cumming confidently declared that "no thoughtful mind can fail to be solemnized while he reads in the daily press the reliable records of a world convulsed, a Church corrupted, and judgment already begun. The proof is full and clear that God speaks in every verse of the Apocalypse, and wields, or restrains, or overrules every fact and complication in living history."[10]

Apart from his ingenious numerical calculations based on Daniel and Revelation, what gave Cumming renewed hope that the end was indeed nigh were yet more pessimistic gleanings from world history. The bloodletting of the American Civil War, widespread cholera epidemics in European and North American cities in 1866, famine in India, chaos in the London financial markets, the slowdown of the Lancashire cotton mills, the speed of communications ushered in by the ground-eating railways, the rapid expansion of scientific knowledge, the steady stream of conversions from Anglicanism to Romanism, the growing weakness of the Papacy, the decline of the Ottoman Empire, the economic and cultural paralysis of Islam, the drying up of the Euphrates River, the successful translation of the Bible into scores of native languages, the control of the Jews over European money markets, the growing pace of Jewish migration to Palestine, reports of Jewish conversions to evangelical Protestantism, the rise of war clouds in Europe between France and Germany, the military expansion of Russia, the renewed popularity of ecumenism, Darwin's fanciful evolutionary theories, and the threatened extermination of the Protestant Church of Ireland under Catholic pressure all persuaded Cumming that the world was about to enter "The Last Woe," with 1867 as his preferred date.[11]

Readers of this text will already know that Cumming's almost inexhaustible demonstration of the "conclusive proofs" of the end of the world proved inconclusive when measured against the inconvenience of a failed prediction, but it would be a mistake to underestimate the cultural power of Cumming's preoccupations and prejudices, not only among Anglo-American evangelicals, but also among the wider population. Cumming's anti-Catholicism, biblical literalism, distrust of scientific discoveries, and ambivalence over Jews (God's unredeemed people) both fed off and contributed to wider social attitudes. His view of Muslims, in particular, has an eerily modern ring: "The extinction of every national and traditional distinction of the Moslem rapidly advances every day. His decay, physically, morally, and politically, is undeniable. Bankrupt in finance, effete in constitution, propped up by pillows provided by France and England, the sick man dies daily."[12]

Cumming's precise delineation of the end of history in 1867 not only was incorrect but also opened him up to the obvious criticisms of failed predictions. Not only did the London press give him a hard time for negotiating a long-term lease for his house and other ideological inconsistencies, but more seriously Cumming's credibility eroded with the passage of uninterrupted time.[13] As early Victorian neuroses about the state of English society and the unfolding of world events settled into mid-Victorian equipoise, Cumming's popularity as a voice for the times diminished, and so too did attendance at his church.

George Eliot's verbal culling of Dr. Cumming came some fourteen years after putting aside her own evangelical faith. That faith was not nourished at home, which has been described as being of the old-fashioned "high and dry sort," but stemmed primarily from her schoolgirl encounter with an Irish evangelical teacher, Maria Lewis, who has been described as having "a kind heart and a good sense of humour about everything except religion."[14] Since Eliot's rejection of evangelicalism came at the relatively tender age of twenty-two, it is difficult to document the nature of her early faith firsthand without recourse to deductions gleaned from her later writings. Nevertheless, from her letters it seems that the defining characteristics of her early commitment were a passion for Bible study, a devotion to evangelical biographies (notably of William Wilberforce and Hannah More), an almost morbid introspection, a genuine concern for the sick and the needy, and a world-denying attitude toward fiction and theater. Her teenage temperament, like many others who grew up within the orbit of evangelicalism in early Victorian Britain, was dominated by moral earnestness, pietistic devotion, and an avoidance of worldly amusements.

Beyond that, it is difficult to know, except to say that there are occasional phrases in her letters that indicate her faith was not without doubts and questionings. The most instructive example in the light of subsequent events comes from a letter to Maria Lewis: "I remember, as I dare say you do, a very amiable atheist depicted by Bulwer in Devereux, and for some time after the perusal of that book, which I read 7 or 8 years ago, I was considerably shaken by the impression that religion was not a requisite to moral excellence."[15] Similarly, other letters reveal that Eliot was more interested in the ethical implications of the New Testament than in its dogmatic content. For her, Jesus was not so much an atoning sacrifice for sin as he was the purest available moral example of humility and love set against a world dominated by egotism and self-interest.

Coincidentally, George Eliot's adherence to evangelicalism in the 1830s corresponded with one of the most divisive and controversial periods in its history, a point often overlooked in her literary biographies, which tend to assume that evangelicalism was an unchanging and monolithic creed. That was not the case. Most historians of the evangelical tradition point to the 1820s and '30s as a time of "crisis," "division," and "revolt." According to Ford K. Brown, "Able young men and women over England who had been brought up in the best Evangelicalism were repelled during these years by something."[16] Many of the sons and daughters of the pioneering generation of English evangelicals, including some of its most distinguished families, shifted allegiance to Anglo-Catholicism, Roman Catholicism, Unitarianism, and skepticism. A section of those who remained in the fold gave the movement a different tone: its political objectives seemed less noble; its piety was less transparently obvious, and its acceptability among English gentlemen scholars declined. Often characterized by a narrow Celtic Calvinism, anti-rationalism, anti-Catholicism, biblical literalism, and social conservatism, evangelicalism morphed from a movement influenced by enlightenment optimism, in which humans could employ activist means to achieve divine ends, to one influenced by romantic pessimism, in which divine action alone could alter the fate of a deteriorating human condition. This "crisis of evangelicalism," to use David Newsome's phrase, was caused partly by pressures from outside, in the shape of the challenges to traditional political, social, and intellectual structures posed by the French Revolution, Irish Catholic nationalism, radical Dissent, and Romanticism. The result was a crisis of authority in which pessimistic evangelicals clung ever more tightly to the inspired Word and the imminence of a divinely instituted millennial kingdom.[17]

Even before her breach with evangelicalism, and long before her essay on Dr. Cumming, Eliot noted the undercurrents within the movement with some alarm. In a letter to Maria Lewis she asked, "Are you fond of the study of unfulfilled prophecy? The vagaries of the Irvingites and the blasphemies of Joanna Southcote together with the fanciful interpretations of more respectable names have been regarded as beacons, and have caused many persons to hold all diving into the future plans of Providence as the boldest presumption; but I do think that a sober and prayerful consideration of the mighty revolutions ere long to take place in our world would by God's blessing serve to make us less groveling, more devoted and energetic in the service of God."[18]

Eliot's contempt for the exotic prophetical speculations of Edward Irving and Joanna Southcote is expressed in the same letter as she declares her enthusiasm for the energetic philanthropic career of William Wilberforce and for John Williams's recently published account of his missionary endeavors in the South Sea islands. The latter clearly fired her imagination. Characteristically, the pious yet intellectually sharp Eliot had little time for the idea of welshing on a world that offered so much scope for devoted service. As Francis Newman put it, "If we are to expect our master at cock-crowing, we shall not study the permanent improvement of this transitory scene. To teach the certain speedy destruction of earthly things, as the New Testament does, is to cut the sinews of all earthly progress."[19]

The mania of prophetical speculation that infected the evangelical mind in the British Isles in the 1820s was not uncontested by the evangelicals themselves. Charles Simeon of Cambridge, who was the most influential clerical leader of the movement, wrote that "the prophecy students were laid aside from a doctrine which fills only with vain conceits, intoxicates the imagination, alienates the brethren from each other, and by being unduly urged upon the minds of humble Christians, is doing the devil's work by wholesale."[20] Eliot would have found no difficulty agreeing with Simeon's opinion, but her rejection of evangelical religion had even deeper roots than frustration with militant millenarians.

While scholars disagree about the precise order of the steps taken in Eliot's journey of intellectual disenchantment with evangelical religion, there is widespread agreement that Eliot's voracious reading introduced her to controversial new ideas on a range of subjects from phrenology to biblical criticism, and from the solar system to Mosaic cosmology. Of particular importance was her reading of Charles Hennell's *Inquiry Concerning the Origins of Christianity* (1838; 2nd ed., 1841), and her friendship with Hennell's married sister, Sara, and her husband, Charles Bray. It is at this point that her letters, though still characterized by moral earnestness and a desire to serve the world in some loving capacity, take on a different tone. In November 1841, almost certainly after reading Hennell's book, she wrote to Maria Lewis, "My whole soul has been engrossed in the most interesting of all enquiries for the last few days, and to what result my thoughts may lead I know not—possibly to one that will startle you, but my only desire is to know the truth, my only fear to cling to error." Later that year she recounted to Lewis one of those ubiquitous conflicts between Church and Dissent that played out everywhere in English provincial culture in the early Victorian period: "What pity that while mathematics are indubitable, immutable, and no one doubts the properties of a triangle or a circle, doctrines infinitely important to man are buried in a charnel heap of bones over which nothing is heard but the barks and growls of contention."[21]

Eliot was now embarked on a journey of uncertain destination. She read Charles Bray's *The Philosophy of Necessity or the Law of Consequences as Applicable to Mental, Moral, and Social Science* (1841), which further persuaded her that a life of loving duty had a moral worth greater than mere devotion to dogmatic religious propositions, which seemed to her to breed such enmity and self-interest. According to her father's journal, she stopped attending church in January 1842. Later that month she wrote a passionate letter to a friend, claiming to be part of "that glorious crusade that is seeking to set Truth's Holy Sepulchre free from a usurped domination." More revealingly she writes, "I cannot rank among my principles of action a fear of vengeance eternal, gratitude for predestined salvation, or a revelation of future glories as a reward, I fully participate in the belief that the only heaven here or hereafter is to be found in conformity with the will of the Supreme; a continual aiming at the attainment of that perfect ideal, the true Logos that dwells in the bosom of the One Father."[22]

Eliot's father, Robert Evans, upset by his daughter's abandonment of churchgoing, interpreted her pilgrimage as one from Anglican orthodoxy to Unitarian heterodoxy under the influence of the Brays, who were themselves Unitarians, but Eliot was at pains to point out to him that there was more at stake than mere denominational migration. She informed him that she could no longer accept the "Jewish and Christian Scriptures" as authoritative. "I regard these writings as histories consisting of mingled truth and fiction, and while I admire and cherish much of what I believe to have been the moral teaching of Jesus himself, I consider the system of doctrines built upon the facts of his life and drawn as to its materials from Jewish notions to be most dishonourable to God and most pernicious in its influence on individual and social happiness."[23] Eliot, although she tried to place herself in an honorable skeptical tradition that included Benjamin Franklin, was all too aware of the unpleasant social consequences that would likely be incurred when the daughter of a respectable family in early Victorian England espoused such views. Her next months were spent in painful separation from her father and wider family as both they and she contemplated the implications of her newly expressed skepticism.

During these months Eliot engaged in further theological reflection, partly under the guidance of Francis Watts, professor of theology at Spring Hill College in Birmingham, who was one of the few Englishmen aware of the issues raised by German higher criticism of the Bible. Although much of her pilgrimage from faith to doubt was self-evidently painful (Mrs. Bray spoke of her long, dismal face), Eliot soon began to see some benefits in her new freedom of thought. She confessed to Watts that she felt inexpressible relief "to be freed from what Finney well describes, that at each moment I tread on chords that will vibrate for weal or woe to all eternity. I could shed tears of joy to believe that in this lovely world I may lie on the grass and ruminate on possibilities without dreading lest my conclusions should be everlastingly fatal. It seems to me that the awful anticipations entailed by reception of all the dogmas in the New Testament operate unfavourably on moral beauty by disturbing that spontaneity, that choice of good for its own sake, that answers my ideal."[24] Unsurprisingly, both the psychological pain of her journey away from evangelical certainty, and the joy associated with intellectual freedom from it, faded over time. She wrote that in the aftermath of the soul's liberation from "the wretched giant's bed of dogmas on which it has been racked and stretched" there is a feeling of exultation followed by the zeal of the new proselyte, but that over time wisdom and reflection produce a kind of equipoise. Eliot came to see that not every opinion had to be contended for, not every error resisted, for the human condition and her own sense of loving duty required empathy, sympathy, and tolerance more than fierce controversy. "It is the quackery of infidelity," she wrote, "to suppose that it has nostrum for all mankind, and to say to all and singular, 'Swallow my opinions and you shall be whole.'"[25]

Eliot's rejection of orthodox Christianity was more gradual than some of her interpreters have suggested. Since the great majority of her early letters were written to ardent evangelicals, the change in her opinions was concealed for as long as possible.[26] The young woman who had come under the influence of Maria Lewis was already a voracious reader who read the Bible from cover to cover and soon found its moral teaching both compelling and disturbing. Moreover, her moral revolt against the implications of religious dogma was far from unique in late eighteenth- and nineteenth-century Britain. Thomas Paine, whose *Rights of Man* and *Age of Reason* were the most influential books among the leaders of Britain's emerging industrial proletariat, also found the teachings of orthodox Christianity morally disturbing. In the *Age of Reason* he recounts a childhood experience of listening to a sermon on the atonement. It struck him that God was both too good to kill his own son and too powerful to be under the necessity of doing it: "I believe in the same manner to this moment: and I moreover believe that any system of religion that has anything in it that shocks the mind of a child, cannot be a true system." Here, then, is a common pattern. In Susan Budd's survey of several hundred committed secularists in Victorian England she found that conversions to Christianity occurred mainly from ages fourteen to seventeen, whereas loss of faith developed in their thirties and forties. According to Budd the most common reasons cited for loss of faith was the conviction that the Bible, church ministers, and religious dogma "were wicked or politically reactionary . . . the biographies suggest that what was crucial was the realization that the Bible, minister, etc., was wrong—i.e. morally wrong."[27] In short, the Bible, having successfully schooled its readership in moral excellence, then became victim of the newly refined moral sensibilities of its readers.

Eliot's journey was somewhat similar. According to Howard Murphy, "Miss Evans did not first read Hennell, and then conclude that, for purely intellectual reasons, she was obliged to discard her childhood religion; rather she first began to suspect that neither her own nor any other form of orthodoxy was 'requisite to moral excellence,' and then was relieved to discover that the Bible could be interpreted in a quite unorthodox sense." Once her new path was chosen, Eliot followed it with characteristic seriousness and devotion. Between 1843 and 1854 she translated Strauss's *Das Leben Jesu,* Spinoza's *Tractatus Theologico-Politicus,* and Feuerbach's *Das Wesen Christenthums.* This extended interaction with the new German theology and philosophy was not all plain sailing. Mrs. Bray reported that Eliot was "Strauss-sick—it made her ill dissecting the beautiful story of the crucifixion, and only the sight of her Christ-image and picture made her endure it."[28]

After she settled in London as the assistant editor of the *Westminster Review* in 1851, Eliot became part of a dynamic intellectual circle that included Utilitarians, early feminists, research scientists, Socialists, and Comtean Positivists. Eliot's own range of intellectual interests and competencies was stunning. In the months before and after she wrote her stinging review of Dr. Cumming's evangelical teaching, her journal shows she was translating Spinoza's *Ethics;* constructing articles on German mythology, French literature, and early English and American feminists; writing critical essays on Liszt, Wagner, Heine, Kingsley, Milton, Carlyle, and Michelet; and reading for pleasure Shakespeare, Goethe, the *Iliad* (in Greek), Longfellow's *Hiawatha,* Herbert Spencer's *Genesis of Science,* and new work on anatomy and physiology.[29] In that context, Eliot's attack on Cumming was not so much a narrow fixation with the religion of her youth as it was part of a much wider encounter with new ideas and their social and political consequences. Although not all of those ideas resulted in the increase of human progress and happiness, as Eliot hoped, there is no denying their excitement for a woman of extraordinary intellectual gifts who had felt muzzled by evangelical religion and English provincial values.

With the old evangelical certainties now well and truly demolished, George Eliot's task was how to create a morally acceptable alternative. The solution for her was a religion of humanity based on sympathy, compassion, and duty. She wrote to Alexander Main that "amid all the considerable trials of existence, men and women can nevertheless greatly help each other; and while we can help each other it is worthwhile to live."[30] Although Eliot is not remembered as a distinguished poet, it is in one of her poems that her religion of humanity is most clearly enunciated.

Oh may I join the choir invisible
Of those immortal dead who live again
In minds made better by their presence: live
In pulses stirred to generosity,
In deeds of daring rectitude, in scorn
For miserable aims that end with self,
In thoughts sublime that pierce the night like stars,
And with their mild persistence urge man's search
To vaster issues.[31]

This conflict between egoism and altruism became the moral and philosophical center of George Eliot's novels, the first of which, *Scenes of Clerical Life,* was published in 1858. Eliot began writing her series of clerical sketches not long after completing her essay on Cumming, and her tone on evangelicalism is unmistakably kinder and more generous. In *Janet's Repentance* she writes, "The first condition of human goodness is something to love: the second, something to reverence. And this latter precious gift was brought to Milby by Mr Tryan and Evangelicalism. Yes, the movement was good, though it had that mixture of folly and evil which often makes what is good an offence to feeble and fastidious minds, who want human actions and characters riddled through the sieve of their own ideas, before they can accord sympathy and admiration."[32] What made Tryan so admirable was not the dogmatic superstructure of his faith, but rather his choice to forsake the privileges of birth and rank to "live in those close rooms on the common, among heaps of dirty cottages, for the sake of being near the poor people." Through that empathetic choice Tryan's noble brand of evangelicalism "had brought into palpable existence and operation . . . that idea of duty, that recognition of something to be lived for beyond the mere satisfaction of the self, which is to the moral life what the addition of a great central ganglion is to animal life."[33] In short, evangelicalism when expressed as a sympathetic religion of self-subjugation in service of a suffering humanity was incomparably greater in Eliot's eyes than evangelicalism as an exclusivist creed of privilege for an already privileged people.

An even more favorable depiction of evangelical religion based on similar assumptions appeared in Eliot's second novel, *Adam Bede,* published in 1859. Eliot's conviction, which she expressed in her *Westminster Review* essay on "Silly Novels by Lady Novelists," that the real drama of evangelicalism was to be found not among its clerical leaders but lower down the social scale, helps explain her enthusiasm for the religiosity of Dinah Morris.

Although Eliot's fictional portrayals of evangelicalism are far more generous than one would expect from the author of the essay on Dr. Cumming, she revisited the darker side of the movement in her greatest novel, *Middlemarch*, published in 1871. In her powerful sketch of an evangelical banker, Nicholas Bulstrode, she presents a character whose outward desire for power and respectability is undermined by a grim personal life stained by hypocrisy and moral mendacity. In her repudiation of the pernicious social effects of Cumming's evangelical ideology, Eliot was at pains to dissociate herself from any personal attack on Cumming's character, apart from that which is implied by his writing, but, when she was released by the imaginative freedom of fiction, Eliot's characterization of Bulstrode points to what she considered to be the real disease of the evangelical temperament. Bulstrode's capacity for social smugness and self-righteousness stemmed from a belief that God was on his side, even when his side was morally indefensible. In short, Bulstrode lived in a liminal state of moral ambiguity in which his public prestige was completely at odds with his intrinsic moral worth. For Eliot, evangelicalism, with its high and undeserved reputation for sanctity, supplied the ideological oil that lubricated the grinding of Bulstrode's bifurcated conscience and prevented him from facing up to the truth of his own life. As his sordid hidden life is laid bare, Bulstrode's "pitiable lot" is that of a man "who knows he is stoned, not for professing the Right, but for not being the man he professed to be."[34] Even as his public persona unravels, Bulstrode, whose entire life was based on public display and private concealment, could not face up to a full confession before God and man (even his own dutiful wife) that would have allowed some oxygen into the asphyxiating roots of his own soul. It is to Eliot's credit as a novelist, however, that she is able to present such a powerful example of evangelical hypocrisy at work without losing all sympathy with the character who embodies it. Bulstrode may be a thoroughly unpleasant character, psychologically trapped in a prison of his own making, but even he has some self-awareness, and his personal tragedy is made more poignant by a wife who, despite all, dutifully sticks by him.

In a passage of revealing symbolism Mrs. Bulstrode prepares herself carefully to adopt a new life of "humiliation" before encountering her newly disgraced husband for the first time. "She took off all her ornaments and put on a plain black gown, and instead of wearing her much-adorned cap and large bows of hair, she brushed her hair down and put on a plain bonnet-cap, which made her look suddenly like an early Methodist."[35] Deserted by his daughters, unable to approach the retributive God of his own construction, and fearful of his wife's loss of respect and affection, Bulstrode waited for the confrontation he most dreaded. In a scene which Eliot carefully controls from descending into sentimentality or cheap restitution, husband and wife meet and collapse into one another with tears of silent shame. Not for the first time, Eliot contrasted one kind of evangelicalism, namely the hypocritical posturing of the pre-fall, corrupt Bulstrode, with another, this time tempered by naked honesty, human pain, and redemptive suffering that reminded Eliot of the style and spirituality of the early Methodists.

Moving from fiction to fact, what can be said of George Eliot's own religious pilgrimage? It is a truism that George Eliot's intellectual biography, beginning with evangelical faith and ending with a humanist creed constructed with many different kinds of materials, mirrors one of the prominent intellectual trajectories of the nineteenth century. Yet it is important to recognize that the evangelicalism she rejected was far from uniform, and her rejection, though superficially complete, was complex and variegated. It is all too easy to assume that her familiarity with German critical theology was the cause rather than the consequence of her ethical revolt against Christian orthodoxy. Moreover, it is equally easy to underestimate the impact of her early evangelical ardor on the rest of her career. It is possible to argue, for example, that the ideas underpinning her mature novel-writing phase were a powerful combination of an enlightened emphasis on human capacity, tolerance, and the pursuit of happiness, and an evangelical emphasis on moral earnestness and spiritual introspection. She rejected an evangelical gospel of grace and a compassionate savior and replaced them with her own mercy and sympathy for human weakness. Although she repudiated many of the distinctive tenets of evangelicalism, her novels are perhaps the clearest examples of that characteristic impact of evangelicalism on Victorian society, its moral earnestness. Some see her as a thoroughgoing determinist in her brilliant evocation of how environment remorselessly shapes human behavior, yet surely no English novelist gives such meticulous consideration to the anxieties and consequences of human choice. She had an enormous capacity for sympathizing with human weakness except her own physical and mental imperfections. She was a theological traveler who found like many before and after her that there was little rest for the skeptic in search of some overarching meaning and sense of purpose.

Perhaps the closest one can get to the settled religious convictions of the mature Eliot is a letter to Francoise D'Albert Durade in 1859. Partly mellowed by the critical acclaim she received from the publication of *Scenes of Clerical Life* and *Adam Bede*, partly occasioned by the personal happiness she found with George Henry Lewes, and partly out of a desire to make amends for her earlier vitriolic antagonism toward the evangelicalism that helped train her moral sensibilities, Eliot writes,

> I think I hardly ever spoke to you of the strong hold Evangelical Christianity had on me from age fifteen to two and twenty and of the abundant intercourse I had with earnest people of various religious sects. When I was in Geneva, I had not yet lost the attitude of antagonism which belongs to the renunciation of *any* belief—also, I was very unhappy, and in a state of discord and rebellion towards my own lot. Ten years of experience have wrought great changes in that inward self: I have no longer any antagonism towards any faith in which human sorrow and human longing for purity have expressed themselves; on the contrary, I have a sympathy with it that predominates over all argumentative tendencies.
>
> I have not returned to dogmatic Christianity—to the acceptance of any set of doctrines as a creed, and a superhuman revelation of the Unseen—but I see in it the highest expression of the religious sentiment that has found its place in the history of mankind, and I have the profoundest interest in the inward life of sincere Christians in all ages. Many things that I should have argued against ten years ago, I now feel myself too ignorant and too limited in moral sensibility to speak of with confident disapprobation: on many points where I used to delight in expressing intellectual difference, I now delight in feeling an emotional agreement. On that question of our future existence, to which you allude, I have undergone the sort of change I have just indicated, although my most rooted conviction is, that the immediate objects and the proper sphere of all our highest emotions are our struggling fellow-men and this earthly existence.[36]

In this way, George Eliot, the slayer of Dr. Cumming, her very personal evangelical dragon, came to lie down, in rhetoric if not in actuality, with the lambs of the humbly religious.

Some of the same tone expressed in Eliot's letter to Durade reappears in the character of Dorothea in *Middlemarch*. Dorothea's spiritual journey, which resonates with Eliot's own earnest striving for religious authenticity, is sharpened by a poor marriage choice that leaves her playing the role of a devoted secretary to her much older husband, Casaubon. The dry and dusty Casaubon is a scholar of religion engaged on a magnum opus called the *Key to all Mythologies*, but his ideas are shown to be both dull and dated. The dreariness of his scholarship is matched only by the crustiness of his temperament. Dorothea is introduced to his cousin Will Ladislaw, an artist and aesthete, whose dislike of his cousin is compounded by his growing attraction to

Dorothea. In one of their early conversations, Eliot places Dorothea against an open window, a symbol of fresh air blowing through the fustiness of her life in Casaubon's estate at Lowick. Will's impetuous comment that her life had become a "dreadful imprisonment" opened up a profound conversation about the nature of life, aspiration, and belief. In response to Will's question about the nature of her belief, Dorothea supplies an answer that is close to Eliot's own convictions: "That by desiring what is perfectly good, even when we don't quite know what it is and cannot do what we would, we are part of the divine power against evil—widening the skirts of light and making the struggle with darkness narrower." In response Will tries to *name* her religion as "a beautiful mysticism," but Dorothea swiftly interrupts him. "'Please not to call it by any name,' said Dorothea, putting out her hands entreatingly. 'You will say it is Persian, or something else geographical. It is my life. I have found it out, and cannot part with it. I have always been finding out my religion since I was a little girl. I used to pray so much—now I hardly ever pray. I try not to have desires for myself, because they may not be good for others, and I have too much already.'"[37]

In this spirit Dorothea reverses the question and asks Will about his religion, which he describes as "to love what is good and beautiful when I see it," but he is more of a rebel than Dorothea. In rephrasing his response Dorothea takes out his characteristic references to beauty and rebellion and concentrates instead on Will's love for the good that she declares to be similar to her own longings.

The interchanges between Will and Dorothea are not the only places in the novel where Eliot, through Dorothea, inserts views about religion that are close to her own. Throughout the novel two clergymen of contrasting types, the Evangelical Mr Tyke and the more pragmatic Mr Farebrother, end up as competitors for local ecclesiastical patronage. There is no mistaking Dorothea's preference. "It is hard to imagine what sort of notions our farmers and labourers get from their teaching. I have been looking into a volume of sermons by Mr Tyke: such sermons would be of no use at Lowick—I mean, about imputed righteousness and the prophecies in the Apocalypse. I have always been thinking of the different ways in which Christianity is taught, and whenever I find one way that makes it a wider blessing than any other, I cling to that as the truest—I mean that which takes in the most good of all kinds, and brings in the most people as sharers in it. It is surely better to pardon too much, than to condemn too much."[38] These comments of Dorothea are close to the heart of George Eliot's mature conception of religion. For her the essence of religion was neither a set of forensic theological propositions nor an assemblage of apocalyptic aspirations. Rather, true and undefiled religion was a life of inclusive love, devoted service to humankind, and forgiveness. Dr. Cumming's evangelical sermons were not entirely free from such concepts, but their overwhelming emphases on Calvinist doctrines, millenarian speculations, and ecclesiastical partisanship could not be further away from the religious ideals of the author of *Middlemarch*. It is scarcely surprising, therefore, that she chose Cumming as the exemplar of all that she disliked about the morals and mores of Victorian evangelicalism.

When George Eliot died in 1880 the evangelical consensus on her life was that she was a great novelist and intellectual who had been led astray while a young woman by the worthless writings of Charles Hennell and later by her illicit relationship with George Henry Lewes. A combination of poor scholarly judgment, personal weakness, and moral frailty conspired to derail her commitment to the evangelical Christianity of her youth. In its place she substituted a moral and religious framework which displaced the supernatural by the natural and love for God by an insipid love for humanity. For all her great talents, evangelicals regarded her life as a sad tale of capitulation to the secularizing dynamics of the nineteenth century. "There seems a slowness on the part of many even thoughtful believers," wrote one evangelical commentator, "to understand that love to God, instead of being inconsistent with love to man, is its deepest and most living root."[39] But for George Eliot the God of evangelicals like Dr. Cumming was neither lovely nor lovable, and could not act as a suitable foundation for her love of humanity.

3 Francis W. Newman—The Road to Baghdad
Evangelicalism and Mission

> But surely the age is ripe for . . . a religion which shall combine the tenderness,
> humility, and disinterestedness, that are the glory of the purest Christianity,
> with that activity of intellect, untiring pursuit of truth, and strict adherence to
> impartial principle, which the schools of modern science embody.
> —Francis Newman, *Phases of Faith* (1850)

Francis Newman, like his better-known brother, John Henry, the eminent
Roman Catholic theologian, underwent an evangelical religious conversion
in his early teenage years.[1] He had grown up as the fourth of six children in
a relatively prosperous English home, the son of a solid and sensible Anglican businessman who later went bankrupt, and a more pious Huguenot
mother. John Henry, who in Francis's mind seemed to alternate between a
model older brother and someone with whom to fight furiously over theology, was born in 1801, Francis in 1805.[2] Francis Newman's account of his
early embrace of evangelicalism is written in the characteristically blunt and
rationalistic style that became his lifelong trademark. As a conversion narrative it lacks both emotional power and mystical imagination, concentrating

Francis William Newman, by (George) Herbert Watkins. Albumen print, oval, 1858 (© National
Portrait Gallery, London)

instead on the bare facts of the case, and the moral consequences accruing from his newly adopted creed.

> I first began to read religious books at school, and especially the Bible, when I was eleven years old; and almost immediately commenced a habit of secret prayer. But it was not until I was fourteen that I gained any definite idea of a "scheme of doctrine," or could have been called a "converted person" by one of the Evangelical School. My religion then certainly exercised a great general influence over my conduct; for I soon underwent various persecutions from my schoolfellows on account of it: the worst kind consisted in their deliberate attempts to corrupt me. An Evangelical clergyman at the school gained my affections, and from him I imbibed more and more directly the full creed which distinguishes that body of men; a body whose bright side I shall ever appreciate in spite of my present perception that they have a dark side also. I well remember, that one day when I said to this friend of mine, that I could not understand how the doctrine of Election was reconcilable to God's Justice, but supposed that I should know in due time, if I waited and believed His word;—he replied with emphatic commendation, that this was the spirit which God always blessed. Such was the beginning and foundation of my faith,—an unhesitating unconditional acceptance of whatever was found in the Bible. While I am far from saying that my *whole* moral conduct was subjugated by my creed, I must insist that it was no mere fancy resting in my intellect: it was really operative on my temper, tastes, pursuits and conduct.[3]

It was characteristic of Newman that as soon as he embraced his new faith he encountered a serious moral problem associated with it, namely how could the doctrine of election be reconciled with divine justice. It was also characteristic of Newman's early evangelicalism that he maintained a fierce devotion to the Bible along with an equally fierce determination to subject the Bible to strict principles of rational accountability. Unsurprisingly, these were the very characteristics that persuaded John that Francis's evangelical faith was built on weak foundations of faith and intellect, and could not possibly endure. He was correct.

Some thirty years after his evangelical conversion Francis Newman published a candid, if rather prosaic, account of his *Phases of Faith*, which his evangelical critics suggested might better be regarded as phases of unbelief or infidelity. Organized into chronological epochs, mirroring the kind of dispensational theology to which he was once exposed, Newman's public confession is self-described as "egotistical in its form, but not in its purport and essence." His stated aim was to strip away all encumbrances of faulty logic, irrational belief, and religious fiction to uncover a purer devotion to a purer God. Characterized by an almost painful moral earnestness, *Phases of Faith* is in part a morality tale, attempting to show that muddled understanding leads inexorably to moral perversion. In that respect, at least, Francis Newman endorsed the very evangelicalism he so resolutely repudiated. As U. C. Knoeplmacher has helpfully observed, in *Phases of Faith* Newman is "not concerned with endearing himself to his readers, but rather wants to serve truth by conducting a self-examination that is as rigorous and objective as the introspective assessment formerly demanded by Evangelical discipline."[4]

Phases of Faith's opening chapter, "My Youthful Creed," allowing for its retrospective analysis, shows that even in his evangelical phase Newman was a stout rationalist with a sharp eye for illogicality or hypocrisy. He was dismayed, for example, by how cavalierly his contemporaries subscribed to the Thirty-Nine Articles of the Church of England. He denied the apostolic succession of Anglican bishops and delineated their tawdry record of moral and spiritual leadership since the Reformation. He repudiated infant baptism (especially baptismal regeneration); he distanced himself from Sabbatarianism and other aspects of the Old Testament's legal codes; he entertained critical questions about the nature of Christ's atonement and the morality of vicarious punishment; he suspected that orthodox doctrines of the Trinity were at best enigmatic and at worst entirely irrational; he found the Apostle Paul's reasoned letters more agreeable than the obscurities of the Gospels; and he regarded the early church Fathers as overrated. If these were the views of Francis Newman in his pious phase, one justifiably might wonder what was to come later. Yet the early record of *Phases of Faith* is misleading. Not only could many of his dissident opinions be explained as a visceral reaction against what he called his brother's "full-blown 'Popery,'" but also his quite genuine evangelical pietism surfaces more commonly not in the filtered memory of his retrospective *Phases of Faith*, but in contemporary letters. For example, in as clear a representation of the nineteenth-century evangelical temperament as one is likely to find, Francis informed his brother that "I cannot keep half measures in religion: unless I would be a profligate, I must be a truly devoted Christian; I must not let a single five minutes in the day lie waste; I must give my whole heart to Christ; I must pray for this *One Thing*, that I may know him & the power of his resurrection." Newman also exhibited the characteristic expressions of evangelical spirituality in his oscillations between joy and melancholy, strength and weakness, glory and anguish, or what he called "this round of sinning & repenting."[5]

Francis Newman was a sufficiently brilliant scholar—his double first in classics and mathematics was regarded as one of the finest ever at Oxford—to have entertained thoughts of a distinguished academic career, but his conscientious refusal to sign the Thirty-Nine Articles effectively prevented him from retaining his Fellowship at Balliol. He therefore ended the first phase of his faith journey at something of a loose end, and with the sober recognition that since he could place no confidence in articles, creeds, or churches, he was left with little to cling to but "the Bible in its simplicity." He also recognized that his unorthodox views precluded him from seeking holy orders in the Church of England, yet his ardor for heroic Christian service remained undimmed. This combination of intense biblicism and desire to save the world he carried with him to a tutoring position in Ireland, where he soon came under the charismatic influence of John Nelson Darby. Darby later achieved fame and notoriety as one of the early founders of the Plymouth Brethren movement and as a promoter of dispensational premillennial theology, which most scholars now believe to be one of the strongest roots of Anglo-American fundamentalism.[6] When Newman first encountered him, however, Darby cut a romantic figure as a roving curate in the Wicklow mountains ministering to Irish Catholics, not as a representative of a privileged Protestant Ascendancy but as an ascetic evangelical saint. Newman concluded "that a dozen such men would have done more to convert all Ireland to Protestantism than the whole apparatus of the Church Establishment." For Newman, who was searching for a model of apostolic authenticity to go with his ardent faith in the Scriptures, Darby was irresistible. Here was someone who shared Newman's romantic conception of primitive Christianity as an otherworldly faith careless of personal comfort, social status, and the trappings of political or ecclesiastical power. As Darby increasingly bent Newman's mind and will to his own, Francis came also to believe in the imminence of the second coming of Christ and the consequent futility of pursuing what he called "earthly objects distant in time." Also influenced by Darby's sister, Susan, Newman's letters from this period are almost obsessed with millennial themes of urgency and making the most of the time. He wrote his brother, "I never gained before so clear an idea of what was meant by a Christian's being opposed to the spirit of the world. It is not *merely* to avoid the pomps & vanities, or *merely* to judge of actions by an opposite rule, but it is to feel that *the time is short,* and to be *looking* for the Lord Jesus from heaven."[7] He piously told a friend that he had spent too long thinking of ways to improve the world instead of thinking of it as a vale of tears from which God planned to gather "a peculiar people, to *suffer* with Christ here, that they may reign with him hereafter."[8] Opinions like these caused his family to worry that, under the influence of his friends in Ireland, Newman appeared to be in danger of capitulating to the worst excesses of religious enthusiasm.

Besides subjecting himself to Darby's dominating influence, Newman experienced one other major consequence in his brief sojourn in Ireland. The hot political topic of the day was the campaign for Roman Catholic Emancipation, which was of course resisted by most Irish Protestants and British evangelicals. Ever the spiritual purist, Newman could not see how the cause of a gospel of love could be furthered by the exercise of discriminatory power by the state. With the early church as his guide, Newman refused to believe that imperial power was an ally of scriptural Christianity and concluded with characteristic logical consistency that it was no more possible to justify Protestant discrimination against Catholics in Ireland than Muslim persecution of Christians in other parts of the world. In his view true Christianity could advance only as fast as its worldly status and ambitions receded. Ironically, therefore, Francis, the evangelical Protestant and lifelong anti-Catholic, was in favor of Catholic Emancipation in Ireland while his brother John Henry, who later became a Roman Catholic cardinal, opposed it.

With such views in place Newman was ready for some grand heroic mission on behalf of the apostolic church he felt called to serve. The stimulus was supplied by his reading of a tract by Anthony Norris Groves called *Christian Devotedness,* which contained an impassioned plea for a less materialistic and more sacrificial brand of Christianity in line with the explicit commands of Jesus to give up earthly treasure and sacrifice all for His sake.[9] Containing little theological or literary eloquence, Groves's short pamphlet made a big impression on those with a high view of Scripture and a low view of the prevailing state of the Christian churches. Newman was ripe for such an influence. Although Groves as a student at Trinity College Dublin associated with some of Newman's circle of friends in Ireland, including Darby, the two men appear not to have met until their planned encounter in Baghdad several years later. The story of how they came to be there is one of the most extraordinary narratives in the history of Protestant missions.

In June 1829 Groves left England for the arduous journey to Baghdad accompanied by his wife, two sons, and an assorted collection of tutors, servants, and associates. Their journey through Copenhagen, St. Petersburg, and the mountains of Georgia and Armenia reads like a picaresque tale of manifold adventures and narrow escapes from the attentions of bandits, but the travails of the journey were as nothing compared to the tragedies awaiting them at their destination. Fortified by a strong sense of providential guidance and shared fellowship, the mission was at first relatively uneventful. Within a year, however, the situation in Baghdad deteriorated. Fighting between rival Arab factions was accompanied by outbreaks of cholera and plague followed by cataclysmic flooding of the Tigris valley. Baghdad's population of some eighty thousand people was decimated, and the missionary expedition was not spared. At first Groves, who had an apparently unshakable belief in the providential ordering of his mission, recorded a series of special deliverances, and his spirits were further lifted by the safe birth of his baby daughter. But the spread of pestilence was unremitting and soon claimed the lives of his wife and daughter. Groves and one of his sons escaped death only by a hairsbreadth. His journal of these events, though not unfeeling or without pathos, is almost astonishing in its calm acceptance of the tragedies unfolding around him. Oscillating between spiritual lessons learnt and an understandable apocalypticism, Groves somehow withstood the ravages of plague and flood, but the whole episode took a frightful toll. "This wretched city," he wrote, "has suffered to an almost unparalleled extent the judgments of God within the last six months. The plague has swept away more than two-thirds of its inhabitants, the flood has thrown down nearly two-thirds of its houses . . . and we are now suffering under daily increasing famine, and we have yet hanging over our heads the revengeful sword of resisted authority and the unprincipled plunder of a lawless soldiery to complete the devastation."[10]

Throughout this long ordeal Groves was repeatedly fortified by the anticipation of a long-awaited party of reinforcements from England, which eventually arrived in the early summer of 1832. Francis Newman was one of the relieving band of missionaries who floated down the Tigris River into Baghdad. How he came to be there is as much a story of intellectual as of geographical pilgrimage. Arising partly from his personal encounters with Darby and from his reading of Groves, Newman had become convinced that the future expansion of Christendom depended not on the kind of Christian apologetics he learned at Oxford, nor on the tired old established churches of European Christendom, but rather on a newly minted heroic church "animated by primitive faith, love and disinterestedness." He wrote, "While nations called Christian are only known to heathens as great conquerors, powerful avengers, sharp traders,—often lax in morals, and apparently without religion,—the fine theories of a Christian teacher would be as vain to convert a Mohommedan or Hindoo to Christianity, as the soundness of Seneca's moral treatises to convert me to Roman Paganism. Christendom has to earn a new reputation before Christian precepts will be thought to stand in any essential or close relation with the mystical doctrines of Christianity. I could see no other way to do this, but by an entire church being formed of new elements on a heathen soil."[11]

Inspired partly by the example of the Moravian missions to Greenland and South Africa, Newman, now in his mid twenties, was ready to test his new understanding of primitive Christianity in the very heartlands of Islam and the Ottoman Empire. In September 1830 he and six others set sail from Dublin accompanied by trunks, chests, bags, a small library, a lithographic press for printing tracts, and a large medicine chest.[12] Their route took them to Bordeaux and Marseilles and then across the Mediterranean to Larnaca before finally sailing to Syria, where they paused in the town of Aleppo. Almost as inflated as the amount of their luggage was their sense of cultural chauvinism. Newman traveled as the self-conscious representative of a civilization that ruled India, and had just built "self-moving engines" for the Liverpool to Manchester railroad. By contrast France was regarded as politically unstable, ecclesiastically disreputable, economically backward, and culturally inferior. The Ottoman Empire was even lower in Newman's league table of world civilizations. But chauvinism did not result in cultural disengagement.

On the journey to Baghdad Newman, an avid and gifted linguist, polished up his Greek, spoke French, took lessons in Arabic, and learned to smoke, which, quite apart from the pleasure of the activity, he thought would make a useful cultural bridge to Arab culture. Soon more substantial religious and cultural barriers to a successful Christian mission presented themselves. Newman records a conversation with a Muslim carpenter in Aleppo that made a lasting impression on him. Armed with his Oxford training and formidable intellect, he set out to prove to the carpenter that the Gospel narratives were authentic and reliable texts. "I will tell you, sir, how the case stands," the carpenter replied, "God has given to you English a great many good gifts. You make fine ships, and sharp penknives, and good cloth and cottons; and you have rich nobles and brave soldiers; and you write and print many learned books: (dictionaries and grammars:) all this is of God. But there is one thing that God has withheld from you, and has revealed to us; and that is, the knowledge of the true religion, by which one may be saved."[13] Newman recognized immediately that his Oxford wisdom had been trumped by a simple declaration of primitive faith, in exactly the same way as a humble European Christian might trump a learned atheistic philosopher, or how the early apostles reacted to the worldly wise of the first century. Newman concluded that "this not only showed the vanity of any argument to him [the carpenter], except one purely addressed to his moral and spiritual faculties, but it also indicated to me that Ignorance has its spiritual self-sufficiency as well as Erudition; and that if there is a Pride of Reason, so is there a Pride of Unreason."[14]

Another encounter in Aleppo, this time with a contentious English unbeliever whom Newman could defeat easily in argument, led him to reflect that if a Muslim witnessed their debates he would have no way of telling which of the disputants was correct, yet here was Newman defending his faith on strictly empirical and historical grounds, which of necessity could not be proved beyond reasonable doubt. It seemed that Newman's original intention of shaking the foundations of Islam with the tools of primitive Christianity had encountered serious problems before he even reached his destination. While in Aleppo waiting for better news from Baghdad, Newman continued to engage Arab culture. He dressed in Syrian gown and slippers, observed local customs and rituals, and started reading the Koran. But Islam perplexed him. He found it hard to reconcile the "stagnant and unprofitable" religious culture he observed in Turkey with Islam's earlier "scientific movement fully comparable to the scholasticism of Europe in the middle ages," and concluded that the Turks must be the culprits. He also thought that if medieval Islamic culture had continued its impressive trajectory of learning and cultivation without interruption it would have imploded from within, thereby making it easier for Christianity to expose its absurdities. It seems not to have occurred to him until later that a similar case could be made for the demise of Christianity, and that the Enlightenment already had achieved within Christendom what he hoped would happen in Islamic civilization. According to Newman Islam was not only intellectually unimpressive, but also liturgically impregnable. The ubiquity and obtrusiveness of Islam's public prayer rituals made him wonder if a less ritualistic and more pietistic kind of Christianity could ever succeed on Islamic soil.

If Islam puzzled him, its sacred text disappointed him. His reading of the Koran, which he described as "shallow and tedious," led him to conclude that Arab minds were weak and captivated by the power of tradition. With a realistic appraisal of the enormous cultural gap between West and East, he wrote, "When I see the vast chasm between Turkish and English thought and knowledge, I am apt to faint into unbelief of heart as to their ever adopting what is here called *English religion*. I should tell you: neither Moslems nor Franks think of us as Christians, but as English." This realization was no trivial matter for Newman, for it penetrated to the heart of his missionary strategy. He wrote, "I always looked to a missionary church formed in these countries; but I did not foresee what I now discern, that it would not be recognized as *Christian* at all, but be esteemed as mere Anglicism, not by papists merely, but by Moslems too." Only a year into his mission, therefore, Newman began to doubt whether anything useful could be accomplished without either an "extraordinary outpouring of the Holy Spirit . . . in which I sometimes believe," or by a new national identity and accompanying religious instruction from above.[15] The former smacked of religious romanticism, the latter of English imperial pragmatism. Neither seemed to offer any realistic prospect of success.

Like a cultural anthropologist on fieldwork, Newman was intrigued by the political, economic, and social characteristics of the Ottoman Empire. He was impressed by the fact that animals were treated kindly, that there were no lunatic asylums or orphanages among the Turkish populations (lunatics were few and regarded as harmless, orphans were adopted by families), and that there was little evidence of drunkenness, prostitution, petty theft, and competitive ambition. He was both attracted and repulsed by the lack of intellectual curiosity, economic energy, and work discipline he observed all around him. Comparing the Turkish and Roman Empires he wrote perceptively that the Turks "crushed material prosperity, but not national spirit. The Romans crushed national spirit, but, for a while, fostered material prosperity." He also thought that the Ottoman Empire had conquered but not assimilated its populations, leaving religion as the chief form of native identity. "Each man's church is here his country: he has no other country. Where a church is a people, fanaticism is undistinguishable from patriotism."[16]

In April 1832, Newman's depleted party at last left Aleppo for the final leg of their journey to Baghdad. It began with a bizarre event that only someone of Newman's ruthless honesty could memorialize. "A strange thing happened to us in quitting Aleppo, which deserves meditation. Mr. P. bought a horse with an amulet hung round his neck. On learning what it was, he cut it off with his penknife, in spite of the entreaties of the late owner, who declared the horse would meet with calamity, if the charm were lost which defended him. Soon after, the poor beast fell down into our area, fifteen feet deep, gashed open his whole side horribly, and had to be left behind, dying or ruined. I find this instructive. We have strengthened these people's superstition."[17]

What self-respecting missionary apologist could tell such a story and then follow it up by concluding that given the unpredictability of chance, challenging native superstitions was a foolish strategy and ought to be discouraged? After this unpromising start, the last leg of the journey to Baghdad proved the most challenging. Beset by bandits, mobs, and robbers, Newman's party experienced many hardships before reaching Mosul and sailing down the Tigris to Baghdad. Newman records very few details of his time there.

Whatever pious thoughts he had about his life as a missionary were deliberately edited out of his *Personal Narratives* of the trip to Baghdad, which was published over twenty years later.[18] With characteristic honesty, but with results disappointing to the historian, Newman wrote in the preface to his book that "the phraseology, especially when religious subjects are approached, is chastened to suit the writer's maturer taste: and on account of the suppressions under this head, and the fullness added to details of secondary importance, the letters, as here exhibited, give an untrue picture of his state of mind at that time."[19]

Although they contain little information about the shaping of his inner religious convictions, and display few poetic descriptions of exotic landscapes (Newman's mind was too severe for that), Newman's letters from his sojourn in the Ottoman Empire are nevertheless riveting reflections of a well-educated English gentleman encountering the Orient, and of a pious evangelical Protestant encountering Islamic culture. A close reading also shows that in honestly facing up to the missiological challenges of spreading evangelicalism in an alien culture, Newman effectively abandoned his romantic and millenarian notion of converting the world through the establishment of a pure missionary church. Unfortunately for him, however, no more convincing strategy took its place. Instead, his personal narratives are peppered with comments like, "I am faithless and see too many difficulties," and "I have no prophecies concerning the future." Although he was not personally disappointed with Groves, whose little work on Christian devotedness had seduced Newman to Baghdad in the first place, Newman seems to have regarded the mission as an overall failure. Attempts to convert Muslims foundered on linguistic, cultural, and religious differences, including the apparently unsolvable problem of how to communicate an inward faith to those accustomed to outward displays of religiosity. As the mission unfolded it seemed that less and less time was devoted to converting Muslims and more time was spent on reviving the dying embers of Baghdad's Christian past represented by small populations of Roman Catholics and Armenian Orthodox. Even here Newman wrote darkly about how different religions with their exclusivist claims and sectarian self-interest had undermined the social solidarity and common humanity of Turkish society.[20] Intellectually unsettled by his observations of how religion shaped culture, emotionally eroded by the deaths of the three women who set out on the long trek to Baghdad, undermined by almost constant illness and discomfort, frustrated by lack of missionary success, disappointed by his failed marriage proposals to a woman he loved back in England (Maria Rosina Giberne), and largely disenchanted with Middle Eastern civilization,

Newman left Baghdad for England in September 1832, ostensibly to recruit fresh blood for the Baghdad mission, but in reality to ponder the consequences of the death of the millennial dream of a pure Christian church planted on foreign soil that had sustained him for the previous five years of his life.

For security reasons, Newman's journey back to England took him on a long detour through Teheran and Constantinople, both of which disappointed him. He thought the Bosporus was beautiful, but Newman the religious puritan could see little architectural or cultural merit in the Constantinople skyline of mosques, to which he claimed "a moral revulsion." He closed the books on his oriental adventure with a comment that showed how far he had traveled, mentally and spiritually, as well as geographically. The man who left Dublin was a vigorous believer in the power of biblical prophecy and the vigor of evangelical spirituality. He left Constantinople unimpressed with the aspirations of the missionaries he met there, and more sanguine about historical "contingencies" than providential power. He wrote, "Some students of prophecy expect the Jews to be the great missionaries, *when* converted. It may be that they are to be converted; but humanly speaking, this is far harder than that the Armenians should imbibe European influences and something of Protestant spirituality. *If* this come about (and it is an object worthy of England, America, Prussia, and Sweden), their wide dispersion and extended connections might make it a historical-theological event of the first scale."[21] Newman's sobering experiences in the Ottoman Empire thus encouraged him to subject evangelical idealism to historical realism.

Although Newman has left a frustratingly thin record of the spiritual consequences of his brief sojourn in Baghdad, which was spent mostly in teaching school and learning Arabic, there is little doubt that the relative failure of his great missionary adventure was a pivotal experience in his life. Unlike Groves, whose unquestioning piety enabled him to shake off the tragedies and disappointments of Baghdad to build a life of devoted missionary service in India, Newman's skeptical intelligence was preparing him for an altogether different destination. Newman did not return from Baghdad a full-blown skeptic, but the whole experience had dampened the ardor of his apostolic enthusiasm. Far from planting a pure Christian church on foreign soil as a light first to Muslims and then to the world, Newman's introductory course on missiology and comparative religion had left him reeling, intellectually and spiritually. Worse was soon to follow.

By a remarkable coincidence Francis Newman arrived back in England on the same day, July 9, 1833, as John Henry Newman returned from his

Mediterranean tour. Both survived almost fatal illnesses, both had their views shaped by observations of how religion worked in unfamiliar cultures, and both were now set on courses that would exacerbate their fraternal disharmony. Francis, for the moment, "clung to his belief in a spiritual invisible church and an inspired, infallible Bible, even as his brother, refreshed and purposive, moved towards the ideal of an Infallible Church, inspired in its interpretation of the Revealed Word."[22] Although Francis soon found a teaching position, and in Maria Kennaway, a loving and pious wife who was also a Plymouth Sister, his return to England ushered in a period of "deep and critical trial to me and my Creed." In the England of the 1830s such trials had relational as well as intellectual and spiritual consequences. In what Francis rather bitterly described as "a sacrifice of personal love to ecclesiastical dogma," his brother denounced him for assuming the priestly office without proper authority by speaking at religious meetings, while John Nelson Darby, who had been his apostolic hero, denounced as heretical Newman's unorthodox view of the doctrine of the Trinity. Newman had come to believe that the conventional Trinitarian formulation of the Athanasian Creed was a kind of polytheistic mumbo jumbo without any scriptural or rational warrant. Newman expected from Darby if not an honest agreement that a coequal tripartite Trinity was against the plain reading of the Scriptures, at least an acknowledgment that good men could differ in their interpretation of nonessential religious dogma. When rebuked by Darby, Newman even signaled his willingness to accept the Trinitarian formulation of the Nicene Creed, which he thought was more credible than that of the Athanasian Creed, but Darby's biblical literalism did not permit him to accept the Nicene Creed, or any extrabiblical source, as a valid authority. The shock to Newman's intellectual and personal universe from his exchange with Darby was palpable. "For the first time I perceived, that so vehement a champion of the sufficiency of the Scripture, so staunch an opposer of Creeds and Churches, was wedded to an extra-Scriptural creed of his own, by which he tested the spiritual state of his brethren." In other words, according to Newman, since the traditional doctrine of the Trinity could not be inferred from a plain reading of the Scriptures, Darby, though he would not admit it, filtered his reading of the Bible through a preselected doctrinal sieve. Condemned by his Anglo-Catholic brother for not allowing the church to be the interpreter of Scripture, and ostracized by his sectarian friend for subjecting Scripture to the test of reason and common sense, Newman could only wail, "Oh Dogma! Dogma! How dost thy trample under foot love, truth, conscience, justice!"[23] Darby soon spread the word that Newman, as the holder of heretical beliefs, was not to be welcomed into the fellowship of the early Brethren assemblies, leaving his erstwhile disciple with little alternative but to forge a new path toward an uncertain destination. Now bereft of much of his family and many of his friends, Newman painfully resolved "never again to count on permanent friendship with any one who was not himself cast out as a heretic." Darby, for his part, was equally wounded by Newman's *Phases of Faith,* which he described as a "guilty book" and "full of evil." His response in *Irrationalism of Infidelity* was to cast doubt on the genuineness of Newman's religious conversion, repudiate his attack on the doctrine of the Trinity, and deny the validity of Newman's rationalistic approach (since it was not informed by faith) to the authority of the Bible.[24] Between the separate spheres of Darby's spiritual submission to the authority of an infallible text (enlightened by faith) and Newman's restless and relentless rationalism, there were no bridges that either man was prepared to cross. A close friendship, which for Newman was also an anchor for his spiritual formation, was at an end.

Newman had returned from Baghdad with a greater sense of realism about Christianity's encounters with other religions, but with his belief in a spiritual church and an infallible Bible more or less intact; he emerged from the furor of his Trinitarian controversy with Darby with the former blown out of the water and the latter sorely undermined. What was left was a diminished Bible and Newman's growing propensity to test all authority against the twin pillars of morality and rationality. In his own words he was ripe for stage three of his *Phases of Faith,* which he entitled "Calvinism Abandoned." With a moral sensibility now sharpened by his sense of how immorally he had been treated by his erstwhile brothers in the Gospel, Newman set about refuting the verities of Calvinism. He had never believed in the doctrine of reprobation, now it was time to subject election, the Fall, eternal punishment, original sin, and substitutionary atonement to the full rigor of his new logic. His arguments are now so commonplace as not to merit detailed attention, but what attracted him to them was the growing conviction that "immoral" doctrines led inexorably to despicable behavior. Not only had he been treated badly by those who disagreed with him over complex points of doctrine, but by extension he attributed all the "execrable wickednesses" of religious persecution through the ages to the predisposition of religious people to subjugate commonsense morality to the interests of religious dogma. "Weakness of common sense, dread of the common understanding, an insufficient faith in common morality," he wrote, "are surely the disease: and evidently, nothing so exasperates this disease as consecrating religious tenets which forbid the exercise of common sense." Likewise, in trying to understand the viciousness with which he was treated by his old Christian brothers, Newman wrote that *"spirituality is no adequate security for sound moral discernment."* In other words, those who devoted themselves most assiduously to church and Bible were not necessarily better exemplars of morality than the "common world of men, who do not show any religious development." "It was pleasant to me to look on an ordinary face," he wrote, "and see it light up into a smile, and think with myself: 'there is one heart that will judge of me by what I am, and not by a Procrustean dogma.'"[25]

Personally wounded by the "spiritual" church, morally rebellious against the whole Calvinistic system, and increasingly isolated from all countervailing tendencies, Newman might still claim "an unabated reverence for the moral and spiritual teaching of the New Testament," but it was only a matter of time before his grim reaping rationality lighted on the Scriptures themselves. In "The Religion of the Letter Renounced" much of what Newman writes about the fourth phase of his faith would be familiar to any student of German higher criticism of the Bible, from which Newman retrieved most of his information. He brought his withering logic to bear on textual errors, pointless miracles, implausible events, scientific impossibilities, and moral infelicities, concluding that "the assumed infallibility of the *entire* Scripture is a proved falsity." Newman italicized the word *entire* because he thought it still possible to find an adequate account of what Christ had taught and accomplished, especially in the Gospel of John, for which he retained a special affection. In subjecting the Bible to such unremitting criticism Newman fully recognized that he could no longer shelter under the epithet of evangelical, or indeed expect cordial treatment from his former evangelical associates. "I now often met persons of Evangelical opinion," he wrote, "but could seldom have any interchange of religious sentiment with them, because every word they uttered warned me that I could escape controversy only while I kept them at a distance: moreover, if any little difference of opinion led us into amicable argument, they uniformly reasoned by quoting texts. This was now inadmissible with me, but I could only have done mischief by going farther than a dry disclaimer; after which indeed I saw I was generally looked on as 'an infidel.'"[26] In addition to the pain of having to take the scalpel to previously sacred opinions, Newman had also to reckon with the fact that the journey he was embarked upon was the one predicted for him not only by his brother, but also by many of his old Oxford acquaintances. Having now abandoned evangelicalism, Newman could only squirm in recollecting how often in the past he had despised the spirituality of others because they were not sufficiently evangelical for his tastes.

With his belief in the inspiration of the scriptural canon in tatters, Newman predictably launched into a rigorous investigation of the whole moral foundation of Christianity. The question of whether moral excellence could be found in Christianity dominated his next phase of faith. For him there could be no satisfying answer to that question based on a simple belief in the power of a church tradition or an infallible sacred text to command obedience. Instead he chose to rely on his inner moral perceptions and the free working of his mind without dogmatic constraints as the final arbiters of what could or should be believed. He then subjected Christianity to the same tests as could be applied to any other world religion and denied that it had an unblemished record in promoting learning and morality, elevating women, extinguishing slavery, resisting tyrannical rulers, ending persecution, and establishing religious toleration. More seriously he came to doubt the credibility of all the New Testament authors when it came to evidence for supernatural occurrences, including the resurrection of Christ. He called the fifth phase of his journey "Faith at second hand found to be vain," meaning that he refused to believe in unlikely events simply because Peter, Paul, or John seemed to have believed them, and then wrote about them in ancient texts of dubious authenticity.

With so much of his old evangelical Christianity now gone, what, then, was left? Newman discovered that he still found pleasure and profit from reading the Scriptures and hymns of faith, even when he knew they contained errors or sloppy logic. He concluded from this that his "religion always had been, and still was, *a state of sentiment* toward God, far less dependent on articles of a creed, than once I had unhesitatingly believed. The Bible is pervaded by a sentiment, which is implied everywhere.—viz. *the intimate sympathy of the Pure and Perfect God with the heart of each faithful worshipper.*"[27] Newman thus felt himself one with the biblical writers, not as authors of infallible texts requiring uncritical obedience, but as fellow travelers in search of love, hope, and the divine presence. Newman basked in what he considered to be the moral superiority of his reformulated beliefs. He felt freer to love all humankind, including the adherents of other religions, not just the members of his own religious tribe; he felt delivered from the implicit selfishness of living his life solely in anticipation of eternal rewards and punishments; he felt liberated from the disagreeable belief that the imminent return of Christ as taught by the Bible rendered useless "all earthly progress"; and he felt released from the mental authoritarianism of "Bibliolatry," which subjected all questions to the "mere lawyerlike exercise of searching and interpreting my written code." Newman's newfound liberation may have unclogged some of the mental capillaries of his erstwhile dogmatic creed, but a close reading of *Phases of Faith* shows that he was certainly not liberated from a pronounced English chauvinism, an unremitting anti-Catholicism, and a fiercely critical anti-evangelicalism. Not surprisingly, the evangelicals lost no time in scolding their scolder.

Coming on top of the publication of *The Soul* a year earlier, the appearance of *Phases of Faith* in 1850 occasioned almost immediate hostility from all those committed to orthodox Christianity. Articles soon appeared in the *British Quarterly Review* and the *North British Review*, and book length refutations followed from David Walther (*Some Reply to 'Phases of Faith,'* 1851), Newman's old apostolic hero, John Nelson Darby (*The Irrationalism of Infidelity*, 1853), and Henry Rogers (*The Eclipse of Faith; Or, A Visit to a Religious Sceptic*, 1852, and *A Defence of 'The Eclipse of Faith,'* 1854, which went through many editions in both Britain and America).[28] Newman, in turn, issued a modified edition of *Phases of Faith* taking account of his critics in 1853, and again in 1860. The 1853 edition contained two extra chapters: "On the Moral Perfection of Jesus" and "Reply to 'The Eclipse of Faith.'" The former was a particularly hard chapter for evangelicals to forgive, and remains so a century and a half later.[29] Newman, by displaying the kind of hard-nosed literalism he despised in his adversaries, subjected the character of Jesus to a withering moral trial. Almost sensing that he was going too far, he accused the Jesus of the New Testament of bombastic dictatorial wisdom in some of his high-sounding aphorisms, a willful sense of obscurity in his parabolic teaching, unhelpful economic extremism in his teaching about selling all and giving to the poor, and of a destructive martyr complex that could produce nothing else but exasperation on the part of civil and religious leaders. His concluding sentence that "in *consistency* of goodness Jesus fell far below vast numbers of his unhonoured disciples" was an affront equally to orthodox Trinitarians and the more radical Unitarians with whom he usually had more in common. In a later comparison that was bound to sting almost all Victorian readers of whatever religious complexion, he stated that the recent history of Mormonism in America showed that the martyr-death of founders of dubious moral worth was good business for their religious cults.

With the controversy generated by successive editions of *Phases of Faith* at its peak, some of the liberal intelligentsia associated with the *Westminster Review* thought it appropriate to offer Newman some support from his many detractors, and Mary Ann Evans (George Eliot) was asked to become his champion. For reasons that are not entirely clear (she was probably busily at work on *Scenes of Clerical Life*), Evans did not fulfill her commission, but an anonymous article titled "F. W. Newman and his Evangelical Critics" did appear in the *Westminster Review* in October 1858. In a review of ten of Newman's books that were published in the 1850s and of the controversies they engendered, the reviewer concluded that although "Mr. Newman may be often mystical, sometimes inconsistent, occasionally obscure" he was motivated by a genuine intellectual desire to get to the truth, whereas many of his opponents "failed in candour, courtesy, generosity, and conscientiousness." Evangelical attacks on Newman concentrated on his denial of biblical infallibility, his subservience of revelation to reason, and his apparent arrogance in setting himself up as the interpreter of the purposes of God without any traditional authority. For example, Rogers observed sarcastically that "when it was impossible for God *directly* to tell man by external revelation that he could *directly* tell him nothing, *He raised up his servant Newman to perform the office.*"[30] Newman's severest critic was his old friend and mentor, John Nelson Darby, who argued that sinful men could not be judges of the authenticity of biblical revelation. Predictably, Darby, whose dispensational millennialism was rooted in a very particular interpretation of the Apocalypse, was outraged by Newman's observations on the dubious canonicity and poetic wildness of the book of Revelation.

Newman was as stung by the criticism of evangelicals as they were by his apparent apostasy. "To any 'Evangelical,'" he wrote, "I have a right to say that while he has a *single*, I have a *double* experience; and I know, that the spiritual fruits which he values have no connection whatever with the complicated and elaborate creed, which his school imagines, and I once imagined, to be the roots out of which they are fed." He was particularly upset with the evangelical claim that he could never have had "the true" faith or he would never have lost it. In response he alleged that many evangelicals loved their opinions more than the truth, and had little interest in subjecting them to critical scrutiny. He also stated, probably correctly, "that if I had been slain at the age of twenty-seven, when I was chased by a mob of infuriated Mussulmans [in Syria on his way to Baghdad] for selling New Testaments, they would have trumpeted me as an eminent saint and martyr." He concluded with some bitterness that if he had been willing to be more stupid or mentally dishonest, or, revealingly, if he had been shown more kindness by his evangelical friends twenty years earlier, he might still be acknowledged by them as a Christian believer. "To try to disown me now," he concluded, "is an impotent superciliousness."[31] Such was the unhappy end of Newman's relationship with evangelical Protestantism that had so captivated him in his teens and twenties when he encountered Darby's apostolic heroism in the Wicklow Mountains and admired Groves's serene piety in the hell of disaster-stricken Baghdad.

Newman's account of his disenchantment in *Phases of Faith* is at once a personal narrative and a logically insistent diatribe against a Christianity based on infallible authority, dogmatic theology, and a narrow spirit. There is no question that it is animated by disillusionment with his evangelical past, an effect made worse in later editions by the bitter controversies resulting from the publication of his dissident opinions. As in his relations with his Roman Catholic brother, Newman had a regrettable habit of berating those who disagreed with him while still claiming the high moral ground. Those who clung to infallible authorities in Victorian Britain, whether of church, creed, or book, he regarded as not just intellectually reprehensible, but morally flawed. His blunt, sometimes brutal, prose had a way of irritating all around him. His biographer stated that sometimes in reading his books one comes across a statement "flung out almost venomously; and one steps back mentally as if a spiritual hiss had whipped the air from some inimical sentence which had suddenly lifted its heretical head from amongst an otherwise quiet group of words."[32] It was not just the evangelicals who disliked *Phases of Faith*. He managed to offend Anglican bishops, Matthew Arnold and his broad church followers, most neo-orthodox Victorians, and the Unitarians. Once roused to argument there was a driving determination in him to go wherever his mind led him regardless of consequences.

But there was another side to Francis Newman. The more pious Newman who went to Baghdad and back under the influence of Anthony Norris Groves's pamphlet on "Christian Devotedness," or who married a deeply religious woman from a Plymouth Brethren background, did not cease to exist because of his feuds with evangelical or Roman Catholic dogmatists. The best place to start to uncover what lay at the heart of his own religious devotion is with a book that was published the year before *Phases of Faith* and that got somewhat lost in the controversies that engulfed him in the 1850s. *The Soul, Her Sorrows and Her Aspirations: An Essay Towards the Natural History of the Soul, as the True Basis of Theology* (1849) is a rather remarkable attempt to locate and nurture the heart and center of human spirituality. In the preface he writes, "By the Soul we understand that side of human nature upon which we are in contact with the Infinite, and with God, the Infinite Personality: in the Soul therefore alone is it possible to know God; and the correctness of our knowledge must depend eminently on the healthy, active and fully developed condition of our organ."[33]

Newman's book is at once a pathology of the soul, a psychology of religious experience, and an analysis of the state of Christianity in Western Europe. More than that it occasionally reaches heights of almost mystical intensity as Newman's usually methodical prose gives way to rhapsody. He begins by outlining how it is that human beings arrive at knowledge of the infinite. Part historical anthropology and part spiritual reflection, the book looks at the way that human connections with the divine had their roots in awe, wonder, admiration, reverence, appreciation of intelligent design, goodness, and wisdom. But his aim is always to go beyond mere evidences or constructive theology, which he thinks sucks spirituality into the contentious world of cognitive debate, to arrive at a communion, a relationship between the human soul and the Divine Nature. It is at this point that the terms *sin* and *holiness* enter the story, for Newman's God is also the God of our consciences who frowns on all wrongdoing. In a chapter that shows how deeply Newman's evangelical teachers communicated to him a sense of the seriousness of human sinfulness, Newman nevertheless forsakes both Calvinistic notions of total depravity (he prefers the eternal imperfection of every created existence) and forensic theories of Christ's atonement to look at how the soul can be perfected in love. At this point Newman's description of the soul's desire for peace, purity, and guilelessness before God is almost a reproduction of Wesleyan perfectionism, and it is to "that glorious hymn-writer Charles Wesley" that Newman looks for illustration of what he means.

> *Yield to me now, <u>for I am weak,</u>*
> <u>*But confident in self-despair;*</u>
> *Speak to my heart, in blessings speak;*
> *Be conquer'd by my instant pray'r*
> *Speak,—or Thou never hence shalt move,—*
> *And tell me, if thy name be Love.*

And again:

> *'Tis Love! 'Tis Love! Thou died'st for me:*
> *I hear Thy whisper in my heart:*
> *The morning breaks; the shadows flee:*

Pure, Universal Love Thou art.
To me, to all, thy bowels move:
Thy nature and thy name is Love.

My pray'r hath pow'r with God! The grace
Unspeakable I now receive:
Through Faith I see Thee face to face,
<u>*I see Thee face to face,—and live!*</u>
In vain I have not wept and strove;
Thy nature and Thy name is Love.[34]

Newman also resonated with the Arminian inclusiveness of Wesley's words, for as surely as God loves one soul, he loves all, not just the elect. He was also impatient with Victorian Christianity's capacity to invent sins that were no sins, such as trivial breaches of Sabbatarian codes, or placing more emphasis on explosive sins of passion than on the "mean and griping conduct" that stems from remorseless self-interest, which more clearly indicates that a man has no stamp of the "Infinite Spirit" upon him.

Part III of *The Soul*, on the "Sense of Personal Relation to God," is where Newman flies into the kind of rhapsody that would not be out of place in the Moravian piety of the eighteenth century. Distinguishing between masculine and feminine piety, he concludes that "women come more easily to pure religion than men," and parallels the soul's love for God with that of a wife for a husband. He gives the soul a female gender, which gives him permission to move into ecstatic descriptions of the relationship between God and the soul, transcending the prosaic rationalism that was Newman's normal style. One passage in particular is worth quoting at length for what it reveals about the way Newman thought an awakened soul, suffused with feminine tenderness and childlike delight, could transform the rational mind.

> The Soul understands and knows that God is *her* [the italics are his] God; dwelling with her more closely than any creature can.; yea, neither Stars nor Sea, nor smiling Nature can hold God so intimately as the bosom of the Soul. What is He to it? What, but the Soul of the soul? It no longer seems profane to say, "God is my bosom friend: God is for me, and I am for Him." So Joy bursts out into Praise, and all things look brilliant; and hardship seems easy, and duty becomes delight, and contempt is not felt, and every morsel of bread is sweet. Then, though we know that the physical Universe has fixed unfaltering laws, *we cannot help* seeing God's hands in events. Whatever happens, we think of as his Mercies, his Kindnesses;

or his Visitations and his Chastisements; everything comes to us from his Love:—and this may be very illogical, (and *possibly* may be a mere illusion), yet we should do such violence to the soul's instinct in *not* thus thinking, that we follow it unreasoningly, and leave others to reconcile the paradox. Thus the whole world is fresh to us with sweetness before untasted. All things are ours, whether affliction or pleasure, health or pain. Old things are passed away; behold! all things are become new; and the soul wonders, and admires, and gives thanks, and exults like the child on a summer's day;—and understands, that she *is* as a newborn child: she has undergone a New Birth![35]

Here is unalloyed pietism, and pietism almost collapses into Wesleyan perfectionism when Newman aspires to a spiritual state in which the soul, even when afflicted with coldness and negligence, spins back to love so swiftly that sin scarcely has time to reign. "This seems to be the state," he writes, "which the Wesleyans (to the scandal of other Christians) have denominated Perfection or Full Redemption, and after which they breathe in many beautiful and touching hymns."[36]

At this point readers are entitled to ask how the Newman of *The Soul*, with all its spiritual passion and noble aspiration, can be reconciled with the Newman of *Phases of Faith*, with its iron skeptical logic and controversial spirit. It would be easy to conclude that these are the dialectical polarities of Newman's personality with which he struggled all his life—and there would be some truth in that—but that would not be a sufficient explanation. Tucked between passages of high spiritual elevation in *The Soul*, there are also passages condemning the mean-spirited dogmatism of much Victorian religion, especially of its evangelical species. In the midst of purple patches about divine love, for example, Newman bristles at those who talk earnestly about such love while effectively believing in a creed that condemns great swaths of the world's population to everlasting punishment. With more than a hint of truth he concluded that the meanest doctrines of orthodox Christianity were brought out only now and again by those who held them "to do mischief in controversy," but that most of the time they lay "buried in dust in a corner of the intellect: it would therefore be unjust to impute to individuals the selfishness inherent in their theoretic creed."[37] He thus exonerates evangelicals from the worst excesses of their own doctrines, while condemning them for only half thinking about the moral implications of their formal beliefs.

The respective poles of Newman's religious sensibilities as expressed in *The Soul* and *Phases of Faith* are brought closer together in the final chapter of

The Soul, titled "Prospects of Christianity," which is really an extended essay on the nature of Christianity, past, present, and future. Anticipating the debates of secularization theorists, Newman's starting point is that while Christianity was making rapid strides through imperial power and missionary penetration in many parts of the world, it was, especially in urban populations, effectively dying in its old heartlands of Western Europe. He predicts that "a real black infidelity will spread among the millions . . . until the large towns of England become what Paris is," while intellectual elites will become spiritually dead Pantheists. According to Newman, a pincer movement of intellectual and popular infidelity would condemn Christianity to a minority creed in Europe, at the same time as it became apparent that it could make no gains among Muslims and Hindus in India and Arabia. This prescient prediction was based on his conviction that modern Christianity was enslaved to what are called "Christian Evidences," namely an attempt to construct absolute authorities at the expense of authentic spirituality. Chief among his targets was the belief in the "Mechanical Inspiration" of an infallible Bible, which he thought delivered Christianity inexorably into the hands of textual critics, whether learned or unlearned. Similarly, by organizing irrational doctrines, such as the Trinity, into a dogmatic and systematic theology, orthodox Christians either damaged the intellect or occasioned needless controversy, or both. Once again displaying his enthusiasm for the early church and its spiritual priorities, Newman states that the Apostles who spread Christianity did not have to defend a sacred text, nor polytheistic doctrine, but rather preached the teachings of Jesus to the souls of humanity. Tying Christianity to existential evidences and propositional proofs, he argues, was forever to condemn it to unprofitable wrestling with advancing knowledge, which is why evangelicals were so pathologically scared of the mind.

While his brother, John Henry Newman, tried to protect the heart of Christianity from encroaching liberalism by appealing to Church, tradition, and the communion of saints, Francis Newman, displaying his evangelical and pietistic roots, chose instead to rely on faith, spirit, and the communion of the soul. He had become convinced from his failed mission to Muslim Baghdad, from his dabbling in German higher criticism of the Bible, and from his observations of the manifold hypocrisies of Victorian Christianity, that a Christianity which tried to convert people by a rational appeal to evidence was doomed to failure from its own irrationality. He wrote, "It is *absolutely impossible* to recover the tens of thousands who have learned to scorn Christian faith, by arguments of erudition and criticism. Unless the appeal can be made to the Conscience and the Soul, faith in Christianity once lost by the vulgar is lost forever."[38] Only by rendering to the mind the things that belong to the mind and to the soul the things of the soul did Newman think that Christianity had any chance of surviving the onslaught of European secularization. Although he comes close to it on occasions, Newman was advocating not that authentic Christian spirituality was at war with the insights of the mind, for they too had to be nurtured in their proper place, but rather that spirituality could not be cultivated by an appeal to "evidences" of ancient events or by belief in mere doctrinal propositions. To rest the heart of Christianity on the interpretation of scantily recorded past events, or on assertions that future advances of knowledge might contradict, was according to Newman a recipe for intellectual fear and endless controversy.

Failing to listen to his diagnosis of where Christianity was headed, Newman believed, would lead to a string of disastrous consequences: the claims of science would be pitted against those of religion, with the former inevitably winning out; theological colleges would teach their recruits to reduce religion to mere logic and literary analysis, thereby further diminishing the spirituality of Christian ministers; and what was left of religion would descend to little more than "black superstition" or a futile war against the advance of new knowledge. By contrast, Newman offers a vision of Christianity's future that is almost Hebraic in its moral grandeur, Wesleyan in its perfectionist theology, Plymouth Brethren in its dispensational millennialism, and pietistic in its contempt for the inanities of formal religion. In a great concluding peroration of the soul Newman asks:

> Do you belief in Sanctification of the Spirit by Peace with God? in the New Birth of the Soul by believing in God? in the free Grace of Him who loved us before we loved Him? in justification of the sinner, in the midst of his sins, by simple Faith in God? in the permanent Union of the believing Soul with God? what know you of the love of God shed abroad in the heart by the Spirit, and of the Hope, that makes not ashamed, thence arising? Or of man's insight into the heart of God, when he has received somewhat of that Spirit which searcheth even the deep things of God? of a Faith that overcomes the World? of a Spirit that guides by a higher rule than Law? Such sentiments and experiences (not propositions) are the true heart of Christianity.[39]

Belief in such a vision of Christianity, according to Newman, would tear down the dividing walls between Christians, Jews, Muslims, and Hindus, rescue English Christianity from its pernicious devotion to the "mechanical Inspiration" of the Bible and the "mechanical consecration" of Bishops, and end the futile search for a suitable authority to pontificate on matters of religious truth. Newman's almost apocalyptic vision of God's spiritual kingdom is not composed of "meat and drink, nor sermons and Sabbaths, nor history and exegesis, nor a belief in the infallibility of any book, nor in the supernatural memory of any man; but it is, as Paul says, righteousness and peace and joy in the Holy Spirit."[40] In this way Newman not only slew the dragons of his evangelical past, but also anticipated the future of religion as defined by spirituality and not by creed, dogma, or tradition. Notwithstanding the survival of denominational labels and theological traditions, many millions of American and European Christians, both consciously and unconsciously, are closer descendants of the kind of spirituality advocated by Francis Newman than they realize.

Although the publication of *The Soul* was greeted by John Henry Newman (who seems not to have read it) and many other churchmen with dismay, it was read and admired by a distinguished cross section of the Victorian liberal intelligentsia including Mary Ann Evans, Frederic Harrison, George Jacob Holyoake, and William Makepeace Thackeray. It was also the subject of conversation at the first meeting of Elizabeth Gaskell and Charlotte Brontë.[41] Together with *Phases of Faith* published a year later, *The Soul* established Newman's reputation as a freethinker with a nevertheless firm commitment to moral theism and spirituality. Although Newman lived for forty-five years after the publication of *The Soul* and *Phases of Faith,* and although he devoted much more ink to the consideration of religious topics, these two works and their attendant consequences are somehow the fulcrum of his life, for they mark the definitive end of the evangelicalism of his youth and the rise of his career as a crusader for manifold social causes. Maisie Ward's famous put-down in her biography of John Henry Newman that Francis "seems to have filled the place of faith with a number of fads" has unduly colored this phase of Newman's life.[42] So too has Mary Ann Evans's more sympathetic but still rather disparaging comment in 1874: "Poor Mr. Francis Newman must be aged now and rather weary of the world and explanations of the world. He can hardly be expected to take in much novelty. I have a sort of affectionate sadness in thinking of the interest which in far-off days I felt in his 'Soul' and *Phases of Faith,* and of the awe I had of him as a lecturer on mathematics at the Ladies' College. How much work he has done in the world, which has left no deep, conspicuous mark, but has probably entered beneficently into many lives." Yet more generously, Basil Willey has observed that "Newman had, what is not unusual to censure in other Victorians, a highly developed social conscience—the last phase, no doubt in the evolution of an escaped evangelical."[43]

The sheer range of Newman's social pursuits, which he fitted around his career as an educator (he was Latin professor in University College London from 1846 to 1863), writer, and public intellectual, is impressive. Many of Newman's passions were organized into opposition to what he considered were the four barbarisms of civilization, namely war, the penal system, the degradation of man (primarily by drink), and cruelty to animals. Newman kept up a lively interest in British foreign and imperial policy, the progress of liberal movements in Europe, temperance reform, and antivivisection. He was an advocate for women's suffrage, administrative decentralization, land reform to benefit small farmers and landless laborers, vegetarianism (which he practiced), university reform, public health, and the abolition of slavery. He took a keen interest in the history of the United States, opposing slavery, defending the North during the Civil War, which was not an altogether popular position in Victorian England, and dreaming of educating freed slaves and their children to be good citizens. He spoke on public platforms, lent his name to worthy causes, and wrote assiduously on a truly remarkable range of issues from political economy to the rise of modern science. His multivolume collection of *Miscellanies* shows a restless, diverse, quirky, and deeply humane intelligence always probing at the roots of ignorance and injustice.[44] As measured by the unforgiving standard of hindsight, Newman was not always correct in his passions, for example in his misjudged writings against compulsory vaccination, but in general he took the side of the poor, the weak, and the unjustly treated. To describe him as cranky and faddish, partly on account of his unconventional attire and strange behavior at social gatherings, is to diminish a great deal of productive effort on a wide variety of fronts. It is also misleading to regard Newman the social crusader as having little to do with Newman the moral theist, for most of his passions grew from his spiritual roots and marked him out as a Victorian prophet, "for like the Hebrew Prophets, he made his life a symbol of his belief in justice."[45] In one of his last published works, Newman, in wrestling with the tricky problem of immortality, supplied one of his clearest statements in favor of a life lived for noble causes. He stated that those who believed that this world was bound for "fiery destruction" because of its intrinsic evil of necessity regard labor for its improvement useless. "Its evil state being inevitable, he not only will not himself struggle for any fundamental change, but will use all his moral and religious influence to induce oppressed classes and nations to submit quietly to outrageous injustice from pretentious authority, under the belief that 'in another world' all will be set right. How very unimportant is the 'the world which passes away.'" Newman, as this statement reveals, was as much a meliorist as a moralist.[46]

Newman's moral earnestness and zeal for social justice also grew out of his youthful evangelicalism, when, under the influence of Darby and Groves, he dreamed of transforming the world into the image of the primitive Christian church. After the controversies provoked by *The Soul* and *Phases of Faith* in the 1850s there is no evidence that Newman ever regretted his decision to sever his connections with the evangelicals who had once inspired him. Indeed, most of his later reflections on evangelicalism express regret about the influence the movement had on him. Of the six years he spent with his new bride in the beautiful scenery of Clifton from 1834 to 1840 Newman later reflected that he had spent too much time in theological reflection to the neglect of the tranquil enjoyment of nature. "I had started from the Puritan idea that it was all under the curse, & enjoyment of scenery was not quite the thing for one 'redeemed *out of* an evil world &c &c.' The waste of time & effort in my whole youth by unprofitable and false theory sometimes appears to me lamentable, and the only advantage is, that I understand & can sympathize with the victims of this theology."[47] In a similar vein, soon after the publication of John Henry Newman's *Apologia pro Vita Sua* (1864), Francis, in one of his many faltering and unsuccessful attempts to patch up his tortuous relationship with his older brother, wrote, "In early years the doctrine of the Evang.s concerning spiritual teaching produced in me the same crude fruit as I daily meet in young persons, who say to me almost in so many words, '*I* have the Spirit of God, & *you* have not.' There is no conscious personal conceit in this, any more than in one who dogmatizes resting on his Church; but the effect of it is more offensive. I know I had plenty in me of this."[48]

Not all evangelicals gave up on the attempt to restore Francis Newman to his "first love," and it is in response to one such attempt that the mature-aged Newman wrote one of his clearest denunciations of evangelical ethics and theology. Partly stung by the idea that he would recant of his skepticism when death approached, Newman repeated his belief in a good and wise God in whose presence he was pleased to dwell. By contrast he had no wish to commune with the evangelical's God of original sin, eternal punishment, and blood sacrifice. He thought these doctrines so morally monstrous that no sane person could believe them unless under a burden to do so by some a priori commitment to the infallibility of a sacred text. Although he repeated his standard arguments about the "self-contradictory, foolish, and barbaric" character of the biblical narratives, there seems little doubt from this and his other writings that Newman's revolt against evangelicalism was primarily on moral grounds. The essence of his reply to his evangelical correspondent was that he could not engage in a serious theological discourse with anyone who simply argued from an infallible text, and that no amount of scriptural quotations could persuade him of the morality of ideas he found fundamentally immoral. "I hold morality to be far more important than theology," he wrote, "earlier in knowledge and more solid in foundation. Babes in science may judge soundly of morality, and by it confute the high pretensions of cursing theologies."[49]

As Newman looked back on his life he came to see that even in his evangelical phase the skeptical future predicted for him by his brother had some validity, and had something to do with the intrinsic nature of evangelicalism. He wrote to Moncure Conway, whose own pilgrimage from Methodist circuit rider to Harvard-educated transcendentalist, loosely paralleled Newman's own faith journey, "I was an Evangelical, but like plenty of Evangelicals beside, both now and then, was resolved to follow the Truth whithersoever it led me; and was always indignant when told 'you must believe this or that,' or you will find it 'will lead you further.' 'If that time comes, I shall go further' was my uniform reply. It was this spirit which led so many of the best brains among the Evangelicals to go further and to secede from the party."[50]

Newman's inexorable quest for the truth certainly explains much of his faith journey, but there are also deeply personal factors at work. Newman's early evangelical phase was largely promoted by the influence of others on his life: his mother; his classics master, the Rev. Walter Mayers; his Irish circle of religious enthusiasts clustered around John Nelson Darby; and his admiration for Anthony Norris Groves. Unquestionably the missionary trek to Baghdad was a shock to Newman. Newman's encounter with Muslim culture in the Ottoman Empire simply blew away his millennial optimism about the future of Christianity in the world order. According to his own record, of even more importance in his disillusionment with evangelicalism was the trail of vituperation he encountered on his return, when his unconventional views on the Trinity became known to his erstwhile co-religionists.[51] Newman was shocked by the antagonism of the "saintly" Brethren, especially Darby, who then repeated the dose after the publication of Newman's *Phases of Faith*. Newman was not treated thus by all the Plymouth Brethren. His wife, whom he adored to the last, was universally admired for her unaffected goodness, and, although the evidence is not conclusive, Newman and Groves seem to have maintained a cordial relationship based on mutual respect.[52]

What Groves made of *Phases of Faith* is not recorded, but somehow

Newman's wife was able to accept his life of skepticism without losing affection for him. As the one genuinely good thing to come out of his evangelical phase, Newman was always thankful for Maria's life, and was devastated by her death. "My dear one lived in a joyful sense of God's presence: she was always saintly without any sanctimoniousness; she was ever alive to human suffering & tenderly sympathized with the afflicted. Towards me she kept a perpetual honeymoon, loving me with the tender ardour of a young girl, & filled with delight at my return every time I entered the house."[53]

Where, then, did Newman end up in his pilgrimage of faith? The record here is somewhat muddied by the statement made by his first biographer, I. Giberne Sieveking, that Newman returned to his earlier faith in Christianity a few years before his death. This opinion was based on her interpretation of some of his last letters along with the recollections of James Martineau, Anna Swanwick, and the Rev. Temperley Grey, who attended Newman during his final illness and spoke at his funeral. Basil Willey, surveying the same evidence, regards Sieveking's opinion as the wishful thinking of a pious Victorian, and that Newman never departed from his settled convictions as a moral theist with an enduring affection for some of the biblical texts. He came to believe that "adoration of God is the universal and final religion," that could unite all the great world religions and end sectarian discord. He wrote similarly to Mrs. Kingsley near the end of his life: "I suppose I must say, 'Alas!' that the older I become [81 last June] the more painfully my creed outgrows the limits of that which the mass of my nation, and those whose co-operation I most covet, account sacred. I dare not (unasked) send to friends what I print, yet I uphold the sacred moralities of Jew and Christian [Hindoo and Moslem] with all my heart. Two mottos, or say three, suffice me:—The Lord reigneth. The righteous Lord loveth righteousness. The Lord requireth Justice, Mercy, and Sobriety of thought, not ceremony or creed."[54]

Newman also expressed his devotion to the Lord's Prayer as the highest and purest of any religion. The most recent biographical treatment of Newman, which has access to some new material, concludes that Newman at the end regarded himself as a Hebrew Christian, and that his fondness for the Lord's Prayer was partly owing to the fact that it contained no messianic claims and no promise of immortality, neither of which Newman could accept.[55] The Lord's Prayer's demonstration of a connection between God and the praying soul, and its expressed desire for God's kingdom on earth, for forgiveness, and for daily bread were at the heart and center of Newman's creed for most of his life. Moreover, there is no evidence that Newman either feared death or was forced to recalibrate his opinions to face it. If anything, Newman's calm acceptance of the death of his wife, most of his family, and many of his friends—the unfortunate consequence of a long life—speaks to the relative lack of tension within him, rather than the reverse.

Newman never did return to the evangelicalism of his youth. Unable to accept the mechanical inspiration of the Bible, morally outraged by some of the doctrines of orthodox Christianity, unimpressed by the moral character of Jesus, and scarred by the way he was treated by his evangelical friends, Newman nevertheless clung passionately to his belief in God and the moral consequences that flowed from it. He was as opposed to atheism, deism, and Roman Catholicism as he was to evangelicalism, but it was the evangelicals who disappointed his expectations, spoiled his youth, and singed his soul. These are not easy things to forgive or forget.

4 Theodore Dwight Weld—The American Century
Evangelicalism and Reform

The terrors of God! The faintest gleam of them smites men with trembling or maddens with frenzy. Oh then whose heart can endure, whose hands be strong when the breath of God sets the Universe on fire and a million worlds burn down at once! My brother I cant [sic] resist the conviction that this terrible rebuke is but a single herald sent in advance to announce the coming of a host. The Land is full of blood. . . . What can save us as a nation but repentance— immediate, profound, public, proclaimed abroad, wide as our infamy and damning guilt have gone!

—Theodore Dwight Weld to Lewis Tappan (1835), on the occasion of the great fire of New York and linking it to the national blight of slavery

Although his personal journey from evangelical firebrand to humanistic firebrand to passive observer was unique, Theodore Dwight Weld's life intersected with many of the most important religious currents of nineteenth-century America.[1] Born in the same year that Napoleon ceded the Louisiana territory to the United States, Weld, the last of the great antislavery patriarchs of the 1830s, died in 1895. Weld, who came from a long line of New England Puritan clergymen, was converted to evangelical Christianity in 1826 at a re-

Theodore Dwight Weld (1803–1895), by Linus Yale. Pencil on gray paper (© The Connecticut Historical Society, Hartford, Connecticut)

vival led by Charles Finney in upstate New York. He died almost seventy years later a member of the Hyde Park Unitarian Society in Boston. In the years between he was an evangelical revivalist, a pioneering abolitionist, a temperance reformer, an advocate of women's rights, a tireless educator, and a writer and orator of far-reaching influence. Along the way he and his wife, Angelina Grimké, the Quaker abolitionist and women's rights activist, dabbled in manual labor educational schemes, flirted with phrenology, followed Sylvester Graham's dietary system, were briefly attracted to Millerite millennialism, and explored Spiritualism through the work of the "Poughkeepsie Seer," Andrew Jackson Davis. In short, there is scarcely a nineteenth-century American religious or reforming tradition that bypassed the Weld–Grimké dynasty.

Weld was raised in a conventional New England home. His father, Ludovicus Weld, was a Harvard-trained Congregational minister in Hampton, Connecticut, and his mother, judging by later letters, was piously solicitous of Theodore's faith and eternal destiny.[2] Beneath the surface of tranquil orthodoxy, however, other forces were stirring, both within and outside the Weld household. Not only did Theodore have a difficult and tempestuous relationship with his father, but also his father's brand of Calvinistic Congregationalism was itself being eroded by the rise of Unitarianism on the one hand and the growth of democratic evangelical denominations on the other. While his father railed against religious enthusiasts and their democratic tendencies, those very tendencies helped secure the disestablishment of Connecticut's Congregational Church in 1818, the year before Theodore set out for Andover to begin his own ministerial preparation. His health collapsed under the pressure of his studies, and he soon embarked on another career as an itinerant mnemonics (the art and science of memory) lecturer. Although he was still only a teenager, Weld's stint as a wandering troubadour for the cause of memory helped break the ties to his father's ancien régime orthodoxy, helped nurture formidable powers of oratory, and exposed him to a rapidly expanding country beyond the white steeples of New England. By the time he returned home in 1824 his father's ministry in Hampton had all but collapsed, and the family had moved to upstate New York. It was an area experiencing rapid demographic, economic, and religious change, symbolized by the opening of the Erie Canal and the arrival of Finney's "New Measures" revivalism.

In this burnt-over district two personal encounters significantly shaped Weld's religious pilgrimage. The first was with a family friend and local schoolmaster, Charles Stuart, the Jamaican born son of a British army officer. Stuart had served with the army of the British East India Company before migrating to Canada and then to Utica, New York. A pious evangelical who later championed the characteristic causes of antislavery, temperance, and Sabbatarianism in England, Stuart struck up an unlikely friendship with Weld. Friendship is perhaps an understatement. Their effusive letters reveal a passionate, devoted love of unusual intensity, except it was rooted more in evangelical pietism than in sexual attraction.[3] It would not require too much psychological imagination to see in the relationship something of the male affirmation that Weld had conspicuously lacked in his own upbringing. The second encounter, equally dramatic, was with Charles Finney, whose methods and style Weld had initially abhorred, but who later became his "father in the gospel" as a result of a powerful conversion experience instigated by Finney's preaching. Weld, who was inveigled into attending one of Finney's meetings by a scheming aunt, first repudiated the evangelist, then became reconciled, and then experienced one of those long dark nights of the soul that resulted in an exemplary religious conversion. After his conversion Weld became one of Finney's most trusted lieutenants in spreading revivalism in upstate New York in the later 1820s.

With two new mentors guiding his spiritual development, Weld threw himself into his gospel labors with a characteristic wild intensity, sometimes to the detriment of his health. In these years two other characteristics of Weld's life soon became apparent. The first was a desire to usher in a new millennium of righteousness, not only by preaching the gospel, but also by preaching an eclectic and wide-ranging message of personal and social reform. He enrolled at Oneida Academy and vigorously pursued a program of hard manual labor, serious study, and earnest service of a multitude of evangelical causes. The Oneida boys, with Weld the acknowledged leader, were millennial storm troopers out to save the infant republic from moribund orthodoxy and moral laxity. Weld farmed the land, studied composition, delivered lectures, organized temperance societies, promoted Sabbatarianism, and exercised general moral oversight. He also built up connections with an emerging evangelical leadership including the Tappan brothers, the New York merchants who bankrolled many of the reforming causes arising out of Finney's revivals.

A second characteristic of Weld's to emerge in these years was a persistent withering dissatisfaction with the limited achievements of religious and moral reform in changing the habits and character of the nation. He subjected everything, even the state of his own soul, to a ruthless examination by the highest standards. Even Finney, who sometimes reported revivalistic news to Weld in a lighthearted fashion, was not spared. On receiving a letter from Finney on the progress of revival in Philadelphia, Weld replied with what amounted to a full-scale spiritual inquisition. He asked Finney how much progress he had made toward the ideal of Christian perfection, castigated him for neglecting personal holiness, and openly criticized him for his attitude to revivals: "*revivals* have become with you matters of such every day commonness as scarcely to throw over you the least tinge of solemnity. I fear they are fast becoming with you a sort of trade, to be worked at so many hours every day and then laid aside. Dear brother do you not find yourself running into *formality*, a round of formality in the management of revivals? I mean of feeling. The machinery moves on, every wheel and spring and chord in its place; but isn't the *main spring* waxing weaker? There has been in your letters a strain of light sarcastic remark . . . oh! Dip not your pen in the gall of sarcasm, but dip it [in] tears and write with a trembling hand and a soul of sorrow."[4]

Later in the same letter Weld excoriated himself for his "wicked asperity of feeling" in his partisan defense of Finney's methods against the criticisms of East Coast Calvinists like Asahel Nettleton and Lyman Beecher, and concluded ruefully that too many of the converts of Finney's revivals rushed back "tumultuously to the beggarly elements of this world." Declaiming Finney's "New Measures" revivals as commercially managed, routinely produced, and temporary in their effects were allegations Finney had come to expect from his opponents, but not from one of his closest friends.

A man unwilling to spare either himself or his "father in the gospel" from such critical scrutiny was unlikely ever to be satisfied with the broader national condition. In 1831, with the Oneida Academy in disarray, Weld accepted Lewis Tappan's invitation to become the general agent of the Society for the Promotion of Manual Labor in Literary Institutions, which involved going on the stump to spread the gospel of manual labor and secure a site for a new model seminary. Although the idea of manual labor seemed superficially otiose, the campaign to introduce it into the curriculum was based on a number of premises: it would make America a less divided society by encouraging "republican equality"; it would promote much-needed discipline and self-control among young men; and it would help young academic women to become less cerebral and more physically robust. Weld traversed huge distances itinerating for the cause, and in the process he nearly lost his life. Weld, by all accounts, not just his own, came perilously close to drowning when his stagecoach was swept away while crossing a swollen river in Ohio. His harrowing, but pious, account of the incident was later published by the American Tract Society and soon became a little evangelistic classic. Physically exhausted, with no hope of rescue, and convinced that he was going to die, Weld later wrote, "I was free from all pain; my whole body totally insensible, and yet as by miracle I seemed to have the most perfect possession of my mind. Then, oh! Then, I felt it in my soul that the religion of the Bible is the religion to die by. Oh! What would have been the horrors of that hour without a hope in Jesus! Not merely to die,—but to die alone, far in a strange land in a wilderness, at midnight,—to die a drowning death—to die without hope. Oh! It would have torn my soul asunder. . . . Oh! If I had possessed more religion, if I had not been such a meager starveling in piety, I should have shouted in triumph, 'Oh! Death,' even such a death, 'Where is thy sting?'"[5] Weld's much-publicized providential deliverance from death in the western wilderness of the new republic added fresh luster to his growing credentials within the evangelical community. Within a year of his close encounter with death he devoted himself to the defining cause of his life, the abolition of slavery within the United States.

Weld's commitment to the antislavery cause arose from a variety of sources including childhood experiences, firsthand observations from his travels, the influence of Charles Stuart (who had become active in the British antislavery movement), his own deeply developed sense of moral blight in the dark corners of American society, and the perceived parallel between spiritual and physical bondage evident in the thought of many nineteenth-century evangelicals.[6] How could those who experienced spiritual liberation go on to endorse physical bondage? As was common among antislavery activists in the early 1830s, Weld initially embraced the idea of colonization, that is, of shipping African Americans back to Africa, but in 1832, after an encounter with a group influenced by the ideas of William Lloyd Garrison, he became an enthusiastic Garrisonian abolitionist. In a letter to Garrison Weld expressed his newfound convictions with characteristic ardor.

> . . . *nothing but crime can forfeit liberty.* That no condition of birth, no shade of color, no mere misfortune of circumstances, can annul that birth-right charter, which God has bequeathed to every being upon whom he has stamped his own image, by making him *a free moral agent,* and that he who robs his fellow man of this tramples upon right, subverts justice, outrages humanity, unsettles the foundations of human safety, and sacrilegiously assumes the prerogative of God; and further, tho' he who retains by force, and refuses to surrender that which was originally obtained by violence or fraud, is joint partner in the original sin, becomes its apologist and makes it the business of every moment to perpetrate it afresh, however he may lull his conscience by the vain plea of expediency or necessity.[7]

There could hardly be a clearer expression of the religious argument against slavery.

Clarity was one thing, unanimity on the issue of slavery was quite another. Weld's vigorous advocacy of abolitionism split open the fragile unity of the Lane Seminary in Cincinnati, where Weld had migrated with many other old Oneida boys to embrace the gospel of manual labor and theological study as preparation for millennial ministry. Viewing the American West as the chosen location, and slavery as the decisive issue, Weld's letters are full of references to the millennium and millennial hope.[8] At this stage Weld was not preoccupied by the kind of prophetical speculation, dispensational chart making, and detailed date spotting that William Miller publicized in the 1830s and '40s, but rather he viewed the United States, and the West in particular, as a providential opportunity to bring in the values of the millennial kingdom. The pernicious obstacle standing in the way was not so much infidelity as it was the great moral blight of human slavery. When the editor of the *Western Monthly Magazine* castigated Weld for introducing political controversy and party spirit into Lane Seminary, Weld mounted a classic defense of the place of social ethics in the theological curriculum, ending with the ringing declaration that "Slavery, in this land of liberty, and light, and revivals of millennial glory—its days are numbered and well-nigh finished. Would to God that they were not the daily enacted horrors of living reality—the legitimate fruits of a system authorized by Law, patronized and protected by republican institutions, sanctioned by public sentiment, and sanctified by religion."[9]

As befitted a crusader for a pure millennial kingdom, Weld's abolitionism was not sufficient in itself but was also the precondition for a more general restitution of black humanity. He worked energetically to turn Cincinnati's black population of some three thousand, three quarters of whom had already secured their freedom, into a model community. He started day, evening, and Sabbath schools; formed Bible classes; and visited African American families who were trying to buy their own children. So harrowing were some of these stories that Weld told Lewis Tappan he "was forced to stop from sheer heart-ache and agony." He later wrote Tappan that, during his eighteen-month residence at Lane Seminary, "my intercourse was with the Colored people of Cincinnati I think I may say *exclusively*. If I ate in the City it was at *their* tables. If I slept in the City it was at their homes. If I attended parties, it was *theirs—weddings—theirs—Funerals—theirs—Religious meetings theirs—*Sabbath schools—Bible classes—theirs."[10] Given the amount of self-criticism that shows up in Weld's correspondence, and his propensity to shun some of the publicity and honors others coveted, there is no reason to doubt Weld's claims about how he spent his time in Cincinnati, or indeed later in

New York City, where he followed similar principles of engagement with the African American community.

Weld's fierce devotion to abolitionism and African American rights, and his ability to carry many of the Lane students with him, led inexorably to a collision with the seminary's trustees and faculty. So profound were the issues at stake that Lyman Beecher's attempt as president to mediate between offended parties stood little chance of success. The majority of the Lane rebels moved on to Oberlin, and Weld once again became an itinerant evangelist, this time preaching the gospel of abolition. The gospel metaphor is not inappropriate, for Weld built into his antislavery preaching many of the revival techniques pioneered by Finney. In the same way as Finney-inspired revivalists considered the established religious denominations to be characterized by religious coldness and indifference, Weld regarded their preference of colonization over abolition as further evidence of their spiritual mediocrity. Even as a roving agent of the American Anti-Slavery Society, Weld was a difficult man to tame, sometimes refusing to cooperate with headquarters over supplying tasty experiences with which to tug the purse strings of abolitionist supporters. Weld, partly out of modesty, partly out of fierce integrity, and partly out of crass indifference to institutional realities, was not a man to bow the knee to organizational pressure of whatever kind. As prophet, pietist, and puritan, Weld, despite his New England roots, often portrayed himself as a western backwoodsman ill at ease with refined folk in the great eastern seaboard cities.[11] He saw himself more as John the Baptist than as Apostle Paul.

While Weld was at the peak of his powers as the abolitionist "thunderer of the west," his life underwent significant changes. First he encountered traumatic opposition to his message in Troy from the very westerners he had courted, then, whether from physical or psychological causes, he lost his booming public voice and never again became a commanding orator, and then he relocated back to his native Connecticut. Perhaps most significantly of all, he began slowly to part company from the group of evangelical activists who had helped sustain his millennial commitment to the cause of reform. The most serious breach was with Finney and was over the respective priorities of gospel proclamation and reformist zeal in transforming the nation. The issue first surfaced in a letter from Lewis Tappan to Weld, criticizing Finney for cowardice in his tepid support for abolition. Although Weld defended his friend and mentor, he wrote Tappan, "The truth is Finney has always been in revivals of religion. It is his great business, aim and *absorbing passion* to promote them. He has never had hardly anything to do with Bible,

Tract, Missionary, Education, Temperance, moral reform and anti slavery." Although at this stage Weld advocated a cheerful pluralism of gifts and tasks all leading to the same destination, the issue of priority did not go away. In part Weld would not allow it. He regarded the sin of slavery as "omnipresent," defiling everything. "It is my deliberate conviction," he wrote, "that revivals, moral Reform, etc., etc., must and [will] remain nearly stationary until the Temple is cleansed."[12]

Finney drove the debate from the other side. He became convinced that the inevitable end of abolitionism, as agitated by Weld and his hothead supporters, would be civil war and military despotism. "Unless the publick mind can be engrossed with the subject of salvation and make abolition an appendage, just as we made temperance an appendage of the revival in Rochester," Finney predicted a bloodbath of unprecedented proportions. This ideological and emotional tug of war between Finney and Weld was played out in the hearts and minds of the Oberlin students whose allegiance was up for grabs.[13]

In the years 1835–37 Weld moved from the West to the East, from being primarily an orator to being a writer, from spending most of his time in company to spending more time alone, and from absorption in the great moral reform of the nation to a serious interest in diet, bodily discipline, and phrenology. Discouraged by the moral mediocrity of the churches, the nation, and even some of his old friends, Weld turned inward, not like his brother in a Wesleyan quest for holiness and perfectionism, but toward control of body, mind, and spirit. If these changes should not be minimized neither should they be inflated, for Weld had been for long an exponent of physical discipline, and he by no means abandoned his passionate commitment to the abolition of slavery. His various passions conflated when he met and married Angelina Grimké, the antislavery daughter of a South Carolina slave-owner who had traveled denominationally from Episcopalianism, through Presbyterianism into Quakerism, and who advocated women's rights with the same fervor as she did her opposition to slavery. Together, Theodore and Angelina, along with her sister Sarah, formed one of the most potent reforming dynasties of the nineteenth century.[14]

The courtship letters and early marriage discussions of Theodore and Angelina are remarkably revealing documents, not only of themselves but also of religious sensibilities and personal identity in antebellum America, but they are beyond our immediate scope. Suffice to say that although marriage and home building eroded some of the time the couple could devote to reforming causes (especially Angelina), a shared passion for antislavery burned on. It reached its apogee in their collaborative work, *American Slavery As It Is: Testimony of a Thousand Witnesses*. Next to Harriet Beecher Stowe's *Uncle Tom's Cabin*, this was the most widely circulated and influential antislavery publication of the nineteenth century. It was based on a simple idea. Weld and the Grimké sisters simply collected firsthand accounts of the cruelties of slavery from thousands of Southern newspapers. As such, it marked a shift in Weld's antislavery stance, from a concentration on the moral imperative to end slavery and the beneficial results that would flow from that, to a more vigorous concentration on slavery as a cruel and wicked institution perpetuated by white Southerners. This shift from moral persuasion to accusation and blame marked a change in tone of the whole abolitionist movement.

Meanwhile the abolitionist movement was itself poised on the edge of rancor and fragmentation over issues of particular concern to the Welds. Issues of nonresistance, women's rights, and Garrison's increasingly anticlerical tone in the *Liberator* forced a split in the movement between Garrison and his supporters in the American Anti-Slavery Society and more conservative abolitionists like Lewis Tappan, who founded the American and Foreign Anti-Slavery Society. Weld was in a particularly difficult position since he and his wife were serious advocates of women's rights but also eager to keep abolition at the center of the reforming crusade. Ideologically they probably had more in common with the Garrisonians, but in terms of friendship and old alliances, they were closer to Tappan and his fellow seceders. Aside from the ideological issues at stake, Weld was saddened by the capacity of erstwhile partners in the reforming cause to engage in vituperative rhetoric against one another. The Welds declared to friends that "we feel *impelled* to stand *aloof* from both of the National A. S. Societies."[15]

With no real institutional base within which to campaign, Weld accepted a position in Washington to help the antislavery wing of the Whig Party mobilize against the gag law, which prevented petitions against slavery from receiving congressional attention. Increased immersion in the complex political and economic processes that embedded slavery in national life appears to have further eroded Weld's confidence in the efficacy of the old methods of religious revivalism and grassroots reform to change things. Instead, he increasingly believed that liberty and slavery were "two great antagonist forces" in the American national condition, and their final conflict was irresistible. In a letter to his friend James Gillespie Birney, Weld outlined the economic, social, and political rationales for his belief in an irrepressible conflict between North and South, closing with the apocalyptic prediction that "*The end must come.*"[16] This opinion was no mere exercise in punditry on

Weld's part, but rather a settled conviction that forced him to reevaluate the whole religious and reforming agenda that had absorbed his life since his religious conversion in 1826. Far from seeing religious revival and moral reform as the twin agencies that would end slavery, Weld darkly suggested that they were only deflection mechanisms holding back a deeply embedded structural conflict in sore need of final resolution.

It would be difficult to overestimate the impact of this growing conviction on Weld's religious sensibilities. In 1826 Weld embarked on a public career as preacher, orator, and educator to revive the church and reform the world. With the American West as his chosen location, and with antislavery as his chosen cause, Weld, with his strong frame, unkempt hair, and commanding oratory, cut a romantic and charismatic figure. Although he lived within and served institutions for a time, they always seemed to disappoint him. His letters are full of the inadequacy of churches. He fell out with the leaders of Oneida Academy and Lane Seminary. He could not find a home within either of America's great antislavery societies. He became disillusioned with the political establishment in Washington. After two decades of remorseless energy, sometimes to the detriment of his own and his family's well-being, Weld had to face the fact that the churches were, in his view, still corrupt and that slavery was still in place. Even the evangelicals who had once inspired him, he soon discovered, had feet of clay. For over fifteen years, which was virtually his entire adult life, Weld had operated within a number of fundamental assumptions, namely, that evangelical religion was a true faith, that the Bible was an authoritative text, that slavery was the greatest moral stain of his generation, perhaps of any generation, that it was the duty of humankind to strive for the millennial kingdom, and that it was the responsibility of those who believed in such truths to propagate them with all possible energy. Religious revivals, great organizations dedicated to reform, revitalized churches, and raw human activism, when yoked to the cause of truth and justice, would cleanse the temple and redeem the nation. By the early 1840s, however, Weld's powerful worldview had been undermined by hard doses of reality. He discovered that churches were prone to mediocrity, reformers to rancorous dissension, and popular sentiment to sleazy manipulation. He came to believe that slavery was not strictly a religious and moral issue that could be dealt with by persuasion and repentance, but rather that it was a structural evil of great complexity, which could be ended only by blood and conflict. The impact of all this on Weld's religious convictions showed up in a letter to Birney only months after he had written to him about his changing views about the end of slavery.

That a vast amount of what passes for truth in the religious world is not taught in the Bible and is utterly contradicted by reason seems clear to me. That the ministry as a body have grasped and are clinging to power and to prerogative that they have no right to—sheer usurpation, is just as plain — that the tendencies of the times to sink the *individual* and exalt the *social* are so strong as to have become utterly morbid—that the body even of good men has rejected truth as the grand author of actual progress in the soul and instituted for it appeals to fear, love of popularity—the pride of caste, etc.—that *association* is employed mainly not as a reflection to gather and flood abroad *truth,* but as a condenser to consolidate public sentiment and to use it as *the* quickener of the soul—the omnipresent and omnipotent motive to action—that mankind are a *great herd* tied together by the horns and fated to stand still, unless they all tilt their hoofs together and in the same direction.[17]

It would be difficult to imagine a more comprehensive indictment of the tactics and strategies of evangelical social reform movements than this statement penned by an erstwhile activist.

A similar pessimism about the power of human initiative to eradicate national evil took a different direction in the mind of his wife, Angelina, who had been left behind on the family farm near Belleville, New Jersey. Angelina, who never had much confidence in churches or reform organizations to effect meaningful change, and who had to cope with an absent husband and a child with serious behavioral problems, became attracted to the prophetical writings of William Miller. Weld was not impressed. He wrote her that "the history of the church shows that with few if any exceptions, great zeal for the study of the prophecies and little *practical spirituality* have gone together. The truth is, the study of prophecy has great witchery over the minds of a certain cast. It powerfully stimulates curiosity, love of the marvelous, the element of superstition, the spirit of adventure, the desire for novelty, etc." Angelina, tired of capitulating to Theodore's "superior" wisdom all the time, and possibly motivated by jealousy of Weld's public role while she festered on a small farm in New Jersey, was slow to give up her enthusiasm for Miller. In particular, the idea that Christ's return, predicted by Miller for 1843, would precede the millennium seemed like healing balm to those who had begun to lose confidence in the power of human effort to reform their society.[18] Whether Angelina's increased "mental excitement" was the cause or the consequence of her interest in Miller's prophecies is hard to tell, but her enthusiasm for Miller was eroded by the evident failure of Miller's prediction and the return of her husband from Washington. As with many others, Angelina "spiritualized" Miller's prophecies, interpreting them not as a physical second coming of Christ, but as a new reign of Christ in the hearts of believers.

Weld's return from Washington not only coincided with the failure of William Miller's predicted date of Christ's return, but also was accompanied by major events in his own life including the death of his father, the birth of his last child, and a major shift in his theological orientation. As we have seen, the seeds of this transformation were in existence long before 1843, but the fruits became more evident in subsequent years. Weld's growing pessimism about the old Finney-inspired agenda was reinforced during the years 1843–44 by a string of disturbing events. First there was the reemergence of the old feud between Weld and the evangelical leadership of the American and Foreign Anti-Slavery Society over the issue of women's rights. The executive committee of the society, apparently without asking him, appointed Weld to be one of the society's representatives at the London Convention. Weld wrote Tappan that he could not in good conscience represent a society that deprived women of their "inalienable rights," and later wrote Angelina that antislavery conventions all too often attracted those "with a passion for distinction and a conspicuous position."[19] Second, Weld was brought face to face with some unpleasant and embarrassing scandals within the evangelical community.

The first surrounded Horace Campbell Taylor, who was a prominent abolitionist, an agent of the Moral Reform Society, editor of the *Oberlin Evangelist*, the Oberlin postmaster, and a leading figure in the Ohio Liberty Party. Taylor's list of moral infelicities included seduction, procuring an abortion, constant mail robberies, and a midnight scourging of a young man for immorality. The Oberlin professor who brought Taylor's peccadilloes to Weld's attention piously proclaimed that he thought Taylor was sorry about all this, which only provoked Weld into a rant about the fecklessness and abject weakness of the Oberlin authorities in rooting out the hypocrisy within their own institution. Against the propensity of Oberlin to keep such matters within the college walls, Weld's characteristic advice was to "Out with the *whole of it* to the world. Make clean work. Proclaim it on the housetops. . . . The knife and the probe are called for, not heartsease and cordials."[20] Not only were Weld's perfectionist sensibilities outraged by the lack of perfection in the very institution that proclaimed it, but also he was furious about a subsequent article in the *Observer* suggesting that "the doctrine of the attainment of holiness in this life produces licentiousness as its legitimate fruits." Weld thought this argument was about as plausible as stating that the atonement was a "bounty upon sin," and declared himself less interested in doctrines than in living.[21]

In the same month as the Taylor scandal broke, an even more unsavory case was reported to Weld. His good friend, Russell Judd, minister of the Free Church in Brooklyn, was accused of the sexual abuse of ten young girls. Weld ruefully wrote that "it is one of the most monstrous and humiliating developments of this age of horrible revelations." While many of his friends thought the whole affair disastrous for the cause of reform and revival, Weld thought otherwise.

> The effect of it [the Judd scandal] upon the cause of truth, righteousness and purity, will it seems to [me] be beneficial. 'Cease from man' is the sermon God is preaching everywhere just now. Ministers are by the mass of professors put in the place of God, and God is showing them that if they put them there He will cast them headlong. Within the last four years, not less than thirty ministers of evangelical denominations have been guilty of the most flagrant licentiousness—i.e. in so many cases it has *come to light*. 'I will be exalted in the earth,' says He who alone is worthy of exaltation. Whoever *consents* to be exalted by the professing church, in any such sense as almost the entire ministry *do consent* to be, and do aim and strive for, him will God *cast down* and those who conspire thus to exalt he will utterly confound.[22]

As letters about scandals, scoundrels, and schisms circulated among Finney's old lieutenants, different personalities chose different paths. Tappan resolved to stay within the churches and the great reforming societies, telling Weld that "reformation must begin at home."[23] Weld agreed, but for him home ceased to be the institutional flotsam and jetsam of Finney's revivals, and slowly became the place where his family dwelt and where his spirit lay in need of restoration. Weld's faith was about to be domesticated, privatized, and made more liberal. In the words of his biographer, Weld largely repudiated the "evangelical vision" that had dominated his life for almost twenty years since his dramatic encounter with Finney, namely the "reform and conversion of the world to bring on the millennial age," and replaced it with a more personal, domestic, and private sense of Christian duty.[24]

Weld effectively signed off on his career as a public agitator for reform in a lecture entitled "Truth's Hindrances," delivered at the Newark Lyceum in 1844. He had clearly girded his loins for a bravura performance of straight talking. A week before delivery he wrote Tappan, "I *reckon* it will be the last time they are guilty of the indiscretion of inviting me."[25] Weld duly spoke as an Old Testament prophet decrying the general wickedness of public sentiment and religious conformity and ending with the ringing declaration that America could never be "free without first being true."

It is hard to find adequate descriptive labels for the next phase of Weld's spiritual pilgrimage. Robert Abzug notes that many of Weld's generation sought escape from a world of sin and mission in more "autonomous and personally ameliorative forms of spiritual life such as Transcendentalism, Perfectionism, Swedenborgianism and Spiritualism."[26] However it is to be described, Weld's change of direction became quickly apparent to all who knew him. One visitor to the Weld farm wrote Tappan that Theodore had become "a Lady Guion Christian," so named after the seventeenth-century French mystic, Madame Guyon. Weld's old evangelical friends, especially Lewis Tappan and Charles Stuart, were saddened both by Weld's apparent heterodoxy and by his absence from the public campaign against slavery. Stuart felt particularly wounded. His love and admiration for Weld knew no bounds, yet he believed that Theodore's rejection of biblical authority in favor of individual conscience made him a "melancholy and anomalous" object in danger of the fires of hell. Indeed, so passionate were Stuart's formulations of evangelical zeal, particularly of biblical authority and eternal punishment, that they almost certainly reinforced the opinions they were designed to counteract.[27]

Although Weld clearly found some satisfaction in his life as husband, father, farmer, and educator, and although his pursuit of private piety took him down some exotic paths, most notably his enthusiasm for the Spiritualism of Andrew Jackson Davis, not all was plain sailing. On the domestic front, Angelina suffered almost constant pain from a prolapsed uterus and hernia, and his relationship with his two sons was problematic for most of his life. The apparently cozy trio of Theodore, Angelina, and her older sister Sarah, the old Weld-Grimké reforming dynasty, was not always full of sweetness and light. Moreover, Weld's various educational ventures followed the same pattern as his own college experiences many years before, that is, early promise followed by crisis, closure, and relocation. Even his new religious direction was not without its pains and difficulties. On one level he had no regrets about abandoning his old public persona as revivalist and abolitionist. For example, he wrote Birney that "creeds have lost all hold upon me, and in the state of mind that exalts them I search in vain for the elements of healthful growth. How speculative notions have usurped the functions of spiritual vitality!" Yet in the same letter he wrote with a hint of wistfulness that "It has become with me a thing as common, to be supposed by my old friends, to be incurably *heterodox*, that I have got quite into the habit of letting all such cases *go by default.* The last mail brought me a letter from an old friend at Oberlin, who says, 'You are often represented from our pulpit as having gone into infidelity'! Such messages I am often receiving."[28]

To be regarded as a heretic and deserter by those who had once looked up to him as their leader in a grand heroic struggle could not have been easy for Weld to bear. At times Angelina sensed that for all Theodore's sturdy manual labor on the farm and his pursuit of inner spiritual vitality, he missed a sense of a greater purpose to absorb his energy. Sensing a deep inner depression in him she wrote, "the fear often comes over me like a dark cloud, that we are not doing the will of God. We are not fulfilling our destiny and yet I cannot see anything definite—don't see any particular thing, to do. . . . It seems to me dearest One—the days of *your* preparation must be over—the time must have come to give up your drudgery. *Don't you feel it is?*"[29] Angelina and Theodore had met at an antislavery convention at the peak of their powers as national personalities in the abolitionist movement. Her image of him had been formed when he was widely regarded as the most charismatic orator in the movement. She could not easily accept that all this was to be sacrificed for a life of toil on an obscure farm.

A new focus for the combined energies of the Weld-Grimké dynasty soon emerged in the shape of the "Weld Institute," a new educational venture begun on the site of the Belleville farm in the fall of 1848. Conceived of as a model educational community, the institute taught a demanding curriculum, embraced nature as well as nurture, and focused on the development of character in a coeducational environment. Not only did the school afford Weld the opportunity of implementing his inner reflections about religion and character in a real environment, but also it helped reestablish connections with some of his old reforming allies who sent their children to the "Weld Institute." However innovative in style and quality, Weld's new institute soon fell victim to the old familiar problems of penury. With almost perfect timing the Welds were offered the chance to run a school at a planned utopian community in Perth Amboy, New Jersey. The Raritan Bay Union, as it was called, soon fell victim to the anticooperative spirit that suffused many of America's cooperative experiments, but the school (Eagleswood) survived and became home for the Welds for a decade. This better endowed version of the "Weld Institute" gave Weld greater freedom to implement a progressive educational curriculum, and became something of a base for the New England literati to deliver lectures and help form the character of a new generation of American leaders.

While the Welds were busily building a model educational community at Eagleswood, the nation seemed to be running headlong into a final conflict over slavery. From bleeding Kansas to the John Brown raid (two of Brown's collaborators were buried at Eagleswood), it seemed clear to the Welds that the hour of destiny had come. On one level the outbreak of the Civil War was a vindication of the position Weld adopted in the early 1840s that sooner or later the forces of liberty and slavery would meet in a decisive conflict, but on another level the old pacifist tendencies of the Quaker-influenced Grimké sisters were brought out by the reported carnage. To some extent Weld distanced himself from the bloodshed and concentrated instead on the moral righteousness of the cause. He wrote Martha Coffin Wright that "I profoundly believe in the righteousness of such a war as this, on its anti-slavery side. You exult, as we do, in this mighty Northern uprising, notwithstanding its mixtures of motives, and base alloys and half truths, and whole lies, thrown to the surface, by the force beneath:—the elements of a vast moral Revolution are all aglow, in the surging mass of a national religious revival, better deserving the name, than anything that has preceded it."[30] For all the grimness of war, Weld was convinced that but for this rebellion "the maelstrom would have dragged us all down."

In a remarkable way the pent-up abolitionist zeal and energy that Weld had locked up in his self-imposed box of private piety was liberated by the war and by Lincoln's Emancipation Proclamation. He accepted Garrison's invitation to address a large meeting at the Boston Music Hall in November 1862, and then he toured New England virtually as an election agent of the Republican Party. Perhaps most satisfyingly for Weld, he was able to take his campaign out west, culminating in a triumphal return visit to Oberlin. Weld's booming voice, the power of which seemed to rise and fall in symmetry with his psychological state as much as with the physical condition of his vocal cords, was back in business. It was nevertheless characteristic of Weld that during the war years Weld gave lectures on the "Cost of Reform," in which he spoke against the narrow iconoclastic spirit of many reformers and the need to rise to a higher spirit of love and forgiveness, even for old and hated enemies.[31]

The emancipation of the slaves and the triumph of the Northern armies in 1865 were the crowning moment of Weld's career, and he duly celebrated victory with his fellow "lane rebels" at Oberlin. On a more personal level, however, the war years brought pain and suffering to the Weld household. Theodore's eldest son, Stuart, refused to fight in the war, believing the North's cause to be fundamentally unjust, while his other son, Thody, displayed symptoms of insanity that were attributed to persistent sexual self-abuse. Also during the war, the family left Eagleswood and moved to the suburbs of Boston, where they spent the rest of their lives. The Welds remained active in reform causes, including holding the government to account over its treatment of the freed slaves and campaigning vigorously for women's suffrage. One of the more bizarre episodes of their later life in Boston was Angelina's serendipitous discovery that her father had three sons with his slave Nancy Weston, a relationship that seems to have started after the death of his legal wife. To their credit the Welds accepted this bombshell with equanimity, and helped advance the careers of Angelina's half-brothers, Archibald and Francis Grimké, who became prominent African American leaders in the late nineteenth century.[32] In terms of his religious development, Weld became a founder member of the Hyde Park Second Congregational (Liberal Christian or Unitarian) Society, the constitution of which contains a clear statement of belief and purpose: "We the undersigned, inhabitants of Hyde Park and its vicinity, that we may quicken in ourselves and others the love of God and the love of man,—a reverence for the brotherhood of the race, for human rights, liberty, equality, and fraternity—irrespective of condition, language, sex, or national descent,—and that we may be helpers of one another in seeking for all, the largest growth in truth and goodness propose to associate ourselves together for the furtherance of the objects aforesaid. Conceding to all the same freedoms of conscience, thought and speech, that we claim for ourselves, we exact no sectarian or theological test of membership, and shall strive for no dead uniformity of speculative belief, as a means of obtaining that living unity with God, which first of all we should seek."[33]

However noble the sentiments, the church did not thrive. When its minister resigned in 1879, one disillusioned parishioner, Dr. W. S. Everett, attributed its lack of success not to poor ministerial leadership, but to the utter vacuity of its beliefs. This criticism was all the more compelling because it came not from an evangelical zealot, but from someone who declared himself to be a supporter of liberal Christianity and Unitarianism. Focusing his attention on the church's constitution, Everett stated that the chief cause of the church's decline was "the indeterminate, perhaps indefinable, character of our faith." According to Everett, the church's constitution expressed no belief in a superintending providence, contained no mention of the Bible, did not acknowledge the existence of a Savior, displayed no faith or hope in a future existence, and said nothing about God or why we should love him. In short, it seemed to be devoted to nothing beyond liberty, equality, and fraternity, as was France when it adopted the goddess of reason and then bathed the streets in blood. In sum, "no religious belief is essential to membership here." Everett pointedly stated that all those who have contemplated mortality or eternity, seen their loved ones die, or "found their reason wanting amidst the tragedies of life, will ask us if this is all we have to give."[34]

Weld, who had grown accustomed to having his heterodoxy exposed by the evangelical zealots he had left behind, was unaccustomed to having his opinions subjected to withering scrutiny by a Unitarian liberal. Weld was stung, and he rose to the challenge in a public letter to the *Norfolk County Gazette* in which he mounted two defenses. His first was that the constitution of the church that Everett found so vacuous was meant only to be the agreed statement of a founding society, and was enlarged by more avowedly theological content on subsequent occasions, such as at the dedication of their meetinghouse. Weld's attempt to sketch in the theological content to which he referred was in truth not very convincing. Weld's second defense was even more disingenuous. He drew a parallel between the Hyde Park society and the Methodist church, whose discipline required only one condition for membership in its societies, "that is a desire to flee from the wrath to come and be saved from their sins; no mention of God, Christ, Providence, Inspiration, Bible, Immorality, Faith, Hope, etc. etc.," yet the Methodists were thriving.[35] Weld was of course technically correct to assert that membership of Methodist societies, as voluntary associations, was based upon a simple declaration of religious seriousness, but aside from the debating points at stake, he could have hardly believed that the statement concocted by John Wesley as a badge of Methodist membership for England's eighteenth-century poor was an exact parallel to the preamble of a constitution written by estimable citizens in a Boston suburb at the end of the nineteenth century.

Weld was angry with Everett, not only because one of his pet projects had been savaged in print by a clever dissident, but also because Weld still regarded himself as a serious Christian believer. In a lecture entitled "Theism and Atheism," delivered to the Unitarian Society in 1876, Weld employed the argument of intelligent design to counteract the materialist logic of evolutionary theory, and spoke about the "new realms of spiritual being that may be revealed to us by the addition of a new sense."[36] Weld's devotion to the idea that humankind was limited in its spiritual quest by a sensory deficiency that would be unlocked by death showed the continuing influence of the works of Andrew Jackson Davis, whose books Weld helped secure for Hyde Park's new library against determined opposition of some of the library's trustees.

As is the way with old age, Weld had to face the deaths of many of his nearest and dearest, including Sarah Grimké and his wife, Angelina, who lingered for six years in a sad state after suffering a severe stroke. In these years of trial, which included the commitment of his son Thody to an asylum, Weld drew consolation from the fact that death was not the end of humankind's spiritual pilgrimage. But Weld was no mere eternal dreamer. Right to the end he lectured and wrote about the evils of intemperance, political partisanship, and, most notably, the lack of Northern interest in the fate of freed blacks, whose freedom had been bought at such a terrible price.[37] Weld died in 1895 and was buried in Mount Hope Cemetery in Boston, close to the final resting place of generations of Welds, who had first come to the New World in search of a more holy place. Whatever one makes of Weld's many foibles, it is hard to resist the conclusion that his life contributed richly to the ideals of his ancestors.

Unlike some of the other figures in this book, Weld's abandonment of evangelicalism was not written down and formally sealed for all to see. Weld was never much of a theological thinker in the conventional sense. He rarely debated (at least in print) with his old evangelical friends theories of biblical authority, the nature of atonement, or the characteristics of the new birth. His conversion under Finney, which, unlike that of many evangelicals, did not become the emotional pivot of his life, was as much a conversion to a millennial mission of national restoration as it was to a personal savior in the classic evangelical sense. What he received from evangelicalism was a deeper appreciation of the nation's sins, especially the great evil of slavery, and a crusading sense of mission. He became captivated by the struggle for the abolition of slavery, a struggle that helped determine his friendships, shaped his education, nurtured his talents, and ultimately supplied his wife. There is no doubt that his religious experience was heavily shaped by the old Methodist doctrine of Christian perfection, a doctrine that is often the midwife of disappointment and disillusionment as messy reality gets in the way of holiness and idealism.

Weld never abandoned his commitment to the holy cause of abolition, but he came to distrust the evangelical machine that campaigned for it. By the 1840s the evangelicalism Weld encountered seemed awash in corruption, full of religious dogma, and increasingly conscious of its growing cultural power. He had a particular aversion to the anniversary meetings of the great evangelical benevolent organizations. In a letter to Angelina written in the mid 1840s he remarked upon "the doings at the so called religious anniversaries this year. What mere mechanism and artificiality! What mouthings, posturings, 'Mr. Presidents,' *making* long prayers at man's bidding! What clappings, fulsome flatteries, ostentatious displays of Rev. Dr.s, and Honorables and Excellencies! with forms, stereotyped rounds of ceremonies, venerations of old usage, idolatry of set times, with *benedictions!* only less pompous than impious—and yet 'religious'! Father forgive them—they know not what they do. And Oh may we whose eyes thou hast opened to see these shadows and fictions, be vitally possessed of those *realities* which are life."[38] No doubt part of this rhetoric stemmed from Weld's repudiation of his clerical and patrician roots in New England, but it was also occasioned by a growing sense of the limits of evangelical cultural power. The apparent failure and fragmentation of abolitionism by the early 1840s, combined with a greater sense of realpolitik stemming from his years as a lobbyist in Washington, persuaded Weld that slavery could not be ended by any number of evangelical or benevolent societies. The sad truth of the matter was that slavery was an institution embedded in economic self-interest and naked racism, which no amount of Finney revivals or reform campaigns stood a chance of breaking. Weld not only became a believer in the concept of an irrepressible conflict, but also saw attempts to prevent it as naïve and counterproductive.

Weld's retreat from evangelicalism was accompanied by a retreat from the public sphere and an embrace of personal piety and communal education experiments. Revealingly, in his design of a school curriculum, Weld relied more on literary classics and physical fitness than he did on the Bible and devotional works. Charles Stuart, the one evangelical who consistently called Weld to account for his growing "infidelity," was appalled by the *"Bible-less"* character of the Eagleswood curriculum and accused Weld of the high crime of fostering infidelity among the young. The more stringent Stuart's letters became, albeit suffused with an almost painful tenderness, the more Weld seems to have switched off.[39] Stuart's reliance on the Bible as his absolute authority for everything simply did not resonate with Weld's evolving sense of political and spiritual authenticity. The same pattern can be seen in his antislavery writings. His first book, *The Bible Against Slavery*, was a rigorous text-based attempt to show that ancient Hebrew slavery as described in the Bible was substantially different from its modern American namesake, and that the Bible could not be used as a proslavery textbook. His second book, *Slavery As It Is*, was a rigorous empirical survey showing that Southern slavery was a cruel and immoral institution. His subsequent antislavery writings concentrated more on slavery as an offense against humanity than as an infraction of God's revealed word.[40]

Detecting changes in Weld's public stances and published writings, though important, is easier than mapping the subtle shifts in his personal piety and religious devotion. A close reading of his letters shows that important changes did take place in these deepest recesses of mind and spirit, but the causes and consequences are not always clear. For example, much of Weld's early correspondence, dating from his most intense evangelical phase, is full of references to his "wretched cold heart," his immersion in prayer, his strong sense of trust in divine providence, and his almost gushing love for Finney, his father in the gospel, and Stuart, his brother in the lord. In the midst of a cholera epidemic at Lane seminary, Weld's reported encounters with a dying saint on the one hand and a dying infidel on the other are classic expressions of evangelical spirituality in the face of death. Weld writes, "I could fill this sheet with the heavenly breathings of this dying saint, but must pause. When I closed his eyes I could not refrain from crying aloud, 'Blessed—Blessed! oh, blessed are the dead that die in the Lord.'" By contrast, the death of the dying infidel is recounted as a fierce and terrifying struggle, in the reporting of which Weld leaves little to the imagination.[41] Over time, the expressed piety in Weld's letters shifts according to circumstances. He is more businesslike and instrumental in his letters about abolition, even to evangelical friends like Lewis Tappan. Yet another shift takes place when he meets the Grimkés and marries Angelina. She brought into the marriage a Quaker spirituality emphasizing anticlericalism, pacifism, women's rights, personal illumination, and a more mystical expression of communion with Christ. After receiving a letter from Weld eulogizing the saintliness and evangelical zeal of his beloved Stuart, Angelina coldly replied that she would find it hard to admire anyone with a military background. At first the Grimkés complained that on issues of spiritual direction, Theodore always seemed to get his way, but over the long term some of the evidence points in the opposite direction. The Grimkés were generally more open to new directions, including phrenology, Millerism, and Spiritualism, and often succeeded in attracting Weld's attention and, sometimes, his support.

In the Weld-Grimké correspondence, it is difficult to follow all the fruits of the consummation of the different spiritual traditions represented in the marriage, but there is no denying their importance. For example, although coming from different directions, Theodore, Angelina, and Sarah reinforced one another's disillusionment with churches and ministers. The Grimkés spoke of churches as "places of spiritual famine," and Weld bemoaned the fact that wherever he traveled he could not find "spiritual fellowship" or "spiritual edification." Equally significantly, Weld's marriage to Angelina required mutual recognition that their views were different on many points not "essential for salvation," such as "the Sabbath, Baptism, The Lord['s] supper public worship, prayer, marriage, the Institution of Government, also the *philosophy* of total depravity and degeneration." In a similar vein, William Lloyd Garrison told Angelina that "bro. Weld's sectarianism would bring her into bondage, unless she could succeed in emancipating *him*." Weld rose to the occasion. He wrote Angelina that with "teachable spirits and by mutual prayer and conference we shall arrive at truth, whether it now lies with one or the other or between us. The bigotry and exclusive views of this adulterous and sinful generation sickens my soul."[42] Weld's experiment with ecumenism within his own marriage was an important testing ground for the later enlargement of his Christian vision. Part of the reason he subsequently reacted against Stuart's evangelicalism was its exclusive dogmatic structure and its narrow sectarian temper.

Yet another shift in Weld's expression of piety occurs in the early 1840s as a result of his disappointment with the splits in the antislavery movement accommodationist churches and hypocritical evangelicals. The letters contain sharper criticisms, sterner judgments, and more hard edged sentences. Weld's inability to find a Christian constituency that thought as he did about the great issues of religion and the fate of the nation drove him inexorably back to the land, manual labor, personal piety, and teaching. Although the changes in Weld's expression of his piety are significant, they should not be overplayed. He continued to believe in the importance of communion with God, love of neighbor, and the need to control his own sinful nature. In a remarkably frank prenuptial confession to Angelina, Weld diagnosed his own sins as selfishness, pride, impatience of contradiction, a bad temper, a severe and gloomy countenance, a tendency to put the worst construction on the actions of others, self-indulgence, laziness, and willfulness.[43] Angelina reciprocated with her own list of shortcomings, and a few months later they were married, two of the greatest sinners in Christendom.

In a sense the most difficult part of Weld's life to explain is not its early and later years. What could be more predictable than someone who started life as the son of a Connecticut Congregational clergyman ending it as a patron of a liberal Unitarian church in a Boston suburb? What lies outside this tidy trajectory are his years spent as revivalist, reformer, and agitator, not in New England, but on the western frontier. Weld may have outgrown or repudiated his early evangelicalism, but there is no denying that it was precisely that phase which gave his life substance and energy. Without the evangelicals he later distanced himself from, Weld might well have become a respectable New England minister or one of the polite organizers of the East Coast antislavery conventions that he later came to despise. Weld did not die an evangelical, but his life was animated by the crusading zeal of the tradition that formed him.

5 Sarah Grimké, Elizabeth Cady Stanton, and Frances Willard—Bible Stories
Evangelicalism and Feminism

As I had become sufficiently philosophical to talk over my religious experiences with my classmates who had been with me through the Finney revival meetings, we all came to the same conclusion—that we had passed through no remarkable change and that we had not been born again, as they say, for we found our tastes and enjoyments the same as ever. My brother-in-law explained to us the nature of the delusion we had all experienced, the physical conditions, the mental processes, the church machinery by which such excitements are worked up, and the impositions to which credulous minds are easily subjected.

—Elizabeth Cady Stanton, *Eighty Years and More: Reminiscences 1815–1897* (1898)

The relationship between the rise of popular evangelicalism during the second Great Awakening and the development of American feminism in the early nineteenth century is a hotly debated topic. On the one hand it has been argued that evangelicalism, particularly the varieties spawned by the rise of Methodism and the revivals associated with Charles Finney, supplied the moral outrage and conversionist zeal that empowered women to act publicly

Sarah Moore Grimké (1792–1873). Wood engraving (The Library of Congress)
Elizabeth Cady Stanton (1815–1902). Photographic print (The Library of Congress)
Frances Willard (1839–1898). Photographic negative (The Library of Congress)

through countless voluntary organizations.[1] Middle and upper class women, so the argument goes, benefited from social and economic changes that freed them from domestic drudgery, were empowered by religious conversions to seek moral change in themselves and their society, and were trained in organizational, fundraising, and public-speaking skills by evangelical churches and voluntary organizations. In this way evangelical religion through its disruptive piety opened a small but expandable crack in the wall of male power and control, allowing countless women to enroll in the great antislavery, temperance, missionary, and suffrage crusades of the nineteenth century.

This tidy explanation is not without its problems, however. Evangelical religion was not the only source of reforming energy among women in the nineteenth century, nor was it a consistently, or even a predominantly, emancipating force.[2] Many of the women leaders of the abolitionist movement, for example, were from liberal Quaker, Universalist, Unitarian, Spiritualist, or other religious traditions that were only marginally influenced by evangelicalism. Many others underwent conventional evangelical conversions early in their lives but later drifted away from, or actively opposed, the evangelicalism of their youth. Still others managed to negotiate sufficient social and intellectual space between themselves and the broad evangelical tradition that they neither benefited from nor fought with that tradition. As a result very few of the major leaders of nineteenth-century American feminism, especially those of a more radical kind, were empowered, sustained, and supported by any of the major evangelical traditions.

The primary purpose of this chapter, however, is not to reenter the debate about the relationship between evangelicalism and feminism, but rather to explore further the theme of enchantment and disenchantment among some feminists who *were* influenced, either positively or negatively, by evangelicalism. Unlike previous chapters the focus this time is not on a single individual, but on a number of women spanning the nineteenth century, namely Sarah Grimké, Elizabeth Cady Stanton, and Frances Willard. The reason for including several such subjects is twofold. First, to my knowledge there is no clear example of an American feminist who has left an extensive record of evangelical disenchantment.[3] That in itself is a revealing statement. Most women who had a profound attachment to evangelicalism at some point in their lives, through either religious conversion or church affiliation, and who later operated at a distance from the evangelical tradition, negotiated and navigated their spiritual journeys without public conflict and hostility. They simply refined and redefined what they thought was central to their religious faith and moral action without too much engagement with the doctrines or dogmas of evangelicalism. A second reason for choosing more than one woman to look at the themes of evangelical enchantment and disenchantment in the emergence of American feminism is that such an approach better illustrates not only the commonality of concerns over issues like biblical hermeneutics and religious dogma, but also the variety of ways women chose to navigate their new terrain. The best place to start is with varieties of enchantment, for, as with the other narratives in this book, the place of enchantment often carries within it the tiny spores of later disenchantment.

The place of evangelical enchantment for many of the leaders of nineteenth-century women's movements was an early conversion experience provoked by the same range of experiences that show up in general surveys of evangelical conversions. Consider for example the experiences of the Grimké sisters, Sarah Moore (1792–1873) and Angelina Emily (1805–1879), who were born into a Southern slaveholding family and became the first female agents of the American Anti-Slavery Society and the first abolitionists to speak to mixed audiences of men and women.[4] The Grimké sisters in their own right, and later in association with Angelina's husband, Theodore Dwight Weld, were virtually a reformist dynasty in the nineteenth century, as they first opposed slavery and then supported women's equality and female suffrage. Brought up in a wealthy South Carolina Episcopal family, Sarah Grimké was denied the college education she craved and was introduced as a young adult to the tiresome round of social engagements befitting an upper crust Southern woman. She later described this phase of her life as one of "dissipation and folly."[5]

By contrast, serious-mindedness, moral duty, and intellectual accomplishment ran through the Grimké family, parents and siblings alike. For Sarah the outer dialectic of Southern balls and dinner parties versus a world of serious purpose became an inner dialectic organized around the push and pull of religious conversion. The catalyst was a Presbyterian minister in Savannah, Henry Kollock, whose fervent preaching produced a repeated tug-of-war between the flesh and the spirit. After one such episode Sarah later wrote that "My whole being was taken captive. I made a full and free surrender and vowed eternal fealty to Jesus. To manifest my sincerity, in my zeal I burnt paintings, destroyed my little library of poetry and fiction and gave to the flames my gay apparel."[6] But on this occasion external fires did not purge the fire within, and Sarah continued a pattern of oscillation between piety and performance. What stoked the flames of the dialectic was not only a contest between religious zeal and social conformity, and, one suspects, between slavery and freedom, but also a gender-inspired contest between a life of purpose and a life of decoration. What pushed Sarah to the next phase were not her further dealings with Henry Kollock, who no doubt sowed some important seeds, but rather an unusually prolonged and isolated encounter with the grim reaper in the shape of her father's death. Sarah not only traveled with her dying father to Philadelphia and New Jersey in search of medical expertise and a better climate, but also met many earnest Quakers along the way. When Sarah returned to Charleston she entered a dark night of the soul relieved only temporarily by an encounter with revivalistic Methodism, which resulted in her making public testimony at a Love Feast. For reasons that she never clearly specified, but which probably had to do with Methodism's naked revivalism and its perfectionist theology, Sarah decided to pitch her tent not with the revivalist populists, but rather with the plain-living and more somber Quakers. It was not an altogether happy choice. Sarah set off for Philadelphia armed with "a call to the work of the ministry," but after fifteen years of struggle for acceptance as a Friend, member, and preacher, Sarah was eventually catapulted out of Philadelphia Quakerism by a very public humiliation at the hands of a leading male elder who could no longer put up with her apparently ponderous public speaking. She landed in the arms of her more radical younger sister, Angelina, and found, in the form of the American Anti-Slavery Society, the noble cause for which she had craved most of her life.

That path was also difficult, and for some of the same reasons. Given the assignment of organizing a National Female Anti-Slavery Society, the Grimké sisters were soon thrust into the public vortex of an East Coast reformist and evangelical culture. Now they were meeting with William Lloyd Garrison, Theodore Weld, the Tappan brothers, and distinguished antislavery activists from Britain. They were part of an argumentative, strong-willed, and self-opinionated culture. As one scholar has pointed out, "not only were there factions within factions and autonomous satellites revolving the main bodies, but personality conflicts abounded."[7] So too did conflicts around strategy and tactics. Emboldened by this company and ever more persuaded from her plain reading of the Bible that slavery was an abomination, Sarah employed her pen for the first time on a public stage in *An Epistle to the Clergy of the Southern States* (1836). The letter is part Bible exposition, part appeal to Christ's sacrificial atonement, part judgment on a national sin, and part ardent appeal to fellow ministers of the Gospel in the South to lead their region away from the moral abyss of an undeniably cruel institution. "God is in a peculiar manner the God of the poor and the needy, the despised and the oppressed," she writes, "he knows the sorrows of the American slave, and he will come down in mercy, or in judgment to deliver them."[8] The tone of the epistle is unmistakably evangelical. Her appeal is to the authority of the Bible, the blood of the cross of Christ, the enormity of human sin, the religion of the heart, the empowerment of the Holy Spirit, and the certainty of an impending apocalyptic judgment and restitution.

> What an appalling spectacle do we now present! With one hand we clasp the cross of Christ and with the other the neck of the downtrodden slave! With one eye we are gazing imploringly on the bleeding sacrifice of Calvary, as if we expected redemption through the blood that was shed there, and with the other we cast the glance of indignation and contempt at the representation of Him who there made his soul an offering for sin! My Christian brethren, if there is any truth in the Bible, and in the God of the Bible, *our hearts bear us witness* that he can no more acknowledge us as his disciples, if we willfully persist in this sin, than he did the Pharisees formerly, who were strict and punctilious in the observance of the ceremonial law, and yet devoured widows' houses. *We have added a deeper shade to their guilt.*[9]

The Grimké sisters were now on a perilous course. By moving across denominations, races, genders, and reforming constituencies, and by publicly speaking to mixed audiences of men and women about the evils of slavery and the inadequacy of colonization as a solution, they were virtually guaranteeing conflict and possible isolation. They were particularly critical of the clergy and their churches, who in their view ought to have known better than to endorse or acquiesce in the sin of slavery. Retribution was not long in coming. Congregational ministers belonging to the General Association of Massachusetts issued a strong attack on Garrisonian abolitionists and women abolitionist agents. This "Pastoral Letter," in essence a thinly disguised attack on the Grimké sisters, was read from the pulpits and printed in the *New England Spectator*. Women were enjoined to be unobtrusive, private, pious, loving, and, out of recognition of their inherent weakness, dependent on men. They were to teach unobtrusively and quietly, and not to "so far forget themselves as to itinerate in the character of public lecturers and teachers."[10] When this thundering pronouncement was made, Sarah had already begun writing a set of letters to Mary S. Parker, president of the Boston Female Anti-Slavery Society on the equality of the sexes and the condition of women. Sarah was now charting a course that embraced antislavery, female equality, and anticlericalism.

Grimké's set of letters to Parker, which later influenced Lucretia Mott, Elizabeth Cady Stanton, and Susan B. Anthony, is one of the foundational texts of American feminism. Although still rooted in a biblical framework, these letters contain some of the seeds of later disenchantment. To begin with, she had lost confidence in predominantly male translations of the Bible, including the Authorized Version, and was willing to state that Paul uncritically absorbed and reproduced some of the prejudices of his day in his writings about women in the church. She had also lost confidence in what she called "Christendom" or "The Christian World," which she thought had, Pharisee-like, substituted a religion based on love and self-denial for one based on the rigid performance of religious duties. Finally, although she paid tribute to Quakers, Methodists, and Christians for allowing women to preach, she was forced to admit that no Christian denomination or tradition upheld "the Scripture doctrine of perfect equality of man and woman, which is the fundamental principle of my argument in favor of the ministry of women."[11] A woman who had begun to think critically about the Bible, who had no confidence in the social record of Christendom, and who believed that no church or tradition upheld her rights to human equality was not likely to live happily ever after within an evangelical or conservative Christian tradition. Ironically, having set out to construct a biblically informed case for woman's rights, the Grimké sisters "managed to alienate themselves, effectively and literally, from virtually every institution that actively preserved traditional biblical interpretations of womanhood."[12]

Grimké's letters to Parker are interesting not only for the light they shed on the state of Sarah's biblical understanding and religious convictions at an early stage in her career as a radical activist, but also because they show signs of a much larger intellectual and cultural engagement with the issue of female equality. She has things to say about history, property laws, marriage, dress, and the state of American culture. She also revisits an old and deeply personal theme about how middle-class women in America could live morally fulfilling lives.

> During the early part of my life, my lot was cast among the butterflies of the fashionable world; and of this class of women, I am constrained to say, both from experience and observation, that their education is miserably deficient; that they are taught to regard marriage as the one thing needful, the only avenue to distinction; hence to attract the notice and win the attention of men, by their external charms, is the chief business of fashionable girls. . . . Fashionable women regard themselves, and are regarded by men, as pretty toys or as mere instruments of pleasure; and the vacuity of mind, the heartlessness, the frivolity which is the necessary result of this false and debasing estimate of women, can only be fully understood by

those who have mingled in the folly and wickedness of fashionable life; and who have been called from such pursuits by the voice of the Lord Jesus, inviting their weary and heavy laden souls to come unto Him and learn of Him, that they may learn of Him, that they may learn the high and holy purposes of their creation, and consecrate themselves into the service of God.[13]

Here is a potent mixture of autobiography, ardent idealism, and earnest aspiration. But what if the midwife to the better life—"the voice of the Lord Jesus"—turned out merely to be a call to yet another disappointing endeavor, or if "high and holy purposes" could be recalibrated to mean antislavery, feminism, and pacifism, rather than Gospel preaching and church service?

The Grimké sisters found themselves at the center of the noisy controversies of the summer of 1837 as reformers waging both internal and external wars over the respective priorities of antislavery, women's rights, and moral suasion versus political action. Although they pressed on regardless, sure of their own convictions on all of these issues, the crucible of public action and controversy took a toll on their health and their religious orthodoxy. Sarah frequently expressed disappointment with institutional churches and their self-serving clergy who could have used their influence for noble causes but chose not to do so. She gave up going to any worship services ("places of spiritual famine"), increasingly convinced that conventional religious meetings of the kind that evolved in the United States had neither biblical nor utilitarian warrant. Her already tense relations with Quakerism were effectively severed in 1838 when she was formally disowned for attending her sister's wedding to a non-Quaker. Nothing could more dramatically confirm her point about the pettiness of institutional religion than this assertion of the power of sectarian boundaries. Disillusioned with churches and their clergy, disenchanted with the trappings of formal and dogmatic religion, and disdainful of the structures of power which maintained them, Sarah Grimké, in common with many other women who were active in the causes of antislavery and women's rights, did not become atheists or secularists. They simply reconstructed their spiritual lives without the aid of formal religious authorities and institutions. How was this accomplished, and how was it expressed?

As Anna Speicher has shown, the best sources for reconstructing the spiritual lives of radical women are the letters they wrote to one another, which serve as the epistles of a spiritual sisterhood unalloyed by a need for public explanation. Sarah Grimké, who was always a much better writer than public speaker, had a talent for distilling to the essence. In her letters to the women's rights activist Elizabeth Smith Miller, she encouraged her to "strive to attain the one thing needful—*Love* to God manifested by love to his creatures." She urged Miller not to spend time searching for rational explanations of religious dogma such as the Trinity: "Let us give up these scholastic doctrines, to those who vainly seek religion thro' the head, instead of the heart. Let us endeavor to illustrate in our lives the belief that God is love, and that religion is an absorption into him, such an absorption, as renders us his representatives on earth. You have the all of religion, in what you say you are sure of—'There is a God and he is a being of love and purity. He requires us to be holy, and our happiness lies in regarding his requirements.' This is all I know and this is sufficient for the present, if more is needed for our advancement, it will surely be given. Doctrines, which occupy so prominent a place in Christianity, have eaten out the life of pure love. Let them go dearest."[14]

Much else flowed from those basic convictions. Speicher has shown how Sarah, in common with many other radical women, continued to criticize the "outsideisms" of religion, including clergy, institutions, doctrines, and rituals, while continuing to value what was loving, intuitive, and affective. More specifically, Sarah developed a more critical perspective on the Scriptures, declaring that "the blasphemies, the monstrosities, the irrationalities of the Bible must be brought face to face with science, reason and common sense."[15] She parted company with conventional Christian doctrines of original sin, substitutionary atonement, and eternal punishment. She continued to believe that her support for radical causes was an expression and reflection of her spirituality, not a denial of it or a detour from it. She found it helpful to think of the deity as having female as well as male attributes, and perhaps unsurprisingly, given her views on individual apprehension of the divine, she eventually embraced Spiritualism.[16]

For Sarah, Spiritualism was not so much a vehicle for experimenting with spirits, mediums, and new realms, but rather it offered a fresh way "to mellow our hearts and produce in us a likeness to God."[17] Her experience of Spiritualism allowed her to recalibrate her view of sin, not as willful disobedience to the divine requiring judgment, but rather as the result of understandable human ignorance requiring forgiveness. Moreover, she claimed that Spiritualism made her less anxious and despondent. Whether through the natural process of aging or owing to a diminution of stress from the highly public and controversial life she once led, or through the quiet cultivation of spiritualist insights, Sarah Grimké seemed to have found the peace of mind that eluded her for most of her early life.[18] Never a conventional evangelical, though deeply influenced by the revivalist movements of the early nineteenth century, Sarah Grimké never abandoned the radical causes she first embraced in the 1820s and '30s, nor did she ever cease to think of her life as one motivated by religious convictions applied to the injustices of humanity. What evangelical religion offered her, however painfully and incompletely, was a means and a way of refashioning her life from one devoted to an endless regime of social engagements and gender inferiority to one of purposeful activity which required the assertion of gender equality. Initially it was her reading of the Bible that supplied the intellectual and moral foundations for her reforming causes, but as time moved on she embraced, albeit mostly on her own terms, first Quakerism and then Spiritualism as loose frameworks within which she could act as a woman with radical religious convictions. Although she navigated her religious transitions as something of an independent spirit she also exemplified one of the strongest cultural shapers of nineteenth-century America, a perfectionist quest for holiness, first in herself and then in the wider society. Whether rooted initially in evangelical piety, Methodist or Finneyite holiness movements, or in older Protestant and sectarian traditions (or more likely a mixture of all three), Sarah Grimké's evolving religious convictions were more the inspiration for, than the casualty of, her career as a feminist and abolitionist.

The more intense phase of Sarah Grimké's religious formation as a young woman began with the classical evangelical pattern of awareness of sin, repentance, relapse into sin, and final conversion. That pattern could, and in her case did, reestablish itself in a modified form even after a significant conversion experience had been duly identified and acknowledged. It was often difficult for individuals clearly to determine what were the preludes, the main event, and the postludes of experiences that had similar taxonomies. While acknowledging the complexity of individual experience, one of the major themes of this book is the way in which intense evangelical conversion experiences could act, both positively and negatively, as engines of individual transformation and empowerment. Whether in reacting against what was later regarded as a bad experience or in embracing religious conversion as the defining moment of a new life of purpose and service, these episodes of deep psychological significance had lasting consequences for those who experienced them. But religious conversions are not easily interpreted: they have social as well as personal contexts; they have prescriptive and descriptive dimensions; they are filtered through memory and self-constructions of meaning; they are written and told as narratives and stories; they are embellished for effect and employed as polemical weapons; they are appealed to as the abiding "truth" of an individual's life and consciously manipulated to incorporate falsehoods; they are comedies and tragedies; and, above all, they obey common patterns but are in the last analysis deeply personal and unique events. Two such conversions, and their profound consequences, will shape the narrative of the rest of this chapter. They were experienced by arguably the two most important female reformers of the nineteenth century, Elizabeth Cady Stanton and Frances Willard, who later became allies and protagonists through their different approaches to the emancipation of women.

Stanton, who has been described as "the philosopher and chief publicist of the radical wing of the woman's rights movement," was the inspiration behind America's first woman's rights convention in Seneca Falls in 1848, where she presented her famous "Declaration of Sentiments," and she devoted herself to that cause through thick and thin for over half a century.[19] Over the course of her long life of public engagement she wrote and published a large corpus of material, but two works published in her last decade when she had effectively retired from public appearances, namely *The Woman's Bible* (1895– 98) and her autobiography, *Eighty Years and More: Reminiscences 1815–1897* (1898), are perhaps the most germane to the role of religion in her life. These works share a common theme, that Christianity in general and its sacred text, the Bible, in particular were profoundly misogynistic shapers of culture. *Eighty Years and More* at first sight looks and reads like a conventional Victorian autobiography of an unconventional life, albeit enlivened by an impish sense of humor and a gift for storytelling. But as with all autobiographies what it unconsciously assumes, or what it carefully or carelessly misrepresents, is often more revealing than what it consciously asserts. In Stanton's case her reminiscences of childhood and girlhood, especially with regard to her early religious life, are complex and psychologically compelling. Recent commentators have shown that Stanton heightened and suppressed aspects of her childhood as part of a polemical reconstruction of her life. Her mother scarcely appears, the deaths of loved ones (apart from her only brother when she was a child) are absent, the fact that her father owned a slave is silenced, her privileged background is complacently minimized, her racism is thinly disguised, and her religious experience is framed as much by a powerful explanatory trope as by a truth-seeking engagement with her own experience.

Stanton's account of the religious aspect of her childhood bears resemblance to a surrealist painting in that the mood and the atmosphere are more important than the precise details. Her gloomy Scotch Presbyterian upbringing became conflated in her mind with the somber experience (when she was only eleven) of the death of her only brother and her father's only son. Seventy years later she still remembered vividly going into the large darkened parlor to see her dead brother and finding "the casket, mirrors, and pictures all draped in white, and my father seated at his side, pale and unmovable." She climbed onto his knee to offer childlike compassion, only to be greeted with the never-to-be-forgotten words, "Oh, my daughter, I wish you were a boy!" After death and disappointment came religion and burial. "Then came the sad pageantry of death," she writes, "the weeping of friends, the dark rooms, the ghostly stillness, the exhortation to the living to prepare for death, the solemn prayer, the mournful chant, the funeral cortège, the solemn, tolling bell, the burial. How I suffered during those sad days!" Later, she easily conflates the emotions of grief and gloom with those of religion and repression. Reflecting back on seventy years of life she counted all her trials and disappointments as light compared with "my sufferings in childhood and youth from the theological dogmas which I sincerely believed, and the gloom connected with everything associated with the name of religion, the church, the parsonage, the graveyard, and the solemn, tolling bell."[20] The solemn tolling bell rings through her prose and her emotions as the lugubrious sound and symbol of the gloomy terrors of Calvinist Christianity.

Stanton's descriptions of the religion of her girlhood reek of patriarchy, coldness, and fear. They are full of chilling scenes and chilled emotions. She trudged to services through the snow-covered Johnstown Hills above the Mohawk Valley, listened to a wordy preacher enclosed in a high octagonal box, sang tuneless and unaccompanied metrical Psalms, and experienced "the cold hospitalities of the 'Lord's House,' there to be chilled to the very core by listening to sermons on 'predestination,' 'justification by faith,' and 'eternal damnation.'"[21] Contrasted with this spiritual and emotional wasteland were her tomboy-like romps through forests and ponds and her encounters with Simon Hosack, a neighbor minister who affirmed her, and taught her Greek and Latin. Here by contrast was a world of learning and knowledge, of emotional warmth and welcome, and of freedom and opportunity. Cold-hearted Calvinism with its terrifying fears offered little competition, but there was to be one last hurrah from the old order in the shape of an emotional encounter with Charles Finney's revivalist and much-modified Calvinism.

Although Stanton's record of what happened does not accord with some known historical facts about Finney's schedule, her impressionistic account of her evangelical conversion acts as a deeper truth in the way she conceptualized her spiritual and intellectual journey. While at Emma Willard's school in Troy, at the heart of the burned-over district of New York State, Stanton encountered "one of those intense revival seasons that swept over the city and though the seminary like an epidemic, attacking in its worst form the most

susceptible. Owing to my gloomy Calvinistic training in the old Scotch Presbyterian church, and my vivid imagination, I was one of the first victims." In
a description that is at once deeply personal and supremely detached, Stanton records the dynamics of the revival experience, from powerful preaching
to the anxiety bench, and from conviction of sin to the prayer of repentance.
She claims to have met and spoken with Finney and supplies a vivid description of his preaching style: "I can see him now, his great eyes rolling around
the congregation and his arms flying about in the air like those of a windmill,"
preaching about sinners being swept down the rapids and into the liquid fire
below.[22] But Stanton's Finney-inspired conversion did not take. The experience literally traumatized her and she was forced to return home for emotional convalescence. She then records what can best be described as a coun-
terconversion narrative in which she goes on a trip to Niagara with her family
and is introduced to some new works of liberal moral philosophy by her
brother-in-law. New ideas led to a new direction: "Thus, after many months
of weary wandering in the intellectual labyrinth of 'The Fall of Man,' 'Original Sin,' 'Total Depravity,' 'God's Wrath,' 'Satan's Triumph,' 'The
Crucifixion,' 'The Atonement,' and 'Salvation by Faith,' I found my way out
of the darkness into the clear sunlight of Truth. My religious superstitions
gave place to rational ideas based on scientific facts, and in proportion, as I
looked at everything from a new standpoint, I grew more and more happy,
day by day. . . . I view it as one of the greatest crimes to shadow the minds of
the young with these gloomy superstitions; and with fears of the unknown
and the unknowable to poison all their joy in life."[23]

Stanton's account of this most personal phase of her spiritual pilgrimage
is not without problems. As Kathi Kern has pointed out, Charles Finney did
conduct a protracted revival in the city of Troy during the Second Great
Awakening, but that revival occurred some four years before Stanton enrolled
in Emma Willard's school. Finney did visit Troy briefly on two occasions during Stanton's school days, and she may indeed have met him, but they occurred after, not before, her conversion to a species of rationalism at Niagara
Falls. Attempts to harmonize Stanton's account of events with known historical facts have not been altogether successful. That she was caught up in a
Finney-inspired revival in Troy during the Second Great Awakening is not in
dispute, but all other contingencies about who was doing the preaching and
how Stanton became involved remain unclear. On one level it does not
matter. As Kern has suggested, "Finney was credited with converting a long
line of abolitionists among Stanton's contemporaries. It was, for her readers,
a recognizable credential. A failed conversion by Finney would have been a

credential of a different sort, a badge of honor among agnostics."[24] What was written as a good story became for Stanton a true story.

Stanton's brief and unhappy career as an evangelical Christian, however flaky some of the attendant details may be, supplied her with a good basis from which to attack the pretensions of the clergy, the corruptions of Christian institutions, the evils of religious dogma, and the dangers of biblical literalism. One important reason for her lifelong commitment to woman's suffrage was her conviction that women had been "too much absorbed in the Church; and to change the current of her feelings by rousing some interest in political questions" was one way of breaking the ties of religious oppression.[25] Space does not permit a full treatment of Stanton's subsequent journey into various forms of religious heterodoxy. She read Voltaire, embraced Auguste Comte's Positivism (albeit from a feminist angle), meandered through the practice of Mind Cure and New Thought, and participated in the free thought movement in both Britain and America.[26] But above all, she relentlessly attacked the conservative Christianity of the Bible as a faith constructed by men to serve the interests of men.

Beginning with a failed conversion to evangelical Christianity in her teenage years, Stanton ended with a feminist version of evangelicalism's sacred text, the Bible, which in her view was the ideological anchor point throughout history of male subjugation of women. In her eighties Stanton assembled a committee of prominent feminists to produce *The Woman's Bible,* which is a set of interpretive commentaries on passages of the Bible relating to women. Stanton's committee, essentially a small group of Theosophists, New Thought leaders, and Freethinkers, was not as eclectic in its religious makeup as Stanton initially had hoped, and it produced a text that managed to alienate not only most men, which did not bother Stanton, but also substantial sections of the women's movement. It was even disavowed by the National American Woman Suffrage Association, over which Stanton had briefly presided. Stanton was left to ruminate on the difficulties associated with substituting reason for superstition in minds once perverted by a false faith. "Women," she wrote, "have been taught by their religious guardians that the Bible, unlike all other books, was written under the special inspiration of the Great Ruling Intelligence of the Universe. Not conversant with works on science and higher criticism, which point out its fabulous pretensions, they cling to it with an unreasoning tenacity, like a savage to his fetich."[27]

One of the women who refused to serve on Stanton's committee to produce *The Woman's Bible,* and who was unhappy with its outcome, was Frances Willard, who like Stanton had undergone a religious conversion in her youth and who later became involved in woman's suffrage through her lifelong passion for the cause of temperance. As the leader of the Woman's Christian Temperance Union (WCTU) Willard was one of the most beloved, famous, and influential American women of the nineteenth century. Although she remained much closer to the center of American evangelical religiosity than did Stanton, her journals reveal that her religiosity, especially later in life, was not without tension and complexity. Her life, from evangelical convert to a leader of the women's movement, makes an interesting comparison with Stanton.

As the editor of her extensive journal has pointed out, Willard's life "epitomized the lives of thousands of other young American women during the second third of the nineteenth century," which helps explain her close relationship to the huge constituency of the WCTU.[28] Born into a western New York farm family, Willard moved with her parents first to Oberlin, Ohio, and then to a farm outside Janesville, Wisconsin. Both her migratory pattern from the northeast to the northwest and then to a suburb of Chicago, and her religious trajectory as an active Methodist, America's largest Protestant denomination in the mid nineteenth century, placed her somewhere near the heart and center of America's religious culture. So too did her evangelical conversion experience.

Willard had been brought up in a Christian household with strong church connections, but had not sorted out her own personal convictions before the summer of 1859, when she was nineteen years old. Several events conspired to force her hand. Her upcoming graduation from North Western Female College presented her with choices about her future life which could no longer be evaded or ignored. Her mother candidly advised her that her weak frame and intellectual disposition placed her in a vulnerable position that could best be secured by seeking the "right path" decreed by God. Willard's journal in 1859 reveals a growing strain of introspection and an accompanying enthusiasm for reading widely and interactively as she sought self-understanding through literary engagement. She wrote little lists of weaknesses, accomplishments, and aspirations.[29] She repeatedly looked at herself in the mirror and composed disconcertingly honest evaluations of her physical plainness. According to her autobiography, which she wrote much later (she kept no journal record of these events), the decisive moment came when she was taken seriously ill with typhoid fever. With the outcome of the illness uncertain, Willard heard two inner voices; one was the voice of divine love and forgiveness urging her to submit, the other was the voice of self-reliance and skepticism urging her to tough it out: "One presence was to me warm, sunny, safe, with an impression as of snowy wings; the other cold, dismal, dark, with the flutter of a bat. The controversy did not seem brief; in my weakness such a strain would doubtless appear longer than it was. But at last, solemnly, and with my whole heart, I said, not in spoken words, but in the deeper language of consciousness, 'If God lets me get well I'll try to be a Christian girl.' But this resolve did not bring peace. 'You must at once declare this resolution,' said the inward voice."[30]

Willard then told her mother ("it cost me a greater humbling of my pride to tell her than the resolution had cost of self-surrender"), recovered from her illness, and took some faltering steps on a new course. At this point the superstructure of the Methodist system, which was designed to promote faith and holiness among its members, supplied the context for Willard's onward Christian journey. She attended the sermons of some of Methodism's greatest luminaries, knelt at the altar for fourteen nights in succession at revival services, joined a Bible class, sought advice from some women mentors, wrestled with her greatest sin (pride), engaged in regular Bible reading and prayer, and in December 1859 firmed up her fever-inspired conversion with a public declaration to lead a Christian life.[31] She began the New Year with resolutions of godliness and good learning and then partook of all the Methodist rituals including Love Feasts, class meetings, regular communion, and probationary membership. What is particularly striking about Willard's religious conversion is how Methodist it all was, including a determination to reform her character and live a life of public usefulness. She committed herself not merely to evangelical Christianity, but decidedly to Methodism "because I like its view of the Doctrines taught in the Bible, better than those of any other of God's militant church, because I have been reared in it, & for me to attach myself to any other would cause great sorrow & dissatisfaction in quarters where I should most desire to avoid such consequences."[32] Here is a trilogy of plain biblical theology, family loyalty, and public expectation that served as the foundation for Willard's life in public service. Although Willard never substantially wavered from the Methodist faith that was worked out in the face of rigorous self-analysis, a near-death experience, and the public rituals of Midwestern, mid-century Methodism, some aspects of her conversion warrant further comment. Not only did Willard view her conversion as a door to a reformed character and a career of public usefulness, but also some of her early postconversion comments are quite revealing. Although she was inspired by the life of Jesus, she was unimpressed by the doctrine of the Trinity, and although she called herself a committed Methodist she disavowed narrow-mindedness and sectarianism. Quoting Galatians 3:28 to herself she declared that in Christ there was neither male nor female, bond or free, so she "resolved to educate in myself an unsectarian spirit—to live against it, write against it, talk against it, always."[33]

Willard's subsequent career as an educator, temperance reformer, supporter of the woman's movement, and American public saint is well known and is in no need of rehearsal, but the trajectory of her religious life, though often assumed to be conventionally Methodist and evangelical, is more complicated than that description permits.[34] To begin with, the first couple of years after her religious conversion were far from easy. She suffered the death of her deeply beloved sister Mary, which produced a long-lasting enthusiasm for a family reunion in heaven, but she also suffered a broken engagement and experienced serious struggles of sexual identity revealed through her passionate love for her friend Mary Bannister. To make matters worse, Mary Bannister married Willard's brother, Oliver. There is no mistaking the confusion and the pain pouring from Willard's pen as she sought to understand what was going on in her heart and head and how it related to her faith. Provoked by the thought of Mary and Oliver together, Willard wrote of her passionate relationship with Mary.

> It is not right or natural—so they say—that you & I should love each other as we *do*. (for it is in the *present tense* & in my wretchedness tonight, be it right or wrong, I *will* say I am *glad*.) Ours is such a love that no two women ever had for each other, before. It is wild & passionate, deep & all-pervading. It is "abnormal." It is *impossible* . . . We can not be together. Fate & circumstance decree it. O *how hard* it is, *My Darling!* my *cherished*, blessed, idolized *Mary!* It touches me—it lacerates my heart in its *tenderest* spot (God forgive me—& not *God* only!—that this *is* so, though I have prayed & agonized & taught myself as best I could to have it as you say it is with you—at least *that* way). It stirs up the very depths of my nature. *You* are wound in with my heart of hearts. Can I help it? Will God damn me for it? Did he send this *Friendship* which I thought my choicest Blessing only to poison it & turn it to a curse? What can I do? What must I do?[35]

Given the available categories for women's sexual identity in the religious culture of Midwestern America in the nineteenth century, it is difficult to write adequately about Willard's relationship with women, but Jean Baker is probably right in concluding that although her relationship with Mary Bannister "was possibly genitally chaste it nevertheless established for all time Willard's sexual identity."[36] Over the course of her life she sustained a series of deep and passionate relationships with other women, and she never married, but her conduct was such that her life did not occasion any public controversy about her sexual identity or behavior. Although her journal does not conceal the depth of her love for some other women, neither does it reveal much about how Willard navigated the relationship between faith and sexual identity along the lines she identified in her first relationship with Mary Bannister.[37]

There were times in Willard's life when her already serious faith nearly morphed into something more deeply pious and evangelical. Along with other members of her family she participated in a Holiness Revival in Evanston during January 1866. Although she was impressed by the leaders, Phoebe and Walter Palmer, she confessed that she did not fully comprehend the doctrine of Holiness (instantaneous, attainable sanctification) and could not see how one could possibly be freed from inward temptation.[38] She had her faith deepened by her encounters with the Palmers, at least temporarily, but she already preferred the practicalities of temperance reform over the sanctification mysteries of Holiness theology. Over a decade later, in 1877, Willard was invited by the famous evangelist Dwight L. Moody to conduct the women's meetings at his evangelical crusade in Boston. Willard accepted the invitation, devoted herself to a crash course in the Bible, and spoke to thousands of women in the Boston churches. But the relationship with Moody did not prosper. Willard insisted on keeping up her temperance activities, partly because she needed the money, and partly because it was the sacred cause of her life. Moody did not want to share her, and events came to a head when Willard was prepared to share temperance platforms with Unitarians, and Moody's evangelicalism would not stretch that far. Willard chafed at separate-sex revival meetings, chafed at being told who she could associate with, and chafed at Moody's autocratic style. In her words "Brother Moody's Scripture interpretations concerning religious toleration were too literal for me; the jacket was too straight—I could not wear it." Although Willard presented her separation from Moody as a great act of self-sacrifice, his brand of revivalist evangelicalism would never have sat well with the more eclectic religious constituencies of the WCTU. She did well to part from Moody, and he from her.[39]

Whatever their initial attractions for her, Willard never became either a Holiness or evangelical revivalist. Her cause was temperance and, by logical extension, woman's suffrage. These causes not only opened up associations with women more liberal in religion and radical in politics than herself, but also gave her both the incentive and the ecclesiastical space to explore more heterodox views. Although the default position of Willard's religiosity was always the Midwestern Methodism she first embraced in Evanston, she was neither blind to new currents of thought nor unwilling to countenance other forms of religion. She adapted almost effortlessly to the implications of Darwinism and biblical criticism, in part because it seemed to erode the traditional biblical mandate for patriarchy. If an end of biblical literalism meant the end of a literal reading of the Genesis story of the rib and its associations with the subjugation of women, then so much the better. She wrote in her journal how evolution, theories of a long earth history, and Higher Criticism had all contributed to her adopting a different view of the Bible from that of her father: "Yet his daughter has lived on & finds Truth in the Bible which is a higher thing than *fact*, and reverences God in the Word as much as he ever did the Word of God."[40]

Many of Willard's later views about Christianity had their roots in earlier thoughts and experiences. Her early determination not to be sectarian ripened into a more mature appreciation of other Christian traditions—Protestant, Catholic, and Armenian—along with a greater enthusiasm for Oriental religious traditions.[41] "I am a strictly loyal and orthodox Methodist," she wrote, "but I find great good in all religions and in the writings of those lofty and beautiful moralists who are building better than they know, and all of whose precepts blossom from the rich soil of the New Testament. No word of faith in God or love toward man is alien to my sympathy. But like the bee that gathers from many fragrant gardens, but flies home with his varied gains to the same and familiar hive, so I fly home to the sweetness and sanctity of the old faith that has been my shelter and solace so long."[42] As the last surviving member of a loving family who all died before her, Willard possessed a curiosity about heaven and the afterlife that stimulated an interest in psychic phenomena and some aspects of Spiritualism. She was also at times attracted to Theosophy and Christian Socialism, but these were outcrops from her Methodist core, not powerful new traditions that commanded her affection and loyalty.

When Willard renewed her journal writing in 1893 after an absence of some twenty-three years, the stimulus was the death of her mother and the dismantlement of Rest Cottage, the emotional and spiritual home of the Willards, mother and daughter. Her first entry for January 1, 1893, is as close as one gets to the heart and center of Willard's mature spirituality. She looked to heaven, because that was where her family were; she looked to her faith as the forging of moral character because that is how she mostly saw it; and she kept her little disciplines of Bible reading and hymn singing, for that was the Methodist way. "We must hold to God, to Immortality, to Duty, to Rewards and Punishment—the necessary outcome of our conduct—and to Christ our elder Brother, Exemplar and Redeemer."[43] Here was fin de siècle Methodism shorn of its revivalism, biblicism, and perfectionism, but holding firm to its sense of duty, morality, and service, for the dignity of human life counted in both this world and the next.

If Willard tried to be kind to the Methodism of her youth, the Methodists were not always kind to her. As Bordin states, she was "dealt several severe blows by a hierarchy that admired her gifts and supported many of her causes, but that could not accept her demands for an equal role in the church."[44] When Willard, who was then president of the WCTU, one of the largest and most influential moral reform movements in American history, was elected as a fraternal delegate to the General Conference of her own Methodist Episcopal Church, an enormous brouhaha ensued at the center of which was the simple fact that Willard was a woman. She was treated even more summarily by the Presbyterians, merely the most recent in a long line of authoritarian snubs by male clergymen over the course of Willard's career. All this provoked the normally nonconfrontational Willard to examine critically the position of women in Protestantism, which was eventually published as *Woman in the Pulpit*. The book was published in 1889, one year after Willard was elected by her own Methodist diocese as a delegate to the 1888 meeting of the Methodist General Conference in New York City. As it turned out, the terminal illness of her mother prevented Willard from attending, but the conference subsequently voted down the rights of women to sit as lay delegates. It was not until 1904, years after Willard's death, that Methodist women, despite being a substantial majority within the church, sat as lay delegates to the quadrennial meeting of the governing body of their own church.

The discriminatory attitudes of the male Protestant clergy, supported by the hierarchical bureaucracies of their churches, radicalized Willard and pointed her toward a more critical biblical exegesis. In *Woman in the Pulpit* Willard's normally polite and conciliatory tone gives way to a harder and more polemical edge. After quoting "the cyclone of absurdities" of Dean Alford's thoroughly male interpretation of Paul's thoroughly male strictures to the women of Corinth, Willard states:

> Now, let any reasonable human being read this exegesis, and remember that two-thirds of the graduates from our great system of public education are women; that two-thirds of the teachers in these schools are women; that nearly three-fourths of church members are women; that through the modern Sunday-school women have already become the theological teachers of the modern church; and that, *per contra*, out of about sixty thousand

persons in our penitentiaries fifty-five thousand are men; that whiskey, beer, and tobacco to the value of fifteen hundred million dollars per year are consumed almost wholly by men; and then see if the said reasonable human being will find much mental or spiritual pabulum in the said learned exegesis. A pinch of commonsense forms an excellent ingredient in that complicated dish called Biblical interpretation.[45]

Willard then explicitly made the connection between biblical hermeneutics and power: "the whole subjection theory grows out of the one-sided interpretation of the Bible by men. . . . It is a whimsical fact that men seem comparatively willing that women should enter any profession but their own. The lawyer is willing that they should be doctors, and the doctor thinks they may plead at the bar if they desire to do so, but each prefers to keep them out of his own professional garden-plot. This is true of ministers with added emphasis, for here we have the pride of sex plus the pride of sacerdotalism."[46]

For both Frances Willard and Elizabeth Cady Stanton, and Sarah Grimké, for that matter, the trail of equal rights for women, whether in church or society, or both, ended with the Bible and its exegesis. Although each woman shared a common criticism of the male dynamics of churches and their ministers, they differed in their approach to the Bible. Willard was willing to use the resources of the Methodist tradition, and even the support of male Methodists who were supportive of the cause of women's ordination, to push for a scriptural exegesis that allowed women to exercise their gifts of ministry within the church. Her beef was not so much with patriarchy in the Scriptures as with the interpretation of those Scriptures by the male leadership of the church in the nineteenth century. Stanton's agenda was considerably more radical, and it is not surprising that Willard refused to participate in Stanton's committee formed to produce *The Woman's Bible*. The situation was not helped by the fact that Stanton, without prior consultation, published Willard's name as a contributor to her revising committee. Willard, correctly sensing that such an association with a largely freethinking project would have damaged her support among the more evangelical wing of the WCTU, withdrew her name. Stanton pressed on regardless, but the absence of evangelical, Jewish, and more conservative women on the revising committee not only reinforced the radical tone of *The Woman's Bible* but also limited its appeal for the majority of women in late nineteenth-century America.

In preparation for the publication of the second volume of *The Woman's Bible* Stanton wrote countless letters to women, asking two questions: "1. Have the teachings of the Bible advanced or retarded the emancipation of women? 2. Have they dignified or degraded the Mothers of the Race?" Stanton was clearly in the "retarded" and "degraded" categories, but she published all sorts of responses reflecting a wide variety of opinions as an appendix to *The Woman's Bible*. Willard's response was characteristically diplomatic. She unequivocally repeated the mantra of the largely female American foreign missionary movement that the nations of the world that treat women with most consideration are all Christian nations. She repeated her convictions that the Bible made possible the development of "a hallowed motherhood," and that it sanctified life, marriage, sickness, and death. Displaying her well-practiced talent for flattery and conciliation, she stated that "No such woman as Mrs. Elizabeth Cady Stanton, with her heart aflame against all forms of injustice and cruelty, with her intellect illumined and her tongue quickened into eloquence, has ever been produced in a country where the Bible was not incorporated into the thoughts and affections of the people and had not been so for many generations." Willard also repeated her belief that men had read their own selfish theories into their hermeneutics, that they had underestimated the progressive quality of revelation, and that they had failed to discriminate between science, history, and ethics in their approach to biblical exegesis, but she still believed that "the Bible comes to us from God, and that it is a sufficient rule of faith and practice."[47] Stanton could not have disagreed more. The grounds of their disagreement were parsed out in the world of ideas and the public shape of the woman's movement in late nineteenth-century America, but their roots go back to their girlhoods when differential experiences of religious conversion and church traditions produced very different intellectual, emotional, and spiritual responses to the American Christianity of the Second Great Awakening. For Stanton orthodox Christianity was forever associated with the dark emotions, which arose from, and were projected upon, her Calvinistic upbringing and her bleak Finney-inspired conversion. For Willard orthodox Christianity was forever associated with the homely virtues of Midwestern Methodism, her mother's unconditional love, and her conviction that Christianity was the friend, not the foe, of moral progress. Both women had nothing but contempt for the hypocritical manipulation of power by the American clerical establishment and the churches they ran. Both came to see that that manipulation was aided and abetted by the Bible. But for Stanton the Bible was patriarchal through and through, not just in the way it had been interpreted but in its very essence. For Willard, the Bible contained the word of God, but men, out of self-interest, simply chose not to read it properly.

Sarah Grimké, Elizabeth Cady Stanton, and Frances Willard, three of the most significant leaders of a cast of thousands of female reformers in nineteenth-century America, started out from religious backgrounds, evangelical conversions, and Christian impulses to redefine the civic structures and public morality of their society. Cultural historian Robert Abzug states that reform moved from "changing habits such as drinking to rethinking the basic theological and social foundations of Western culture," leading partly to the "collapse of the evangelical Christian cosmos."[48] The sacred text upholding that cosmos for most nineteenth-century Americans was the Bible, so it is not surprising that first Grimké and then Stanton and Willard began to read that text through some new lenses. Some were supplied by new developments in science and biblical criticism, but mostly their new readings were inspired not by scholarship, but by their experiences as women confronting male hermeneutics and ecclesiastical structures. The degree to which they were radicalized and secularized depended largely on the strength of their emotional and spiritual attachments to the faith of their youth and the churches of their early adulthood. Stanton became the most radical, Willard the least, and that was also reflected in how far they were willing to push a new feminist exegesis of the Bible. Evangelicalism's sacred text did not emerge unscathed from the early history of the women's movement, nor did the evangelical faith of some of its most famous leaders.

6 Vincent van Gogh—A Hard Pilgrimage
Evangelicalism and Secularization

> It must be good to die, conscious of having performed some real good and know-
> ing that one will live through this work, at least in the memory of some, and will
> leave a good example to those who come after. A work that is good may not be
> eternal, but the thought expressed in it is; the work itself will certainly remain in
> existence for a long, long time.
> —Vincent van Gogh (on the death of the painter Charles Daubigny), 1878

Consider the following two extracts from the published letters of Vincent
van Gogh.[1] The first is taken from his only surviving sermon, preached in the
Richmond Methodist Church in the autumn of 1876 during van Gogh's intensely evangelical phase, when he still retained ambitions to be a Christian
minister in a populist evangelical tradition.[2] The second, written over a
decade later, is a piece of worldly advice to his sister Wilhelmien (Wil) from
an older brother whose religious framework and spirituality had changed in
many important respects. The sermon is worth reproducing at some length,
not only to hear van Gogh's very distinctive voice, but also because in both its
content and metaphorical structure it represents themes that were central to

Vincent van Gogh, self-portrait dedicated to Paul Gauguin. Oil on canvas, 1888 (© President and
Fellows of Harvard College)

van Gogh's Christian pilgrimage, especially in his years of deeply pious engagement from 1873 to 1880.

Psalm 119:19. I am a stranger on the earth, hide not Thy commandments from me. It is an old belief and it is a good belief, that our life is but a pilgrim's progress—that we are strangers on the earth, but that though this be so, yet we are not alone for our Father is with us. We are pilgrims, our life is a long walk or journey from earth to Heaven. . . .

There is joy when a man is born into the world, but there is greater joy when a spirit has passed through great tribulation, when an angel is born in Heaven. Sorrow is better than joy—and even in mirth the heart is sad—and it is better to go to the house of mourning than to the house of feasts, for by the sadness of the countenance the heart is made better. Our nature is sorrowful, but for those who have learnt and are learning to look at Jesus Christ, there is always reason to rejoice. It is a good word that of St. Paul: as being sorrowful yet always rejoicing. For those who believe in Jesus Christ, there is no death or sorrow that is not mixed with hope—no despair—there is only a constantly being born again, a constantly going from darkness into light. They do not mourn as those who have no hope—Christian Faith makes life to evergreen life. . . .

Yet we may not live on casually hour by hour—no we have a strife to strive and a fight to fight. What is it we must do: we must love God with all our strength, with all our might, with all our soul, we must love our neighbours as ourselves. These two commandments we must keep, and if we follow after these, if we are devoted to this, we are not alone, for our Father in Heaven is with us, helps us and guides us, gives us strength day by day, hour by hour, and so we can do all things through Christ who gives us might. . . .

The heart of man is very much like the sea, it has its storms, its tides and its depths; it has its pearls too. The heart that seeks for God and for a Godly life has more storms than any other. . . .

What is it we ask of God—is it a great thing? Yes, it is a great thing, peace for the ground of our heart, rest for our soul—give us that one thing and then we want not much more, then we can do without many things, then can we suffer many things for Thy name's sake. We want to know that we are Thine and that Thou art ours, we want to be Thine—to be Christians—we want a Father, a Father's love and a Father's approval. . . .

Our life is a pilgrim's progress. I once saw a very beautiful picture: it was a landscape at evening.[3] In the distance on the right-hand side a row of hills appeared blue in the evening mist. Above those hills the splendour of the sunset, the grey clouds with their linings of silver and gold and purple. The landscape is a plain or heath covered with grass and its yellow leaves, for it was in autumn. Through the landscape a road leads to a high mountain. Far, far away, on the top of that mountain is a city whereon the setting sun casts a glory. On the road walks a pilgrim, staff in hand. He has been walking for a good long while already and he is very tired. And now he meets a woman, or figure in black, that makes one think of St. Paul's word: As being sorrowful yet always rejoicing.[4]

Here is van Gogh's conceptualization of the Christian life as a pilgrim's progress (Bunyan was a favorite author), as a storm at sea, as a search for a father's approval, as a commitment to love, as a desperate search for peace and rest, as a constantly being born again, and as an oscillating experience of sorrow and joy, yet with sorrow as the purer and more noble state. Characteristic also is the tangible and colorful description of the pilgrim's walk (from darkness to light, and from death to life) through a landscape that is more than mere scenery, but somehow encapsulates the essence of the journey itself. These images, metaphors, and assumptions about the nature of Christianity and his engagement with it appear again and again in van Gogh's correspondence throughout the 1870s. Darkness, death, sorrow, and rejection stood on one side, while light, rebirth, joy, and acceptance stood on the other.[5] Somewhere in this dialectic van Gogh's own oscillating temperament sought rest and hope.

Compare the sermon with his brotherly advice to his sister Wil written only a few years before his death.

Well, what shall I say about your little literary sketch about plants and rain? You see yourself that in nature many flowers are crushed underfoot, get frozen or scorched by the sun; and further that not every grain of wheat, after ripening, returns to the earth, there to germinate and become a new plant—but that the great majority of grains of wheat do not attain their natural development, but go to the mill—isn't this true?

Now as for comparing mankind to grains of corn.

In every man who is healthy and natural there is a *germinating force* as in a grain of wheat. And so natural life is germination.

What the germinating force is in the grain of wheat, love is in us.

Now I think we are apt to stand staring with a long face, and at a loss for words, as soon as we are frustrated in our natural development and see this germination made impossible, and find ourselves placed in a situation as hopeless as that of the wheat between the millstones must be.

If things go like that with us, and we are absolutely bewildered by the loss of our natural life, there are some among us who, though wanting to submit to the course of things as they are, yet do not want to relinquish their self-consciousness and self-respect, and insist upon knowing what is the matter with them, and what is really happening.

And if with good intentions we search the books which it is said shed light in the darkness—though inspired by the best will in the world, we find extremely little that is certain, and not always the satisfaction of being comforted personally. And the diseases which we civilized people labor under most are melancholy and pessimism. . . .

Is the Bible enough for us?

In these days, I believe, Jesus himself would say to those who sit down in a state of melancholy, it is not here, get up and go forth. Why do you seek the living among the dead?

If the spoken or written word is to remain the light of the world, then it is our right and our duty to acknowledge that we are living in a period when it should be spoken and written in *such* a way that—in order to find something equally great, and equally good, and equally original, and equally powerful to revolutionize the whole of society—we may compare it with a clear conscience to the old revolution of the Kristians.

I myself am always glad that I have read the Bible more thoroughly than many people nowadays, because it eases my mind somewhat to know that there were once such lofty ideas. But because of the very fact that I think the old things so beautiful, I must think the new things beautiful *à plus forte raison. À plus forte raison,* seeing that we can act in our own time, and the past as well as the future concern us only directly. . . .

To return once more to your little piece of literature; I find it difficult to assume, for my own consolation, or to advise others to assume that there are powers above which interfere in things personally in order to help and comfort us. Providence is such an extremely queer thing, and I solemnly assure you that I most decidedly do not know what to make of it. . . .

And most of all I consider it alarming that you think you will have to study in order to be able to write. No, my dear little sister, learn how to dance, or fall in love with one, or more than one, of the notary's clerks, officers, in short all who are within your reach—play any number of pranks rather than take up study in Holland. It serves absolutely no other purpose than to make one dull-witted, and so I don't want to hear it mentioned.

As far as I myself am concerned, I still go on having the most impossible, and not very seemly, love affairs, from which I emerge as a rule damaged and ashamed and little else.

And in my opinion I am quite right in this, because I tell myself that in the years gone by, when I should have been in love, I gave myself up to religious and socialistic devotions, and considered art a holier thing than I do now.

Why is religion or justice or art so very holy?

It may well be that people who do nothing but fall in love are more serious and holier than those who sacrifice their love and hearts to an idea.[6]

Here is a similar hymn to the supremacy of love, the same infatuation with the material rhythms of nature, the same sense of weary melancholia about the realities of life, but the tone and the content are very different. Here the Bible is insufficient, providence is opaque, the powers above are inscrutable, conventional religion is next to useless, and Jesus is not so much someone to believe in as he is a creative life force.

These two extracts are respectively the clearest available enunciations of his early evangelical piety and his later reflections on religion. They raise a number of questions. Why was van Gogh so attracted to evangelical piety in his late teens and early twenties, and what was the nature of that pietism? Why did it not last, and with what did he replace it? How did these transformations affect his art, and how do they relate, if at all, to broader changes in the secularization of thought in late nineteenth-century Europe? The questions are compelling, but the answers are to some extent elusive, for van Gogh, though a prolific letter writer, is not always the most consistent interpreter of his own life, and his writings betray the same temperamental oscillations that plagued his life, leading eventually to his tragic suicide in the summer of 1890.

Although there is widespread agreement among scholars that van Gogh's religious transformation from a largely uncritical acceptance of the Dutch Reformed religion of his parents (his father was a Reformed pastor associated with the Groningen School of Dutch piety) into a more intense evangelical pietism began with his job transfer to London in June 1873, there is little consensus about what caused it.[7] Many have followed the first "memoir" of van Gogh's life, written by his sister-in-law, Johanna van Gogh-Bonger, who ascribed the change in his religious sensibilities to the consequences of his unrequited love for the daughter of his landlady, Eugenie Loyer.[8] Others have drawn attention to the possible psychological impact on van Gogh's parents of the stillborn child a year before his birth, or to the supposed melancholic results of a Calvinist upbringing, or to the results of separation from his family in a strange country. By their very nature, none of these interpretations can be conclusively validated or invalidated by an appeal to van Gogh's letters. What the letters show is that his job transfer from the Goupil galleries in The Hague to their London branch was accompanied by a sense of loneliness, separation from his family and his beloved Dutch countryside, increasing disillusionment with the commercial grind of the art market he was required to serve, and an expanded reading program that included Michelet's *L'Amour,* Ernest Renan's *Life of Jesus,* and George Eliot's *Adam Bede.* Van Gogh also seems to have been rocked by the death of his young relative Annette Haanebeck and, over a concentrated period of time, by the deaths of several other relatives and acquaintances. Within this phalanx of reasons for his intensified religious piety the painful rejection by Eugenie Loyer, the first great love of his life, stands out, not only because of the emotional fidelity with which he wrote about it, but also because a similar argument can be made for his final retreat from conventional Christianity, which was partly a result of his second great unrequited love, this time for his cousin, Cornelia (Kee) Vos, in 1881.[9]

Whatever the precise dynamics of these factors in van Gogh's life, the period between his two great loves is characterized by both frequent changes of location and profound piety, which are linked in some kind of melancholic symbiosis. He moved first to London, then to Paris, back to London, then back to Paris, then to Ramsgate and on to Isleworth (a London suburb), then to Dordrecht, Amsterdam, the Borinage in Belgium, and then to Brussels and The Hague. Even within these moves there are changes of lodgings, jobs, and friends, and various visits to home (which had also changed location). The emotional toll of all this was not inconsiderable, since it is clear from his correspondence that he hated partings, including the ultimate parting of death. Clearly, spatial or emotional stability were not the defining characteristics of van Gogh's period of affinity with popular evangelicalism. What were?[10]

One approach is to look at the detectable change of religious tone in his letters throughout 1875, especially those to his younger brother and confidante, Theo, to whom he acts as a kind of self-appointed spiritual adviser. In April he quotes Renan with approval: "Pour agir dans le monde il faut mourir à soi-même. Le Peuple qui se fait le missionaire d'une pensée religieuse n'a plus d'autre patrie que cette pensée" (To act well in this world one must sacrifice all personal desires. The people who become the missionary of a religious thought have no other fatherland than this thought). In August he tells Theo about the sermons he had listened to and encourages him to become a regular churchgoer. In September he writes about obtaining "wings" over life, death, and the grave, and cites his father as model of faith, prayer, and Bible study. Later the same month he quotes passages from the Sermon on the Mount, "blessed are the poor in spirit, blessed are the pure in heart," and then "narrow is the path which leadeth unto life, and those that find it are few." He concludes with what seems to have been his favorite Bible verse from 2 Cor. 6:10, when Paul, after describing the manifold hardships of ministry, talks about being "sorrowful, yet always rejoicing." In October he sends Theo a copy of the *Imitation of Christ* by Thomas à Kempis and quotes "some very beautiful English hymns." His choices are revealing:

Thy way, not mine, O lord,
However dark it be:
Lead me by Thine own hand
Choose out the path for me

Nearer, my God, to thee
Nearer to Thee.
E'en though it be a cross,
That raiseth me;
Still all my song shall be,
Nearer, my God, to Thee,
Nearer to Thee.

Oft in sorrow . . . oft in woe
Onward, Christians, onward go:
Fight the fight, maintain the strife,
Strengthened with the bread of life.

Later that month he tells Theo that he has taken under his wing a young Englishman, Harry Gladwell, a fellow employee of Goupil, who, like Vincent, was a lonely young man of uncouth appearance: "Every evening we go home together and eat something in my room; the rest of the evening I read aloud, generally from the Bible. We intend to read it all the way through."[11] Socially isolated in an apartment in Montmartre, Gladwell and van Gogh became unlikely partners in faith, sharing breakfast in the early morning and Bible reading late at night.

Van Gogh's pilgrimage of faith was not an easy one. His propensity for melancholia and extremism seemed to draw him to biblical texts and devotional literature that emphasized the narrowness of the path, the hardships of the journey, and the single-mindedness required of the pilgrim. But there is another defining characteristic of van Gogh's piety that was to have an immense influence on not only his Christian pilgrimage, but also later on the development of his painting. Van Gogh came to believe that the most authentic expressions of Christianity were those carried out in sacrificial service of Christ's poor. For example, while in England the two authors who made the most impression on him were George Eliot and Charles Dickens. In particular, Eliot's portraits of Mr. Tryan the evangelical minister who sacrificially ministers to the humble poor in "Janet's Repentance," and of *Felix Holt, The Radical* (van Gogh's favorite novel), who chooses the simple life of an artisan, made a lasting impression on him. So too did Dickens's emotionally affective descriptions of the English urban poor. Van Gogh was also deeply influenced by John Bunyan's *Pilgrim's Progress,* Thomas à Kempis's *Imitation of Christ,* the religious poetry of the great English hymnodists, and Charles Haddon Spurgeon's sermons.[12] What particularly attracted van Gogh to Bunyan was his highly visual portrayal of "the subversive theme within Christianity" that Christ came primarily to the poor who have "a natural spiritual advantage in this theology of self-denial, humility, and worldly renunciation." Hence the "pilgrims who emulate Christ are strangers and outcasts, divested of material possessions and social status."[13] Bunyan's subversive identification of sin with the values of aristocratic worldliness was meat and drink to van Gogh's soul.

The devotional and institutional expressions of van Gogh's evangelical piety follow on naturally from his voracious reading of the Bible and his picture of Christ as a messenger to the poor. Although he continued to love art (there is a rich collection of drawings from this part of his life), nature, and literature, there are some hints in his letters that he found it hard to reconcile his aesthetic sense with the apparently exclusive claims of religious devotion he read in the Bible. He came to believe that the latter trumped the former, but this belief brought with it profound inner struggles that he was unable to resolve. He seemed continuously wrapped up in the old Calvinist dilemma of how to subject everything—culture, nature, and the human will—to the lordship of Christ. As a result of van Gogh's inability to find compatibility, accommodation, or resolution, his passions for religion, art, and nature sometimes seemed more competitive than integrated.

Throughout 1875 van Gogh's piety deepened in inverse proportion to his commitment to the world of art dealing, and it came as little surprise to him that he was asked to leave his employment early in 1876. However frustrating it had come to be for him, the end of van Gogh's seven-year employment in the art world had profound consequences. The career to which he had been apprenticed at the age of sixteen was over, and with it went an important element of vocational stability, financial independence, and familial respect. Over the next three years he taught school in Ramsgate and Isleworth, took a job as a bookseller's clerk in Dordrecht, studied for university entrance exams in Amsterdam as a preparation for ministry, entered missionary training college in Brussels, and was appointed evangelist to the Belgian mining district of the Borinage.

It was in these years that van Gogh's absorption in evangelical religion was most intense. During his sojourn in England he attended church and taught Sunday School at Turnham Green Congregational Church, but he also attended prayer meetings and preached at the Wesleyan Methodist Church in Richmond. It was there that he preached the celebrated sermon quoted at the beginning of this chapter. In his sermon he describes life as a pilgrimage, a journey from the mingled joy and anguish of childbirth to an eternal destination in the heavens. The dominant metaphor he uses for the journey is sailing on a river in the midst of a storm. Just as Jesus was able to reassure his frightened disciples by calming the storm on the Sea of Galilee, so too God acts on the believer's life to bring calm and peace, love, and charity. Even so, van Gogh relentlessly portrays life as a violent storm, an arduous uphill pilgrimage, and a vale of tears, for even "the calms are often treacherous." It is the pilgrim's lot, as a stranger on the earth, to strive and to suffer, to be "sorrowful yet always rejoicing." The overall tone of the sermon is of youthful ardor and lofty aspiration, tinged with a strong sense of the hardships to be expected in terrestrial life. It ends with van Gogh's quotation of two old sayings retrieved from memory: "Much strife must be striven, much suffering must be suffered, much prayer must be prayed, and then the end will be peace," and "The water comes up to the lips, but higher comes it not."

Perhaps even of more importance than his sermon for understanding the nature of van Gogh's piety during his sojourn in England is the recently discovered scrapbook of his favorite texts that he presented to Mrs. Annie Slade-Jones, the wife of the clergyman/schoolteacher in whose school he taught. The first page, written in Dutch, contains extracts of Psalms, hymns, and poetry. "This is followed by the one English page, which includes several verses from Corinthians ('Though I speak with the tongues of men and of angels . . .'), three favorite hymns ('Tell Me the Old, Old Story,' 'O Sacred Head Once Wounded' and 'Tossed with Rough Winds, and Faint with Fear'), along with two Longfellow poems ('The Secret of the Sea' and 'Afternoon in February'). Also included are some of his favorite German poetry and French writers. Apart from this scrapbook, van Gogh also filled the edges of many of his prints with Bible verses which he seems to have memorized.[14]

Van Gogh's stint as teacher and preacher for the English Congregationalists and Methodists did not last long, however. Loneliness, financial exigencies, and lack of clear prospects necessitated a change of direction. Under family pressure he took a job as a bookseller's clerk in Dordrecht. The change of location, if anything, only intensified his fierce religious devotion and his determination to enter some form of Christian ministry. On weekdays his consuming passion for Bible study—before, during, and after work—was noted by all who knew him, and on Sundays he attended Dutch Reformed, Jansenist, Roman Catholic, and Lutheran churches. All the while, according to his roommate, "he got more melancholy . . . religion occupied all his spare time and thoughts."[15] This close association between fervent piety and deep melancholy almost always characterized van Gogh's religious pilgrimage. He wrote Theo that he was drawn to the Bible, that he read it daily, that he wanted it to be a light unto his path, that he hoped it would change his life, but also that he was "sometimes lonely and sad, especially when I am near a church or a parsonage." Nevertheless, he was still determined to become a Christian minister, drawing comfort and inspiration from the fact that "as far as one can remember, in our family, which is a Christian family in every sense, there has always been, from generation to generation, one who preached the Gospel. Why shouldn't a member of that family feel himself called to that service now?"[16]

Standing in the way of van Gogh's aspiration to become a Christian minister was the uncomfortable and, to him, outrageous reality that he would have to take a course of theological study at the University of Amsterdam. As it turned out, despite the tuition arranged by his family, he was unable even to clear the preparatory examinations in Latin and Greek. His letters to Theo from Amsterdam are dominated by the grind of academic study, his fear of failure, endless perambulations around narrow streets and canals (described always through an artist's eye), frequent sermon tasting, more intensive Bible study, more close encounters with death (including a moving account of the drowning of a young boy), and another revealing meeting with his fellow pilgrim Harry Gladwell, who also loves "the man of sorrows, and acquainted with grief." Despite the rigor of the study of ancient languages, and perhaps because he did not approach it rigorously enough, van Gogh seemed more absorbed with paintings and books than with theological preparation. In Delaroche, Michelet, Carlyle, and Dickens he detected "something of the resurrection and the life" and confessed, "I should like to read more widely, but I must not; in fact, I need not wish it so much, for all things are in the word of Christ—more perfect and more beautiful than in any other book."[17]

Meanwhile, as with many who find their principal task unappealing, van Gogh spent more time planning and arranging his studies than actually doing them. After yet another planning session with his tutor he told Theo of the oppression he felt taking "Greek lessons in the heart of Amsterdam, in the heart of the Jewish quarter, on a very close and sultry summer afternoon, with the feeling that many difficult examinations await you, arranged by very learned and shrewd professors."[18] As the year unfolded he became increasingly aware that the preparatory examinations for entry to the University of Amsterdam were going to present a formidable challenge. To his studies in Latin and Greek were added new challenges from algebra and mathematics, history, and geography. He told Theo that his desire was to finish his studies as quickly as possible so that he could be ordained and "perform the practical duties of a clergyman," which is where his heart really lay. Revealingly, van Gogh describes his studies variously as "a dog gnawing at a bone," as a "race and a fight for my life," and as an exercise in "good courage for what must follow." As the sore struggle continued, van Gogh's letters are often illuminated by brilliant descriptions of paintings, books, and city scenes, sad indications that his mind was working furiously, but alas not in the direction required by the entrance examinations. Just before Christmas 1877, van Gogh, the struggling tutorial student, painted a verbal picture of the Amsterdam skyline for his brother:

> Twilight is falling, and the view of the yard from my window is simply wonderful, with that little avenue of poplars—their slender forms and thin branches stand out so delicately against the gray evening sky; and then the old arsenal building in the water—quiet as "the waters of the old pool" mentioned in the Book of Isaiah—down by the waterside the walls of that arsenal are quite green and weather-beaten. Farther down is the little garden and the fence around it with the rosebushes, and everywhere in the yard the black figures of the workmen and also the little dog. Just now Uncle Jan with his long gray hair is probably making his rounds. In the distance the masts of the ships in the dock can be seen, in front the Atjeh, quite black, and the gray and red monitors—and just now here and there the lamps are being lit. At this moment the bell is ringing and the whole stream of workmen is pouring toward the gate; at the same time the lamplighter is coming to light the lamp in the yard behind the house.[19]

Van Gogh's descriptive powers were unfortunately superior to his capacity to master Greek verbs. Early in 1878 he opened up to Theo the possibility of failure, and in the same letter expressed his admiration for an artless evangelical clergyman from Lyons whose simple devotion to the local factory workers made a deep impression on him. In a similar vein, van Gogh's Greek and Latin tutor, Mendes da Costa, commented on his greater concern for simple and marginalized people than for the delights of classical conjugations. Da Costa was particularly disturbed by what he called van Gogh's "mental masochism," namely his capacity to engage in self-chastisement as acts of atonement for neglecting his scholarly duties. According to da Costa, he, van Gogh, and his father all came to a mutually agreeable conclusion that enough was enough, and that he should cease his increasingly futile preparations for admission to the University of Amsterdam.[20]

Van Gogh's retrospective explanation for abandoning his preparations for theological study is rather different. He told Theo that the real reason for his change of plan was that he no longer wanted to take his parents' money for a course of action in which he had completely lost confidence. "You understand," he wrote, "that I, who have learned other languages, might have managed also to master that miserable little bit of Latin—which I declared, however, to be too much for me. This was a blind, because I then preferred not to explain to my protectors that the whole university, the theological faculty at least, is, in my eyes, an inexpressible mess, a breeding place of Pharisaism."[21] Was this the comment of a failed student trying to rationalize a past humiliation, or was it the honest opinion of a man who had seen the inner sanctum of a theological education and did not much like it? If the latter, van Gogh would be one of thousands of nineteenth-century seminarians who neither admired their teachers nor cared for what they were taught.[22]

However, the real reason for van Gogh's termination of study is probably more complex. The letters plainly show that his heart was not in the project right from the start. He wanted to be a clergyman but did not want to spend irreplaceable years of his life in what he regarded as arid and irrelevant academic study before he could minister to needy people.[23] He repeatedly told his tutor that John Bunyan's *Pilgrim's Progress*, à Kempis's *Imitation of Christ*, and the Bible were far more important guides than any amount of classical and historical texts.[24] In short, he wanted to minister to humble people and saw no advantage in theological study as a means to that end. Having neither the desire nor the aptitude for rigorous study of ancient languages, he withdrew and told himself that he did not so much fail in his studies as much as he failed to see the point of them.

After a brief sojourn at his father's parsonage in Etten, van Gogh left for the Training School for Evangelists in Brussels, a course of study that would take three years, not six as in Amsterdam, and where the teachers "require less knowledge of ancient languages and less theological study, but they value more highly fitness for practical work and the faith that comes from the heart."[25] For van Gogh it represented another new start, in another new city, under the supervision of yet another religious institution. For him the deadly combination of academic study, separation from family and friends, financial privation, and religious intensity had not worked before, and, alas, was not to work again. To make matters worse, a new problem emerged. He recognized straight away that the key to being a successful evangelist was to become a "popular orator," with a capacity to speak fluently, persuasively, and rousingly.[26] He tried to prepare for his new vocation by writing out lengthy sermons on the parables, a course of action not likely to produce the spontaneous oratory that would be required of him.

Not surprisingly, the old melancholia soon returned. Occasional visits from his family, designed to lift his spirits, had a seesaw effect on his temperament, with a convivial high always followed by a deep low. After a happy day in Brussels visiting galleries with Theo, he walked the working-class districts at night. He saw the street cleaners coming home with carts drawn by old white horses, which brought to mind a series of aquatints on "The Life of a Horse," the last of which was of an old, emaciated animal bound for a knacker's yard surrounded by skulls and skeletons. For van Gogh this "very melancholy scene" was a metaphor of life and death. He wrote Theo "that whenever we see the image of indescribable and unutterable desolation—of loneliness, poverty and misery, the end or extreme of all things, the thought of God comes into our minds. At least it does with me." In the same letter he announced to Theo that his probationary study in Brussels had not resulted in an official nomination, but that he nevertheless intended to pursue his vocation as an evangelist among the coal miners of the Borinage in southern Belgium. What after all could better represent "the end or extreme of all things" than to work among those for whom "daylight does not exist" and who experience "thousands of ever-recurring dangers?" If God was indeed to be found in the depths of desolation, van Gogh expected to find the divine presence in the deep coal pits of the Borinage.[27]

As with his withdrawal from his studies in Amsterdam, van Gogh's account of his failure to secure a nomination from the Brussels training school for evangelists is somewhat at odds with the recollections of others. While his explanation to Theo focused on his lack of financial resources, others drew attention to his lack of submission, poor scholarly aptitude, and self-absorption.[28] Whatever his failings as a student, however, he threw himself into his mission among the Belgian miners with characteristic zeal and determination. As was the way with van Gogh, the early signs were encouraging. He thought the countryside picturesque ("Maris could make a wonderful picture of it"), evoking fond memories of Brueghel's paintings and Dürer's etchings. He seemed to enjoy the religious meetings and Bible classes, and the opportunity to speak about "the great Man of Sorrows who knows our ills." He regarded the people as simple and good natured, "those who leave are homesick for their country; on the other hand, homesick foreigners may come to feel that they belong here." His letters display a strange kind of exotic enthusiasm for life underground and those who lived it. There was, of course, another side. The people were emaciated, victims of firedamp explosions, mining accidents, futile strikes, polluted lungs, typhoid, and fever. Who can look at his evocative drawing *The Bearers of the Burden* (1881) with its image of mining women bent double under the burden of carrying heavy sacks of coal set against the gray desolation of a mining landscape, and not sense the awful drudgery of that occupation, or taste the coal dust?[29]

All surviving accounts of van Gogh's sojourn among the miners of the Borinage pay tribute to his fierce, almost manic, self-denying approach to his mission. He subjected himself to every privation, identified with every human need, and lived without all comforts, even access to his beloved art. In his limited spare time he read *Hard Times* and *Uncle Tom's Cabin*, novels appropriate for someone becoming more aware of the structures of human oppression. Although his letters from this period often record a sense of fulfillment and satisfaction, the manic intensity of his ministry to the poor exhausted van Gogh and increasingly alarmed his family. The scene was set for yet another psychologically painful transition, only this time his commitment to evangelical religion was to be the casualty, not the facilitator, of a new direction in his life.[30]

The end of van Gogh's career as a missionary evangelist to the Belgian poor, as was the way with Vincent, came in three painful bumps. The *official* end came in July 1879 when his hard-earned endorsement of his mission to the Belgian miners was withdrawn. The annual report of the Union of Protestant Churches in Belgium stated, "The experiment that has been tried by accepting the services of a young Dutchman, Mr. Vincent Van Gogh, who believed his calling was to preach the Gospel in the Borinage, has not given the results we had expected. Mr. Van Gogh has certainly shown admirable qualities in his care for the sick and the wounded; many times he has shown devotion and a sense of sacrifice; he has kept night watches with people who need it, and even gave the best part of his clothes and linen away. If he had also had the gift of the word, which is indispensable to anyone who is placed at the head of a congregation, Mr. Van Gogh would surely have become an accomplished evangelist."[31]

Van Gogh's services were no longer required by the Belgian evangelicals because apparently his actions spoke louder than his words. He found a temporary six-month assignment as an evangelist in the coal-mining town of Wasmes, but that too ended in the same way and with the same set of criticisms. Another stint as an independent evangelist in the nearby town of Cuesmes, also ending in tears, was to be his swan song as an evangelist to Christ's poor. It also prepared the way for his own personal repudiation of the evangelical gospel he once felt called to preach. "There may be a great fire in our soul," he wrote, "yet no one ever comes to warm himself at it, and the passers-by see only a wisp of smoke coming through the chimney, and go along their way."[32]

Why, then, did van Gogh's rejection by the evangelicals lead to his rejection of the faith they represented? While serving in the Borinage did van Gogh find out, like many other nineteenth-century evangelical missionaries to the working classes, that the evangelical dogma of the time seemed irrelevant to those whose lives were pressed by more urgent physical needs, or was there more to it than that?[33] Although he never addressed the issue directly in 1879, there are abundant clues in his subsequent correspondence that offer the beginnings of an explanation.

No doubt piqued by a sense of rejection, and schooled in the evils of hypocrisy by his readings in Shakespeare, Dickens, and Harriet Beecher Stowe, Vincent developed a passionate cynicism for those in authority, especially those in religious authority. In the same way that he lost respect for commercial art dealers in Paris and London, and self-serving theological educators in Amsterdam, he grew disenchanted with the evangelical leadership he encountered in Belgium. "I must tell you," he wrote Theo, "that with evangelists it is the same as with artists. There is an old academic school, often detestable, tyrannical, the accumulation of horrors, men who wear a cuirass, a steel armor, of prejudices and conventions; when these people are in charge of affairs, they dispose of positions, and by a system of red tape they try to keep their protégés in their places and to exclude the other man." Comparing the spirituality of evangelical worthies to that of Shakespeare's drunken Falstaff (very Dickensian), van Gogh concluded that they were incapable of normal human emotions or of anything approaching clear sightedness.[34]

A similar distrust of religious professionals shows up a year later, when, after yet another bout of unrequited love, this time with his cousin Kee Vos, he wrote that the object of his love was in a mental prison imposed by the "Jesuitism of clergymen," which no longer had a hold on him because he knew some of "the *dessous de cartes*": "For me that God of the clergymen is as dead as a doornail. But am I an atheist for all that? The clergymen consider me so—so be it—but I love, and how could I feel love if I did not live and others did not live. Now call it God, or human nature or whatever you like, but there is something which I cannot define in a system though it is very much alive and very real, and see that as God, or just as good as God."[35]

Van Gogh's criticism of the religious professionals he had once sought to emulate was accompanied by a more inclusive and less mutually competitive view of religion, art, literature, and spirituality than was the case in his evangelical phase. "I think that everything which is really good and beautiful—of inner moral, spiritual and sublime beauty in men and their works—comes from God, and all which is bad and wrong in men and their works is not of God, and God does not approve of it." In this way van Gogh was able to move beyond what was at times an antithetical view of religion and art to one that sought unity in all "the many things one must believe and love." Thus he could find something of Rembrandt in Shakespeare and something of the Gospel in Rembrandt and so on. Nevertheless, resolutions of old warring members did not come easily to van Gogh, and not all was resolved. He recognized that he had spent five years of his life "more or less without employment, wandering here and there," and that he was still without a suitable vocation, financial resources, familial respect, or his own family. He described himself as a caged bird imprisoned by adverse circumstances, a damaged reputation, and insufficient redeeming love. Even if his cage had not sprung open, something substantial changed in him in the years 1879–80. After parting company with the Belgian evangelicals, never again are his letters dominated by endless scriptural quotations, pious instructions, and a desire to find some form of sacrificial Christian service. Van Gogh, the evangelical Protestant, was buried somewhere in the coal mines of the Borinage.[36]

The person who emerged from the Belgian "black country" was just as much a tortured soul as the person who entered it, but never again was the torture prescribed for him by some form of intense biblical Christianity. Van Gogh came to believe that love was the more excellent way and that art, for better or worse, was his passion. In 1880 he wrote, "the best way to know God is to love many things. Love a friend, a wife, something—whatever you like—and you will soon be on the way to know more about Him."[37] There is a similar message in the letter to his younger sister Wil quoted at the beginning of this chapter. In the midst of much brotherly advice about how his sister should ease up on piety and discover instead the joys of living, loving, dancing, and looking afresh at nature and its colors, he wrote, "people who do nothing but fall in love are more serious and holier than those who sacrifice their love and hearts to an idea." This was not a sentence that could have shown up in one of van Gogh's sermons a decade earlier.

Taken together, it seems clear that van Gogh abandoned his melancholic commitment to evangelical Christianity because he was disillusioned with its institutions, its theology, its practitioners, and its effects. He had become a believer, not in a body of dogma carried forth by professional clergymen, but in the transcendent power of life, love, nature, and the pursuit of happiness. He would not have appropriated descriptive labels such as atheism, agnosticism, or infidelity for this new faith, for it was based not on rationality, but on sense and experience, on impressions and expressions.

Van Gogh's abandonment of evangelicalized and institutionalized Christianity was certainly not an abandonment of all interest in the sacred. In a brilliant book on the strange "collaboration" between van Gogh and Gauguin in the town of Arles in Provence in 1888 Debora Silverman advances the thesis that in their search for an authentic expression of sacred art van Gogh drew on his Dutch Reformed heritage while Gauguin drew on his Roman Catholic background.[38] Challenging the interpretation that van Gogh grew up in a quintessentially dull and limited Calvinist household of fictional stereotype, she shows how van Gogh partly imbibed from his parents a love of nature and art, and also a connection to modernizing theological trends within the Dutch Reformed tradition. Despite the vicissitudes of his faith and practice, these things went with him to the end of his life. When in Arles van Gogh equally repudiated the culture of agrarian festivals and popular "superstitions" of French Catholic peasants and also the overt attempts by Gauguin and Emile Bernard to import Catholicized images into their paintings. Van Gogh was impatient with what he thought were crude and inauthentic attempts to paint representations of the crucifixion, the Garden of Gethsemane (as an expression of human despair), or other biblical images and stories. But Silverman is not content to leave it there. She shows how van Gogh sought other ways to convey the sacred that resonated with his Dutch Protestant heritage including an emphasis on the sanctity of labor and an attempt to "express divinity in the labor forms of paint as woven cloth, plowed earth, and crumbled brick." In this way van Gogh sought the infinite in and through the materiality of nature and nature's workers. But he also retained an unconventional view of an afterlife—if after all a caterpillar can become a butterfly why couldn't a painter-butterfly have another life (van Gogh's comparison)—and he retained a fascination with Christ, not as a martyr or a religious teacher, but rather as a life-giving artist. He wrote Bernard that "Christ alone—of all the philosophers . . .—has affirmed, as a principal certainty, eternal life, the infinity of time, the nothingness of death, the necessity and raison d'être of serenity and devotion. He lived serenely as a greater artist than other artists, despising marble and clay as well as color, working in living flesh."[39] Artists, however great, made only objects, but Christ made "living men" through "pure creative power." These quasi-theological musings of van Gogh were given artistic expression not in conventional biblical art, but in paintings like *The Sower* (1888), which combines an earthy, heavily textured celebration of lowly labor with "blazing, incandescent sunlight, which seems to blast through and saturate every pore of the canvas surface." "In this combination of grounded peasant work and immaterial irradiation," writes Silverman, "van Gogh identified a new theory of art and attitude toward reality that he connected for the first time to 'symbolism' and to the aspiration for a modern sacred art."[40]

Van Gogh and Secularization

As was the case with George Eliot, van Gogh's personal pilgrimage from evangelical Christianity to a deeply personal philosophy based on love and creativity is worthy of much wider application in late nineteenth-century Europe. In that sense their biographies are as revealing of the secularization of the European mind in the nineteenth century as they are of their own personal journeys. The best place to start this analysis is with some of the paintings van Gogh produced in the mid 1880s. The two hundred or so paintings that survive from van Gogh's Dutch period (1881–85) have been studied mostly as rather rough experiments in the creative evolution of a major artist whose really important work came later. By contrast with the remarkable brightness of color and light characteristic of his later paintings, when a combination of Gauguin's influence and the southern French countryside lightened his palette if not his spirits, van Gogh's early work is Dutch dark.[41] At first sight the canvases look as if they were painted in forty shades of gray, but on closer inspection they are as much experiments with color and light as they are with subject matter and technique. Mostly still lifes, scenes of peasant life, and portraits of peasant women, van Gogh's early work was produced under those most common of early adult pressures—vocational agnosticism, familial expectations, and financial duress. More out of economic necessity than filial devotion, van Gogh spent some of these years at his parents' home in Nuenen, where his father was pastor. By this stage van Gogh had become a religious disappointment to his parents, a trajectory sadly complicated by the sudden death of his father in 1885.[42] Three paintings from around that time, one painted before the death of his father and two completed shortly afterward, are strikingly illustrative of major themes in the history of European secularization. For convenience these paintings will be examined not in chronological order of completion, but in the chronology of secularization to which they refer.

The first is *The Old Church Tower at Nuenen ("The Peasants' Churchyard")*, which depicts the remnants of a twelfth-century church surrounded by an old burial ground marked by simple wooden crosses. Influenced perhaps by Millet's *Church at Greville* (1871–74), Van Gogh's church tower is at once a simple study of one of the enduring legacies of Christendom, an old church surrounded by the parish dead, and a symbol of something yet more profound. Van Gogh's intention was to show "that *for centuries* peasants have been laid to rest in the same fields in which they toil during their life—I wanted to express how perfectly simple death & burial is, as simple as the falling of autumn leaves—just some earth dug up—a little wooden cross. The fields around—they make a final line against the horizon, where the grass of the churchyard ends—like a horizon of the sea. And now this ruin tells me how a creed and a religion have moldered away, even though they were so well established—how, nevertheless, the life & death of the peasants is and remains the same: always sprouting and withering like the grass and the flowers that are growing in this graveyard. *Les religions passent, Dieu demeure*, as Victor Hugo—whom they've also just buried—once said."[43]

In short, van Gogh thought he was painting a relic of Christendom, the remaining stump of a culture in which church and people were indissolubly linked together in life and death. Even the stump was crumbling, however, for in an almost surreal testimony to the death of a culture the old church tower at Nuenen was disappearing almost as fast as van Gogh could paint it. The spire was demolished before his early watercolors could be turned into oil on canvas, and his final version only just outpaced the sale of the rest of the tower for building scrap. Indeed the whole history of the old church at Nuenen bears a striking resemblance to the narratives constructed by historians to describe and explain European secularization. The Romanesque church was built in the early medieval period when the task of Christianizing the populations of Europe was painstakingly and monumentally undertaken, parish by parish. While historical debates still rage about the kind of Christianity appropriated by van Gogh's dead peasants, there is no denying the fact that for most inhabitants of medieval and early modern Europe, parish churches were somewhere near the center of village life. In a surprising act of symbolic solidarity, Nuenen's medieval church collapsed in 1792, just a few years after Christendom received its most telling blow from the hands of the French revolutionaries. Enthusiastic attempts were made to patch up Nuenen's old church tower in 1803, just as Europe's Catholic and Protestant churches made heroic efforts to recover from the damage inflicted on the Christendom model by events in France, but both the Nuenen church restorers and the churches of Europe recognized that nothing would ever be the same again. The French Revolution had altered forever the terms on which established churches could exercise ecclesiastical power and social control in Western Europe.[44]

Van Gogh painted another ecclesiastical site during his brief sojourn in Nuenen, and it too is suggestive of wider themes in the history of European secularization. His *Congregation Leaving the Reformed Church in Nuenen* shows the church of the local Reformed congregation to which his father had ministered since 1882. Built in the early nineteenth century, a century that saw more churches built or reconstructed in Europe than any other, the little Reformed church of van Gogh's father catered for Nuenen's minority Protestant community. In early sketches for the painting and, as X-rays have shown, in the final canvas itself, van Gogh painted a lone peasant with a shovel over his shoulder trudging past the church in winter. In contrast to the wooden crosses dotted all around the medieval church tower at Nuenen, van Gogh's lone peasant seems disconnected with its modern counterpart. For reasons that may never be clear, van Gogh painted over the lone peasant, replacing him with a procession of predominantly female churchgoers, most of whom are respectably dressed and some of whom are in mourning clothes. Why? Was it because the painting was intended as a present to his mother, who disliked its drab, wintry, and isolated appearance? Was it because it seemed to be such an obvious copy of Millet's *Church at Greville*, which also has a lone peasant walking past a church? Was the painting reworked by van Gogh as a more fitting memorial to his recently deceased father? Hence the introduction of warmer autumnal colors and the mourning attire of some of the women. Whatever the reason for the changes, there is no doubt that van Gogh's portrayal of his father's small Protestant church with its mainly female worshippers in a predominantly Catholic village serves as an excellent symbol of late nineteenth-century European religion. Religious pluralism, confessional pride, respectability (see also van Gogh's painting of *The Vicarage at Nuenen*), and feminization, which historians interpret as both the signs and the engines of European secularization, are all on display.[45]

The third and best-known of van Gogh's religious trilogy painted at Nuenen is his *Still Life with Bible*. It has a disarmingly simple composition—an open Bible, a modern novel, an extinguished candle, and a flowing tablecloth—but the painting is redolent with more profound thoughts and meanings. The Bible belonged to van Gogh's father and lies open at chapter 53 of the book of Isaiah, the passage about the suffering servant that Christians see as prefiguring the life and death of Christ. Like many artists and intellectuals of the later nineteenth century, van Gogh had come to have ambivalent views about the Bible. On the one hand he regarded it as gloomy and parochial, but he also admired its grandeur and longevity. He remained intrigued by the person of Christ. Jesus, he wrote, was the only "solace in the otherwise so dispiriting Bible, [. . .] which pains and perplexes us so deeply with its narrow-mindedness and contagious stupidity—the consolation, [. . .] like a pit surrounded by a hard rind and bitter fruit, that is Christ." Van Gogh's simultaneous rejection of the Bible's "bitter fruit" and his fascination with "the man of sorrows acquainted with grief" pointed not only to an inner tension, but also to a kind of generational religious war with his father, who was disturbed by his son's growing infidelity. This too, as readers of diaries and fiction will know, is one of the great themes of nineteenth-century European literature.

In van Gogh's still life the open Bible is deliberately juxtaposed with a copy of Emile Zola's recently published novel, *La Joie de vivre* (1884). Van Gogh later told his sister that he read Maupassant, Rabelais, Rochefort, and Voltaire for laughs, while he read Zola to satisfy his need "for being told the truth" or "life as it is."[46] Hence the juxtaposition of the Bible with Zola's novel may not be as straightforward a contrast between biblical melancholia and modernist liberation as it first appears, but is rather almost the reverse. The suffering servant is after all as much a tale of redemption ("he will see the light of life and be satisfied") as it is of suffering, and Zola's novel, despite its title, is a cold-eyed treatment of the human condition in all its complex realism. Put another way, van Gogh admired the Bible for its "lofty ideals" and its connections (however expressed) with the past and the future, while Zola brought him face to face with the present, the only time that human beings can directly "take action" and alter their condition. It is also possible to see a connection between Isaiah's suffering servant and Pauline Quenu, the most admirable character in Zola's novel. Despite being an orphan who was abused by almost everyone around her, she emerges as a redemptive figure, "the incarnation of renunciation, of love for others and kindly charity for erring humanity."[47] Thus, van Gogh's still life painting is not so much a contrast between a gloomy Bible and the modern joy of life as it is an expression of van Gogh's frequently articulated view that it was the responsibility of artists and writers to express the truth of life for their own generation. In that sense the Bible was not redundant, it was simply not enough.

Van Gogh's *Still Life with Bible,* though it looks dark and static to the untutored eye, was painted "in *one rush,* during a single day" and is really a riot of free brushstrokes and experiments with new colors.[48] It is also a recognition that modernity, in the shape of Zola's naturalism, was a necessary addition to the "old beauty" of the Scriptures, which could never again be taken at face value by a new generation of critical Europeans. Van Gogh was astute enough to recognize that Zola's new realism would not diminish the sum total of "pessimism and melancholy" in modern civilization, but his still life, quite as much as a demolished medieval church tower, marks an important transition between Christendom and modernity. The extinguished candle in van Gogh's painting, whether intentionally situated or not, rests beside the open Bible, not Zola's *La Joie de vivre.*

Van Gogh's little religious trilogy has profound implications for understanding the trajectory of European secularization. The old certainties of the classical sociologists and social historians of religion who thought that the explanation for the decline of the social significance of religion lay in inexorable processes of urbanization, industrialization, and societalization, all conveniently subsumed within the catchall concept of modernization, have come under pressure in recent years. Since these processes were held to be unilinear and irreversible, the standard view was that secularization was the inevitable consequence of modernity. The stubborn resistance of the religious history of the United States to line up with the theory, coupled with the worldwide expansion of Pentecostalism and religious fundamentalism of all shapes and sizes, seemed to indicate that all was not well with the theory. But what are the alternatives, and how do they relate to van Gogh's paintings? In particular, is it possible to construct an alternative master narrative that would have explanatory appeal beyond a small group of secularization cognoscenti?

One creative attempt, by Hugh McLeod, the distinguished English historian of European secularization, seems to fit snugly into van Gogh's trilogy.[49] McLeod divides the history of modern European religion into three epochs characterized by three metaphors: the register, the ticket, and the Web site. McLeod's thesis is that the central theme of European history since the eighteenth century has been emancipation. The three eras of religion he identifies are the era of the confessional state (when parish registers kept records of all inhabitants), the era of collective emancipation (when groups formed voluntary associations, including churches, and were issued membership tickets), and the era of individual emancipation (when individuals could create their own religious identities as one would design a Web site). Van Gogh's paintings similarly depict the era of the confessional state (parish church and graveyard for all), the era of collective emancipation (religion as a voluntary activity for some), and the era of individual emancipation (the freedom of individual expression evident in new movements of art and literature).

Van Gogh's own life and work is but a poignant example of much wider trends in the history of European thought. As his own personal worldview changed from inherited Calvinism to self-liberation, his art likewise shifted from realism to impressionism and then to postimpressionism. A close look at his letters shows any number of factors promoting these changes. They include his early geographical mobility from a small Dutch village to major European cities such as Paris, London, Brussels, and Amsterdam; his literary excursions into the works of the French Enlightenment and those of the French naturalists; his close encounters with the grinding poverty of the English and Belgian working classes during the industrial revolution; his growing sense of the intellectual and emotional poverty of orthodox Calvinism and evangelicalism; his conviction that clergymen, ecclesiastical institutions, and professional theology were light-years removed from anything he had once found attractive in the Christian faith; his growing belief that the glories of nature operating on the senses offered more to humankind than did speculative philosophies about the operation of providence; his indebtedness to fellow artists, like Gauguin, whose interest in the exotica of the tropics introduced a new world where space was not mapped by parish churches; and, above all, his deepening conviction that for good or for ill humankind had no ultimate authorities upon which to rely apart from their own fidelity to nature, to honest labor, and themselves. All this is secularization of some sort, but how does it happen and what are its mechanisms, even in the life of a single person, never mind the collective history of European civilization? Van Gogh's life and work, for all its blazing uniqueness and quirky singularity, offers more insights into this disturbingly difficult question than we mere social historians might care to admit.

Where then did van Gogh's own religious pilgrimage end? In some of his later letters to Theo and Emile Bernard, the young painter with whom he struck up a close friendship, van Gogh writes of his interest in the religious views of Tolstoy and George Eliot, the religious significance of Japanese art, and his complete impatience with contemporary artists who painted biblical scenes in the style of medieval romances. After reading a review of Tolstoy's

My Religion, van Gogh speculated on a new kind of religion that might have the same effect "of comforting, of making life possible, which the Christian religion used to have," and which might transcend the "disasters that are all the same bound to strike the modern world and civilization like terrible lightning, through a revolution or a war, or the bankruptcy of worm-eaten states." Van Gogh's next sentence referred to his study of Japanese art, the unaffected simplicity of which he found compelling. "Isn't it almost a true religion which these simple Japanese teach us, who live in nature as though they themselves were flowers? . . . and you cannot study Japanese art, it seems to me without becoming much gayer and happier." He was particularly impressed by Japanese artists' intense concentration on nature, their clarity and simplicity, and their unhurried and uncluttered appreciation of beauty. By contrast, he told Bernard that attempts by Gauguin and others to insert biblical scenes into natural landscapes was "counterfeit" and "affected." He confessed that he was more inclined to bow down in worship before a painting that expressed the profound truth of "peasants carrying home to the farm a calf which has been born in the fields." The same Vincent who had been alienated by the pharisaism of the artistic and religious establishments he encountered was equally uneasy with any artistic expression that seemed to treat nature with any hint of emotional or aesthetic falsification. He wrote Bernard that there were other ways of treating anguish than painting the Garden of Gethsemane, or gentleness by painting the Sermon on the Mount; rather, "modern reality has got such a hold on us that, even when we attempt to reconstruct the ancient days in our thoughts abstractly, the minor events of our lives tear us away from our meditations, and our own adventures thrust us back into our personal sensations—joy, boredom, suffering, anger, or a smile." His bald conclusion was that apart from the discreet and sensitive paintings of Judeo-Christian motifs by Millet and Corot, "Biblical pictures are a failure."[50]

Van Gogh, who spent much of the decade of the 1870s studying the Bible with passionate intensity, came to believe that nature offered a better window into spiritual reality than did ancient words, however beautiful some of them undeniably were. Yet it would be a mistake to conclude, as some have, that his encounter with biblical Christianity was an entirely negative experience for him. The almost frightening zeal with which van Gogh pursued his religious mission was the consequence, not the cause, of his manic personality. The terrible isolation caused by his frequent moves around fast-growing modern cities, and his inability to find the loving and satisfying relationships he craved, exacerbated his self-confessed melancholia. In those circumstances, the Bible seemed to offer him an explanation for the difficult "pilgrimage" of life and a personal model of self-sacrificial love. In the midst of loneliness the text offered one kind of relationship, and the God it pointed to offered another. His painful discovery that those who held the keys of access to Christian institutions were not up to the standard of the faith they professed, paralleled a similar disenchantment with commercial art dealers and artistic establishments.[51] As his disenchantment with conventional Christianity grew, not even his fascination with the "Man of Sorrows" could survive his increasing conviction that the old Christian narratives, however glorious in their time, could no longer speak with authority to the human condition in the late nineteenth century. He turned instead to the profound mysteries of nature, which helped unleash his creative energies in a quite remarkable way. But even in this phase of his career, van Gogh, the passionate Bible student and good Samaritan to the Belgian poor, remained fiercely determined to avoid fakery and infidelity. Both in his paintings and in his instructional letters to Bernard, something of the evangelical missionary lived on in Vincent van Gogh, not least in his excoriation of those who cheapened both Scripture and nature by their crude attempts to force them together in acts of artistic prostitution. He was still capable of celebrating the legacies of Rembrandt and Delacroix, the only painters of religious art to escape his censure, with a strange late painting of an angel; but van Gogh's angel looks more like a young Dutch peasant than it does a heavenly body. Even in this very rare exploration of a religious theme, van Gogh was resolutely unwilling to descend to idealized abstraction or sentimental piety.[52] That same fierce integrity of purpose that characterized his evangelical devotion earlier in his life went with him to the grave. But there was one more twist to the story. Because van Gogh took his own life he was refused a church burial by the Catholic Church in Auvers.[53] Vincent's body was carried in a hearse supplied by the local villagers, and he was buried beside the wheat fields he has immortalized in paint. It seems appropriate that the erstwhile servant of Christ's poor was buried by them, while the representatives of the institutional religion he came to loathe looked the other way.

7 Edmund Gosse—Father and Son
Evangelicalism and Childhood

Let me speak plainly. After my long experience, after my patience and forbearance, I have surely the right to protest against the untruth (would that I could apply to it any other word!) that evangelical religion, or any religion in a violent form, is a wholesome or valuable or desirable adjunct to human life. It divides heart from heart. It sets up a vain chimerical ideal, in the barren pursuit of which all the tender, indulgent affections, all the genial play of life, all the exquisite pleasures and soft resignations of the body, all that enlarges and calms the soul are exchanged for what is harsh and void and negative. It encourages a stern and ignorant spirit of condemnation; it throws altogether out of gear the healthy movement of the conscience; it invents virtues which are sterile and cruel; it invents sins which are no sins at all, but which darken the heaven of innocent joy with futile clouds of remorse. There is something horrible, if we will bring ourselves to face it, in the fanaticism that can do nothing with this pathetic and fugitive existence of ours but treat it as if it were the uncomfortable ante-chamber to a palace which no one has explored and of the plan of which we know absolutely nothing. My Father, it is true, believed that he was intimately acquainted with the form and furniture of this habitation, and he wished me to think of nothing else but of the advantages of an eternal residence in it.
—Edmund Gosse, *Father and Son* (1907)

Sir Edmund William Gosse, by John Singer Sargent. Oil on canvas, 1886 (© National Portrait Gallery, London)

Edmund Gosse's epilogue to his book *Father and Son,* from which this quotation is taken, was written in the first decade of the twentieth century.[1] The book, which carries the subtitle *A Study of Two Temperaments,* is an exploration of the relationship between Gosse's father, the distinguished Victorian naturalist Philip Henry Gosse, and Edmund, his only son, who later became one of England's most influential literary figures.[2] The book not only is regarded as Gosse's finest literary achievement, but also is viewed as one of the most compelling dissections ever written of the pernicious effects of evangelical religion on family life, particularly the relationship between parents and children. But there is more to it than that. *Father and Son* also stands as a bridge between the morals and values of Victorian civilization and those of the twentieth-century world. The traffic moving over the bridge includes the role of evangelical religion, the emergence of modern science (particularly evolutionary biology), the construction of personal identity, and the structure of family relationships. In that sense *Father and Son* is more than just a finely written exploration of the relationship between a particular Victorian father, who happens to be an eminent natural scientist, and his young son, who happens to be a poet and man of letters; it stands as a lasting monument to the religion and culture of Victorian England.

The book's generic significance helps explain why it was welcomed with such enthusiasm by early twentieth-century artists and writers, and why so many found in it echoes of their own childhood experiences. Richard Gilder wrote, "my own experience (how many must have told you that!) was somewhat similar," a sentiment echoed by Rudyard Kipling, who wrote, "the delicacy of the psychology, the inferential revelation of the milieu, and, above all, the wonderful realization of your father, have given me very deep delight. I don't say pleasure because the thing is too near certain of my own experiences to only please."[3] In an even more dramatic way than Samuel Butler's *The Way of All Flesh,* a satirical repudiation of Victorian religion by a disgruntled son of a religious father published only four years earlier, Gosse's *Father and Son* captured the imagination of an Edwardian intelligentsia in transition from one set of values to another. His book had a similar galvanizing effect on his contemporaries as George Orwell's socialist fiction of the 1930s and Jack Kerouac's *On the Road* in the 1950s and '60s.[4]

Gosse was acutely aware that his book was more than a mere account of a peculiar childhood. *Father and Son* opens with the thunderous statement, "This book is the record of a struggle between two temperaments, two consciences and almost two epochs. It ended, as was inevitable, in disruption. Of the two human beings here described, one was born to fly backward, the other could not help being carried forward."[5] However confidently stated, Gosse's declaration of his book's content and purpose is not altogether sufficient, nor is its genre entirely clear. Although *Father and Son* fits most conveniently into the genre of biography and autobiography, the combination of which is itself unusual, it is also partly a work of social and intellectual history. Those familiar with the biographical and autobiographical tradition in English literature will know that it is a complex tradition embracing everything from medieval religious hagiography expressed through the lives of saints to more modern attempts to penetrate to the heart of personality and identity.[6] Culture and cultural expectations shape conceptions of what is important about human life and therefore what is worth telling about any given life. Gosse's *Father and Son* is a conspicuously ambiguous example of a complex tradition of biography that embraces works as widely divergent as those by Augustine, Rousseau, Boswell, and Mill.[7]

Gosse's aim is to tell the tale of his repressive childhood as a defense for what he called, in the book's last sentence, "a human being's privilege to fashion his inner life for himself."[8] Yet even that ambition is circumscribed by all sorts of limitations, including a sense of decorum about revelations the Edwardian reading public might regard as filial infidelity, and a residual sense of honor and respect for parents who, however unwisely, clearly loved their son. *Father and Son* is therefore a complex work, full of historical details about a puritan provincial family in Victorian England that whet the appetites of social and intellectual historians, but also a work that is suffused with intense emotion, sometimes openly expressed, sometimes covertly expressed, and sometimes deliberately suppressed. Above all, it is a book written from the perspective of the son, not the father or the mother.

There is yet more to be said about the literary genre of *Father and Son,* for Gosse makes the grand claim at the start of the book that his narrative is "scrupulously true. If it were not true, in this strict sense, to publish it would be to trifle with all those who may be induced to read it." Yet this claim is fundamentally unreliable. Not only is Gosse constructing his childhood narrative through the filtered memory of a much older man, but the book itself gives any number of clues that, in order to survive as a child in such an intense religious atmosphere, Edmund Gosse was forced to create an alternative self who could create illusions, negotiate space, tell lies when necessary, and even observe himself when he was praying. When Gosse talks about "fashioning" his inner life for himself he is testifying to the fact that "the self has become something discovered, revealed, or created by the autobiographer." In this modern sense, autobiography is partly "an activity of self-conscious reflection upon the nature and process of interpretation itself."[9] Hence, Gosse's appeal to absolute truth is both naïve and disingenuous, but it does illustrate the fact that Gosse knew he was doing something rather unusual, and that his portrait of his father in the context of Edwardian England sailed dangerously close to the wind of indelicacy, if not indecency. Only an appeal to truth and fidelity could assuage the criticism that Gosse fully expected, namely that he had deliberately and self-consciously besmirched the reputation of his own father.

When *Father and Son* slides back and forth from biography to autobiography, the perspective is always that of Edmund Gosse, the man of letters, not Philip Gosse, the natural scientist.[10] What gives the book its peculiar power is that Gosse is able to write about the evils of a repressed childhood without appearing to lose all affection for the father who propagated them, or without capitulating to overt bitterness. There is no doubt that Gosse carefully selects his language to convey the impression of a dreary (one of his favorite words) childhood and an inflexible, dominant father. Although the father is portrayed as a man with winning and redeeming features, Edmund's choice of words leaves the reader in no doubt that his religiously motivated desire for control verged on the tyrannical. In terms of admiration and respect, therefore, what Edmund concedes to the father with one hand is often quickly taken away with the other, often by a careful choice of word or phrase. For example, Edmund detected a slight thawing in his father's mood after his second marriage, when the son was temporarily given more freedom to mix with his friends. He writes, "It was a remarkable proof of my Father's temporary lapse into indulgence that he made no effort to thwart my intimacy with these my new companions. He was in an unusually humane mood himself."[11] "Unusually humane" is a particularly devastating compliment, and there are many such examples, perhaps too many, in *Father and Son*. Although in general it is the father's religion, not the father, that is the real villain of Edmund's childhood, the son's word selection refuses to allow the reader to forget how disagreeable was his father's domestic tyranny, whatever its motivation. However justified, Edmund clearly saw himself as a victim, and his sense of victimhood is embedded deep within the text.

The purpose of this chapter, however, is not to attempt a new critical reflection on *Father and Son*, however sorely needed that may be, but rather to look at what the book reveals about the way in which an intense form of evangelical Protestantism shaped the lives of the Gosse family. Although *Father and Son* is a prime source for such an endeavor, due attention will be paid to other sources and wider frameworks. The aim is not so much to arrive at a judgment on the literary merits of an important book, but to discover more about the way a particular version of evangelical religion worked on family, identity, and personality. In so doing the emphasis will be as much on the father and the mother, and their shared devotion to the evangelical sect of Plymouth Brethren, as on the son. Although insignificant numerically, the Plymouth Brethren sect, an offshoot of the Church of Ireland originating in Dublin in the 1820s, is widely regarded as one of the most important roots of modern Protestant fundamentalism, particularly in its dispensational premillennialist theology. Literary critics of *Father and Son*, who simply assume that the Plymouth Brethren sect is a nasty and narrow version of a generic Calvinism, often fail to take into account its very particular emphases in the shaping of the religious culture of the Gosse family.[12]

Father and Son was published in London in 1907 to immediate acclaim from Gosse's literary contemporaries. In one of the more insightful comments of that year, Henry James wrote Gosse that "*F. and S.* is extraordinarily vivid and interesting, beautifully done, remarkably *much* done and deserving to be called . . . the very best thing you have ever written. It has immense and unfailing *life*, an extraordinary sort and degree, quite, of vivacity and intensity, and it *holds* and entertains from beginning to end—its *parti-pris* of absolute and utter frankness and objectivity being, it strikes me, brilliantly maintained—carried through with rare audacity. You have thus been in a position to write a book that must remain a document of the first importance— à consulter—about the pietistic passion and the religious rage."[13]

James acknowledged that writing a book of such transparency about the private relationship between a Victorian father and his son stretched the conventional boundaries of public taste, but that Gosse's candor, tenderness, and lack of bitterness would deflect and dissipate all charges of filial disloyalty. In light of our previous discussion it seems obvious that James overestimated the extent of the "utter frankness and objectivity" of Gosse's work. Not only did a postmodernist generation regard such claims with justifiable hermeneutical suspicion, it is also clear from Gosse's biographers that he either misremembered or deliberately distorted some aspects of his recorded experience. For example, in *Father and Son* it appears that the family spent most of Edmund's early childhood in a small dark house in London, when in reality they spent almost as much time by the seaside in Wales, Devon, and Dorset.[14] Similarly, the reader gains the impression from Edmund's epilogue to *Father and Son* that the son completely repudiated his father's religion quite early in his career in London, when in reality Edmund was still teaching in a Plymouth Brethren Sunday school until well into his twenties. Moreover, Gosse was a notoriously unreliable writer whose career almost came to a grinding halt when one of his books on seventeenth-century English poetry was subjected to withering empirical criticism by John Churton Collins. Although Collins's motives for his ferocious display of literary stalking, footnote by footnote, were not above reproach, there is no denying the fact that he exposed in Gosse a disturbing casualness about historical exactitude.[15]

It was not just that Gosse was more careless about historical facts and events than someone of his stature had any right to be, but also that he was prone imaginatively to inflate events with which he was personally associated to make a better story. Consider, for example, his three different versions (one in his private journal, and two in published accounts) of his first encounter with the Victorian poet Augustus Charles Swinburne, in which the dates, times, and events are irreconcilable. Moreover, each of his accounts differs in tone and style from Swinburne's own record, and from one another. The actual encounter took place in the British Museum reading room, where Swinburne had gone to look up some references and where Gosse was employed as a junior assistant. Swinburne wrote that during his visit he "fainted right out and in falling cut my forehead slightly." Gosse's accounts of the event not only are internally inconsistent over the time and date of the incident, but also inject a much greater sense of human drama than Swinburne's casual reference. Gosse writes, "This afternoon about two o'clock I was walking through the Reading Room when I saw a crowd of people in the passage by which readers enter. I heard someone had had a fit and on coming near recognised from the published portraits, the poet A. C. Swinburne. His great forehead, though bandaged, was bubbling with blood, and all his hair matted and gory. . . . He had struck his forehead so violently against the staple of an iron ring as to make a gash one and a half inches long and penetrating to the bone."[16] The important issue at stake here is not to catch Gosse out by some historically exacting form of source criticism organized around a trivial event, but rather to show that he had a lifelong propensity to record events in highly colored ways, especially when he was associated with them. Virginia Woolf, who combined great insight with uncommon acerbity, wrote of Gosse that "the narrowness, the ugliness of his upbringing; the almost insane religious mania of his father; the absence from his home of culture, beauty, urbanity, graciousness—in fact, of all those elements in life to which Edmund Gosse turned as instinctively and needed as profoundly as a flower the sun. What could be more natural than that the flower once transplanted, should turn, almost violently, the other way, should climb too high, should twine too lavishly, should—to drop these metaphors—order clothes in Saville Row."[17] In short, Gosse, whose background was hardly prepossessing, once he emerged from his father's clutches, discovered he had an ego, chased honors and the honorable with indecorous enthusiasm, and was always interested in presenting himself in the best possible manner. None of this undermines the artistic brilliance of *Father and Son* as a remarkably successful work of biography and autobiography, but it is well to be reminded at the outset that the story is told by the son, and the son is not without his foibles. However fine *Father and Son* is as a work of art, it would be a mistake to assume too easily that it is a work of marble detachment and pure objectivity. It is not, nor should one expect it to be.

It seems perverse to begin an analysis of the religious structure of *Father and Son* with the role of the mother, who dies in only the third chapter of the book, but her life and death, though occurring before Edmund reached the age of seven, cast a long shadow over those she left behind. Gosse's mother, Emily Bowes, the daughter of wealthy Bostonians who had fallen on hard times, met his father at the little Plymouth Brethren assembly in Hackney, East London. Ironically, in the light of the future history of the Plymouth Brethren, Emily was attracted to the sect because of its ecumenical emphasis on recovering the love and simplicity of the primitive church, unencumbered with ecclesiastical paraphernalia and petty differences between churches. She was elegant, intelligent, sociable, and deeply pious. She fought a lifelong battle against an attraction to imaginative fiction, which she thought worthless, and was a prolific writer of religious tracts that had a remarkably wide circulation. She also had a talent for using her tracts to evangelize strangers, much to the embarrassment of her son. Edmund remembers her as emotionally the stronger of his parents, deeply devoted to raising a Christian son who would perhaps be the Charles Wesley or George Whitefield of his generation. Gosse's account of his mother's uncompromising attempts to nurture his piety is a vivid example of why so many historians now see feminine religiosity and maternal transmission as the most potent forces in sustaining evangelical religion.[18]

There is no doubting that the Gosses were happily married, with a shared faith, a shared devotion to biblical and prophetical literature, and a shared determination to raise Edmund as a child of God. All came crashing down with the tragic news of Emily's diagnosis with breast cancer, a disease Edmund could not bear even to name in *Father and Son,* though it was written half a century later. Gosse's account of his mother's illness and death is one of the finest and most moving evocations in all literature of a much-loved parent's death seen through the eyes of a young child: "We had no cosy talk; often she was too weak to do more than pat my hand: her loud and almost constant cough terrified and harassed me. I felt as I stood, awkwardly and shyly, by her high bed, that I had shrunken into a very small and insignificant figure, that she was floating out of my reach, that all things, but I knew not what nor how, were coming to an end. She herself was not herself; her head, that used to be held so erect, now rolled or sank upon the pillow; the sparkle was all extinguished from those bright, dear eyes. I could not understand it; I meditated long, long upon it all in my infantile darkness, in the garret, or in the little slip of a cold room where my bed was now placed; and a great blind anger against I knew not what awakened in my soul."[19]

Emily's approaching death was made all the harder because of her sense that she would not be around to fulfill her solemn duty of raising Edmund as a faithful Christian disciple. At the very end she urged Philip Gosse to "take our lamb and walk with me," which was an obvious appeal for her husband to devote himself to the task she could never complete. Edmund writes, "Thus was my dedication, that had begun in my cradle, sealed with the most solemn, the most poignant and irresistible insistence, at the death-bed of the holiest and purest of women. But what a weight, intolerable as the burden of Atlas, to lay on the shoulders of a little fragile child!"[20] Gosse, with equal justification, might have concluded that the real weight of Atlas's burden fell not on the child, but on the father. Both in the text of *Father and Son,* and in the private letters that were exchanged between them, it seems clear that Emily's death not only removed a loving and softening presence from the household, but also bound father and son in a terrible compact to fulfill the dying wish of a woman they both loved and could not easily live without. For the father the compact necessitated redoubled efforts and constant vigilance to produce the desired end; for the son it required either complete conformity or painful rebellion. Equanimity was not possible for either; that was the mother's unintended legacy to both.

The months after the mother's death are revealing both of the new psychological dynamic in the relationship between father and son and of the characteristics of the domestic piety fostered by an austere Victorian evangelical. Father and son studied the Scriptures daily, with the former adding learned theological footnotes on the Epistle to the Hebrews, while the latter tried unsuccessfully to absorb the complexities of law and grace, sacrifice and redemption, and faith and works. They sang hymns together, but only those coming out of the evangelical tradition, particularly those written by Charles and John Wesley, Charlotte Elliott, and James Montgomery. The hymns and poetry of the High Church tradition, composed by John Henry Newman and

John Keble, despite their beauty and spirituality, were studiously avoided as products of popery. The Plymouth Brethren's distinctive emphasis on dispensational theology with its almost obsessive interest in the end-time was reflected in their readings in Revelation. "Hand in hand," Gosse writes, "we investigated the number of the Beast, which number is six hundred three score and six. Hand in hand we inspected the nations, to see whether they had the mark of Babylon in their foreheads. Hand in hand we watched the spirits of devils gathering the kings of the earth into the place which is called in the Hebrew tongue Armageddon."[21]

Only those who have grown up under the sacred canopy of premillennial dispensational theology can testify to the power of this mental framework in shaping the imagination, in interpreting past, present, and future events, and in organizing all information around the coming of the end-time. One of its most common characteristics is a fierce anti-Catholicism, with the Roman Catholic Church portrayed variously as the Antichrist, the Scarlet Woman, and the Whore of Babylon. All current events and all newspaper reports were read through the thick filter of biblical prophecy. Together father and son rejoiced in "any social disorder in any part of Italy, as likely to be annoying to the Papacy."[22] In this way prophetical interpretation, religious particularity, and political orientation were fused in a biblical synthesis impervious to critical debate.

If the death of the mother was one major event in the shaping of the father's temperament and his relationship with the son, the publication in 1857 of Philip Gosse's *Omphalos* was another.[23] By the late 1850s Philip Gosse had built quite a reputation as a distinguished naturalist. His extensive publications, including *A Naturalist's Sojourn in Jamaica*, *A Naturalist's Rambles on the Devonshire Coast*, and *The Aquarium*, marked him out as a careful observer, cataloguer, organizer, and illustrator of the natural world. Philip Gosse, through the popularity of his works, was at least partly responsible for the seashore and aquarium crazes of mid-Victorian England. As an admired author on natural history, and as a frequent attendee of meetings at the Royal Society, of which he was a Fellow, Philip Gosse was on speaking terms with some of the great figures of British science including Charles Lyell and Charles Darwin. As ideas of a long earth history, natural selection, and the mutability of species began circulating with increasing intensity in the 1850s, culminating in the publication of Darwin's *The Origin of Species by Means of Natural Selection* (1859), Philip Gosse felt compelled to make a contribution. He was motivated not by fame or fortune, but by a high-minded attempt to reconcile the apparent contradiction between his Bible and his fossils, or, in

Edmund's words, to deal with the "peculiar agony in the paradox that truth has two forms, each of them indisputable, yet each antagonistic to the other."

The theory Philip Gosse came up with was the Law of Prochronism (literally, before time), in which he argued that when the world was created it carried within its physical makeup evidence of long existence. Hence, Adam had a navel, but never had an umbilical cord, and the Garden of Eden had fully grown plants and trees. When the world was created, Gosse suggested, it "presented, instantly, the structural appearance of a planet on which life had long existed." According to Edmund, his father waited in a "fever of suspense" for the publication of his book, which he thought would bring all the "turmoil of scientific speculation to a close, fling geology into the arms of Scripture, and make the lion eat grass with the lamb." As it turned out no publication could more decisively have rebounded on its own intention. The scientific elite derided it as completely implausible, Christians thought it made God look like a trickster, and the press lampooned it as an attempt to show that "God hid the fossils in the rocks to tempt geologists into infidelity." Philip Gosse's hard-won reputation as a natural scientist was destroyed almost instantly. In words eerily resonant of his own butchery later at the hands of John Churton Collins, Edmund Gosse writes, "my Father was not prepared for such a fate. He had been the spoiled darling of the public, the constant favourite of the press, and now, like the dark angels of old, so huge a rout encumbered him with ruin."[24] Philip Gosse paid a high price for working in unassisted solitude, for his devotion to an inerrant Bible, and for stepping beyond his limitations as a scientific observer into the murky waters of natural theology and philosophy. In a passage of savage insight, which must make all fathers look nervously on their clever children, Edmund writes that in truth his father was not a philosopher: "He was incapable, by temperament and education, of forming broad generalizations and of escaping in a vast survey from the troublesome pettiness of detail. He saw everything through a lens, nothing in the immensity of nature. Certain senses were absent in him; I think that, with all his justice, he had no conception of the importance of liberty; with all his intelligence, the boundaries of the atmosphere in which his mind could think at all were always close about him; with all his faith in the Word of God, he had no confidence in the Divine Benevolence; and with all his passionate piety, he habitually mistook fear for love."[25]

Critics generally assume that Philip Gosse's narrow religion made him a narrow scientist and a narrow father, but what is equally likely is that in all aspects of his life he had an ineluctable propensity to embrace positions that had a cut-and-dried rationality. In that sense his belief in biblical inerrancy, his commitment to memory of virtually the whole Bible, his literalistic interpretation of texts, his highly programmatic dispensational premillennialism, his passion for collecting, dissecting, and cataloguing natural species, his incapacity to forge flexible relationships, and his desire for control all point to the possibility that his choice of religion was as much a symptom as a cause of his temperamental narrowness of spirit. It is also a well-attested, if counterintuitive, fact that many of those who had a particular attraction to prophetical calculations in the nineteenth century were deeply rationalist in their methods. They consulted histories of civilization, dug deeply into texts, and constructed charts, maps, and diagrams of immense complexity and sophistication.[26]

Within the space of a year, Philip Gosse lost a wife he loved and a reputation he valued. In response, according to Edmund, he manifested "a first tincture of that heresy" that was to afflict him later on, namely anger with the God who seemed to tease him with cruel misfortune and who stood idly by while his reputation was ground into dust. Although his brooding melancholia was temporarily relieved by a successful remarriage, a partially restored reputation as a natural scientist, and many happy seashore rambles with his son, there is no denying that Philip Gosse never fully recovered from the shattering events of 1857. What did not change, however, was his driving determination to safeguard the eternal destiny of his only son, to whose story we must now turn.

From the biographical details we know about Edmund Gosse's childhood, it is clear that the vivid memories recounted in *Father and Son* are selected less for their typicality and factual accuracy than for their symbolic and emotional importance in the son's quest to forge a personal identity separate from that prescribed by his father and the Plymouth Brethren. These little episodes of self-realization are humorously and humanely recounted by Edmund Gosse. Their evident charms help alleviate an otherwise somber book. Edmund's prayer that God would deliver a large painted humming top he saw in a shop window, his experiment in religious idolatry by worshipping a chair to test whether God would punish him, and his claim that God had told him it was his will for him to go to a party that his father disapproved of, are all classic stories of childish subversion of pietistic categories. Equally engaging are Gosse's recollections of his encounters with his father's little Plymouth Brethren assembly in Devonshire—his "kidnapping" by the eccentric Miss Flaw, his evaluations of the women showing an interest in his father, and, above all, his baptism. Baptism by total immersion upon declaration of religious conversion is the central religious ritual of the Plymouth Brethren and opens up all the privileges of full membership including participation in the weekly sacrament of the breaking of bread. Gosse regarded his public baptism as the central event of his whole childhood, made all the more remarkable by the fact that at ten years old he was uncommonly young for such an experience, which of course conferred upon him celebrity status. Gosse's mock heroic description of the event, which included the unscripted prelude of a woman who fell into the baptismal pool fully clothed and was "held upright in the water by the inflation of the air underneath her crinoline which was blown out like a bladder," is full of self irony. "The scene was one which would have been impressive," he writes, "not merely to such hermits as we were, but even to worldly persons accustomed to life and to its curious and variegated experiences. To me it was dazzling beyond words, inexpressibly exciting, an initiation to every kind of publicity and glory. There were many candidates, but the rest of them,—mere grown-up men and women,—gave thanks aloud that it was their privilege to go where I led. I was the acknowledged hero of the hour."[27]

Edmund Gosse's baptism, whatever its liturgical and psychological vagaries, led to a temporary truce in the spiritual war of attrition with his father. Public baptism was, after all, the mechanism by which the Plymouth Brethren marked the conversion of the believer. The father's deathbed promise to his wife had been fulfilled; eternal life had been secured, or was it? Looking back on the events of his baptism and public profession of faith, Gosse writes that the whole business had more to do with intellectual assent, communal imitation, and liturgical conformity than with mystical rapture and personal deliverance from one life to another. It seemed that two personalities resided in the same body, the one conformist and speaking the pious words of salvation, the other "a hard nut of individuality" that knew deep down that nothing beyond mere public display had ever taken place. Gosse's bifurcated religious persona, and the fact that he was conscious of it, not only made further conflicts with the father over self-realization inevitable, but also supplied an intriguing inner dialectic through which he could process his experience. For example, one side of his personality had to confess to the other that his private prayers, when no audience was present, were mere mechanical addresses, empty of language and devoid of "real unction." Similarly, he was intrigued by the fact that a rough working-class couple who had shown up to scoff at his baptism had been so moved by the experience that they were set on the road to their own conversion, albeit through the strange mechanism of a vision of the devil and an induced miscarriage. Gosse, impressed by their story and feeling personally implicated in their plight, saved his money and paid a philanthropic visit to their cottage. His money was swiped with ungracious zeal by the husband, and Gosse was left to trudge home without either his cash or the couple's appreciation. As a result, "the infant plant of philanthropy was burned in my bosom as if by quick-lime."[28] Although Gosse made his visit in secret, it is clear from his own writing that he did not want the result to be secret. Both in the telling of the story to his father and in his memory of the incident, it seems that Gosse the pious giver (let not your right hand know what your left hand is doing) was in conflict with Gosse the benevolent, but unappreciated, bourgeois.

Another pecuniary incident of a more serious kind, one of those unseemly financial scandals that periodically waft around evangelicalism, seems to have had a lasting effect on Edmund's religious sensibilities. A local Plymouth Brother had taken in a wealthy old man as a lodger, and exploited his position illegally to change his will. As a result the old gentleman's son, who was living abroad, was disinherited in favor of the Brother, who subsequently donated some of the money to all sorts of missionary and religious causes. Even at his criminal trial the Brother defended his actions without apparent remorse. Gosse believed that the Plymouth Brother was not a religious hypocrite in the conventional sense, but that he seems to have thought it was genuinely better for the money, however fraudulently it had been gained, to be used in "religious propaganda than in the pleasures of the world." This unsavory incident drove Gosse to the same conclusion that many evangelical deserters came to embrace through manifold different routes, namely that religion, especially of an exclusive kind, was no guarantee of acceptable, never mind pure, ethics.[29]

The question of ethics surfaced again, only in a more profound way, in the conversations between father and son over the issues of God's justice and eternal punishment. In common with most evangelical Protestants, the father believed that eternal salvation would be denied to Catholics, Unitarians, and anyone else who deviated from the strict evangelical conception of personal salvation. The notion that all the inhabitants of Austria, for example, were doomed to eternal punishment, or that the holy life of an aged nun would count for nothing in the salvation stakes, struck Edmund with grim force. "Little inclined as I was to be skeptical," he writes, "I still thought it impossible, that a secret of such stupendous importance should have been entrusted to a little group of Plymouth Brethren, and have been hidden from millions of disinterested and pious theologians."[30] It was not the strict soteriological issues at stake, however, that most disturbed Edmund as much as the apparent contradiction between his father's gentleness toward all living creatures and his iron insistence on eternal punishment. "He who was so tenderhearted that he could not witness the pain or distress of any person, however disagreeable or undeserving, was quite acquiescent in believing that God would punish human beings, in millions, for ever, for a purely intellectual error of comprehension. My father's inconsistencies of perception seem to me to have been the result of a curious irregularity of equipment. Taking for granted, as he did, the absolute integrity of the Scripture, and applying to them his trained scientific spirit, he contrived to stifle, with a deplorable success, alike the function of the imagination, the sense of moral justice, and his own deep and instinctive tenderness of heart."[31] No matter that his father would not have been happy with the formulation that human beings would be condemned to eternal punishment for a mere error of comprehension, the point remains that Edmund came to see not only that his father was a better man than his beliefs, but also that his beliefs were the very source of his father's most disagreeable characteristics.

Of even more significance than theological discussions in driving Edmund to the point of separation from his father's controlling influence was his love for art and literature, a love that became the dominant passion of his adult life. Ironically, some of this was nurtured within his father's system through his acquaintance with the Hebrew Scriptures, evangelical hymnody, Latin poets, maps of Caribbean islands, and a profound love of nature. The father taught the son to walk, look, observe, and write about all aspects of nature. It was the father's recitation of Virgil, in whose verse he delighted, that revealed to Edmund "the incalculable, the amazing beauty which could exist in the sound of verses . . . and the magic of it took hold of my heart for ever."[32] The father allowed him to read Dickens, took him to see Holman Hunt's *Finding of Christ in the Temple,* read Sir Walter Scott's epic poetry aloud to him, and permitted his second wife, a watercolorist of some note, to introduce Edmund to painting. There were of course strict limits. Scott's poems were allowed, but his novels were not; Greek sculpture (too beautiful to be wicked according to Edmund) was ruled out because it celebrated pagan deities; Shakespeare was forbidden, though interestingly Edmund had to read Shakespeare in school for national examinations, a trivial but significant example of how secularizing tendencies could penetrate religious sects via public prescription; Southey, Coleridge, and Wordsworth were permitted, but Marlowe's erotic "Hero and Leander" sent both father and his second wife into a tailspin of disapproval. This climate of permission and repression acted as a tease to Edmund, whose private adventures with literature are recounted with the kind of zest that some adolescents save for sexual exploration. The father, who spent part of his early life in Jamaica, allowed him to read *Tom*

Cringle's Log, a picaresque romance situated in the tropics, which particularly fired the son's imagination. The adventures, mutinies, exotic locations, and descriptions of the "boundless tropical ocean" nurtured in the young Edmund "a belief that I should escape at last from the narrowness of the life we led at home, from this bondage to the Law and the Prophets."[33]

Unwittingly and unconsciously, the father's passion for the natural world, his delight in the cadences of Latin and Hebrew poets, and his own history of world travel helped subvert his religious system, which largely depended upon the establishment of clear boundaries between the sacred and the profane. It was the father, for example, who introduced Edmund to the magical underwater world of the sea, and even brought it into the home through his construction of aquaria. Edmund writes that there were "two, and sometimes three aquaria in the room, tanks of seawater, with glass sides, inside which all sorts of creatures crawled and swam; these were sources of endless pleasure for me, and at this time began to be laid upon me the occasional task of watching and afterwards reporting the habits of animals."[34] In his book *The Aquarium* Philip wrote that the naturalist's life is a happy one because it drew "him out of the narrow sphere of self into a pure and wholesome region of joy and wonder."[35] But for Philip there was a difference between wonder, as a divine gift to humans in their contemplation of God's creation, and imagination as a concept grounded in self and the self's ability to create entirely fictional worlds and new possibilities.

Nevertheless it is possible to argue that the categories presented by Edmund in *Father and Son* of a prosaically unimaginative father and a vividly imaginative son need some subversion. Not only was the father capable of a certain kind of biblically rooted imagination in his extravagant conceptions of Eden and Eschatology (the beginning and the end of time), but also Edmund's poetry was influenced by Parnassian ideals of formal coherence, methodical precision, and exact description.[36] Some of the passion for observing and cataloguing of the naturalist father lived on in the verses of the poetic son. But that is not how Edmund saw it in *Father and Son*. For Edmund the world of imagination, aesthetic pleasure, and adventure was contrasted with the drabness of evangelical religion, as exemplified by his memorable account of a Victorian Sabbath with its five religious meetings interspersed with short interludes for rest, prayer, and Bible reading. In temperament and in spirit, Edmund thought of himself as more a Hellenist than a Hebraist, while he regarded his father as the reverse.

With his imagination allegedly starved of acceptable outlets, it is scarcely surprising that Edmund began to focus on the one area where Plymouth

Brethren theology, without apology, soared heavenward, namely the anticipated Second Advent of Christ. He began to write poems about the return of Jesus and the rapture of the saints, and then, if his memory is to be trusted, Edmund recounted the pivotal moment of his youthful religious pilgrimage. On a warm summer afternoon he lay on a sofa gazing out over a beautiful vista of gardens, foliage, and twinkling sea. The sky was unusually beautiful, the atmosphere uncommonly still. Clearly affected with emotion, and partly dreading his upcoming move to London, Edmund hoped that the Second Coming was at hand. "Come now Lord Jesus," he cried, but soon the mundane sounds of schoolboys returning to their dorms and the tea-bell shattered his mystical illusion. He writes, "'The Lord has not come, the Lord will never come,' I muttered, and in my heart the artificial edifice of extravagant faith began to totter and crumble."[37] In a strange irony, Edmund's fatalistic resignation that the Lord would never come in the clouds as he had been taught paralleled a much more turbulent scene on his father's deathbed many years later. There are many hints in *Father and Son* that the father expected the Second Advent before his own death, and was repeatedly disappointed as his calculations proved wrong. Edmund suggests that disappointment gradually translated into anger. According to his account of his father's death (if Edmund's account can be taken at face value) related many years later to Harold Nicolson, the father died miserably, turning against his God in the anger of abandonment, and "reviling Him for treachery."[38] The belief in the imminent Second Coming of Christ, accompanied by the rapture of the saints who would not taste death, was perhaps the most imaginatively compelling, and potentially most disastrous, of all the dogmas the father embraced with such rationalistic fervor.

The impression conveyed by Edmund Gosse in *Father and Son* is that his rebellion against his father's religious control accelerated after he left home and school for his first job as a junior assistant at the British Museum. The father's assiduous attempt to maintain control through what Edmund called the "torment of a postal inquisition" was frightening in its intensity and counterproductive in its results. Nevertheless, the religion that had been so systematically inculcated throughout his childhood was not immediately overthrown. In London Gosse continued to attend a Plymouth Brethren assembly, taught Sunday school, lodged with two elderly Brethren ladies, and associated himself briefly with the philanthropic work of the evangelical Dr. Barnardo in the East End. Yet the great flow of his life was beginning to find different channels. The British Museum afforded him an ideal environment to pursue his interests in poetry and Scandinavian languages and literature. It also offered him an entrée into London's literary and artistic culture. He dressed well, spoke well, and networked assiduously to get noticed. He discovered the power of flattery. He began to associate with important poets like Swinburne and with the pre-Raphaelite painters. No doubt part of the reason for his father's saturation campaign of letter writing was a sense that his son was cultivating the kind of society that would not promote the ideals of the Plymouth Brethren. He was, of course, correct.

A direct clash between father and son seemed inevitable, and it came in 1873. The immediate provocation was the father's latest musings on prophecy. He had become convinced not only that the Second Coming was imminent, but also that not all Christian believers would be raptured, "but only those who are watchful, and practically ready; only those who are, in habitual affection, in separation from the world, in circumcision of the heart—wholly His."[39] Through the inexorable winnowing of the father's soteriology, it now seemed that even those whom he regarded as genuine Christian believers, already a tiny minority of humanity, would be further divided between the watchful and the casual, between the wise and the foolish virgins of the New Testament parable. Those "left behind," including genuine but careless Christian believers, would have to suffer the fiery trial under the earthly rule of the infidel Antichrist. What father who resolutely believed such things, and who assumed he had a special God-given insight into the prophetical literature, could resist importuning his only beloved son to believe likewise? He wrote Edmund, "oh! to be left behind to endure that terrible tribulation, which assuredly is coming soon: when if the thoughts of many deeply taught are correct, the only choice possible will be, either open apostasy and demon-worship, or—the axe of the executioner!"[40] Edmund, whose literary stake in the world had increased, and who seemed on the brink of a dazzling career on planet Earth, had every reason not to wish for a rapture. His return letter to his father in March 1873 is the most comprehensive statement of his religious views as a young independent adult.

In his own personal and very short statement of faith he writes, "I believe in Christ, the God-Man, who gave his blood to take away the sins of the world. Beyond this I do not know that I have any creed." In a point-by-point rebuttal of some of his father's most cherished beliefs, Edmund declared that he did not believe in the verbal inspiration and complete accuracy of the Bible, did not accept that he should separate himself from an ungodly world, and did not share his father's narrow delineation of who would be saved by Christ's atoning sacrifice. As is the way with religious discussions, of more interest than the bald theological issues at stake are the underpinning assumptions of Edmund's evolving beliefs. Comparing his father's microscopic approach to science with Darwin's more broad-ranging ability to construct a grand narrative, Edmund stated that he read the Bible not, as his father did, for particulars, but for the "meaning of the great scheme of salvation." Similarly he could not accept that the Bible was a Koran-like inflexible lawmaker for culture (his comparison), but rather that it gave general guidelines that each generation had to interpret for itself. What was said to Corinth 1,850 years ago, he writes, is not meant to apply directly to England in the nineteenth century, any more than the Southern planters' conviction that slavery was divinely sanctioned in the Scriptures should be accepted by everyone else. Revealingly, Gosse's argument in this section of his letter is full of English Protestant chauvinism. How could Paul's letter to pagan Corinth be applied directly to "England, where the glorious Gospel has, down all the ages, formed the very marrow of the best thought of the nation?" Gosse may have thought his father's scheme of salvation too narrow, but he amply absorbed the anti-Islamic, anti-Catholic, and anti-foreign sentiments of his time and place. Gosse's God may not have been a Plymouth Brother, but he was assuredly an amiable and cultivated English Protestant.[41]

At the heart of Gosse's remarkably frank epistle to his father was the same basic idea that informed *Father and Son*. He was stung by his father's contemptuous dismissal of his poetry and prose as "incurably worldly," as if by comparison the pursuit of natural science was essentially godly because it dealt with the divine creation. In an almost adolescent plea for intellectual and creative space, Edmund writes, "you are the most difficult Father to satisfy in all the world." He was also at pains to point out to his father that he was no hypocrite, living one life among the Plymouth Brethren of Tottenham and another among the literati of the city of London. "Everybody who cares to know, in London, knows I am a superintendent of a little Dissenting Sunday-School; and everybody who cares to know at Brook Street knows I am a poet, critic and *littérateur*. You only have found these things inconsistent."[42] But the father's stream of nervous criticism did not cease. An article by Edmund in *Fraser's Magazine* provoked another attack followed by one of Edmund's sharpest retorts. "You insist, more than any professional theologian I have ever met," he writes, "on your own insight into theology. Why is it that practically you narrow the channels of God's grace to the mere streamlets that can run through your garden? I cannot understand how you can possibly regard the truth as a thing so *borne*, so stereotyped, so whimsical. You permit the enjoyment of nature in the fields and by the shore; you forbid the exactly kindred pleasure found in the society of one's own friends."[43] This letter also contains some of Edmund's most pointed statements about mutual tolerance, respect, and filial freedom, themes that were later developed more powerfully in *Father and Son*.

Edmund Gosse was in his twenties in the 1870s, and his opinions were clearly following the zeitgeist of the period when poets and novelists began self-consciously to break away from the narrow constraints of Victorian values. On the progressive side in this Victorian culture war, as Edmund became more tolerant, more cultivated, more expansive, and more poetic, his religious convictions were modified to suit his changing environment. The sympathies of most modern readers flow with him and his quest for intellectual and moral freedom from the terrible narrowness of his father's religious convictions.[44] Most critics who write about Gosse are themselves women and men of letters who find in him an important prototype of the cause of intellectual and religious liberalism. Similarly, it is almost impossible to defend the father, so extreme were his positions on almost everything to do with religion, especially those distinctively Brethren emphases on separation from the world, the imminence of the Second Advent, and a view of the Bible that was rooted in inerrancy and literalism. But there was one aspect of the father's mental universe that proved over time to be right. He clearly saw, especially in those early years in London when Edmund was assiduously seeking to carve out a literary reputation, that his son's association with the literati could not be combined for long with his devotion to what Mathew Arnold called the dissidence of Dissent. The Edmund Gosse who loved intelligent society, who delighted in his London clubs, who flattered those more important than himself, who loved critical acclaim, and who positively exulted in his appointment as Clark Lecturer in literature at the University of Cambridge, was not the man who would patiently nurture the Plymouth Brethren gathered in self-conscious separation from the world in Tottenham. All this points to a contrast between father and son never referred to in the critical literature. In a religion of few charms, it is easy to overlook the fact that the Plymouth Brethren actually set out as a form of primitive Christianity emphasizing the priesthood of all believers against nineteenth-century emphases on clergymen, hierarchies, and denominations. The anti-sacerdotalism of the Brethren therefore has an implied democratic and populist dynamic. In Brethren assemblies there are no ordained clergymen. Every believer has the right to speak at meetings, except women, who are victims of a literalistic interpretation of the Pauline epistles on the subordinate role of women in churches. Theoretically, at least, the Plymouth Brethren are committed to the idea of Christian brotherhood regardless of class, education, and status. Hence the father in *Father and Son,* despite his status as one of Britain's most distinguished natural scientists, patiently ministers to a group of quirky, eccentric, and poorly educated Brethren as one of them. There is no doubt that the father derived some pleasure from the control and public visibility he had in the little assembly at Marychurch in Devon, or that his ministry over time added a more cultivated membership, but there is also a noble side to his devoted ministry, which rarely seems to have descended to condescension or chauvinism toward this quaint group. To be fair, Edmund recognizes some of this when he writes, "I wish that I could paint, in colours so vivid that my readers could perceive what their little society consisted of, this quaint collection of humble, conscientious, ignorant and gentle persons. In chronicle or fiction I have never been fortunate enough to meet with anything which resembled them. The caricatures of enmity and worldly scorn are as crude, to my memory, as the unction of religious conventionality is featureless." To Gosse's credit, this is as good an account of popular rural religion in nineteenth-century England as exists anywhere, but it was not the life he coveted for himself.[45] Whereas the father was more or less content to cast his religious lot with the rural poor, Edmund had other aspirations.

From Gosse's biographies and letters it is difficult to be precise about the dates and events marking out his separation from the Plymouth Brethren assembly and Sunday school in London, but references to them simply dry up in his correspondence, eradicated by Gosse's increasing commitment to writing, socializing, and traveling. Even his relationship with his father seems to have mellowed somewhat. With both father and son absorbed in happy marriages, and with Edmund able to carve out sufficient space to pursue a successful literary career, the old struggles for mastery lost some of their energy. It is hard to know from the surviving evidence whether the father simply accepted the uncomfortable fact that he could no longer control his adult son, and therefore it was pointless trying, or whether he simply mellowed with age and derived some paternal satisfaction from his son's evident success as a poet and writer. The latter was certainly Edmund's interpretation. No son who has dearly loved a father ever forgets the "terror" (Edmund's word) of the first clear sign of impending mortality and separation. After such an encounter Edmund wrote to his closest friend, the sculptor Hamo Thornycroft, "It is strange and pathetic that the approach of old age and weakness have softened his temperament. He was, as I think you know, rather severe and unbending to me when I was a child, and I went about the empty house in some dread of him. But now he is clingingly affectionate, and apologetic for the trouble that he brings. I parted from him yesterday with tears in my eyes."[46]

Although the old dogmas were softened with age, they were not abandoned. The father never lost interest in the defining tenets of the Plymouth Brethren, including a fierce attachment to the doctrine of the Second Advent, a belief that led the father late in life to exchange the microscope for the telescope in a bizarre attempt to watch for the returning Lord to whom he had devoted his life. There is a grim irony in the fact that his final illness was the result of bronchitis contracted while peering at the stars from an open window on a cold January night.

The death of the father in 1888 had probably less impact on Edmund's religious sensibilities than did the father's cessation of his "postal inquisition" over a decade before. As the father's power of control ebbed, Edmund's surviving religiosity seems to have ebbed with it. His letters rarely raise the issue of religion except here and there to complain of John Henry Newman's evaluation of his poetry or to inform his interest in seventeenth-century poetry and biography. Evan Charteris, who immersed himself in Gosse's public and private writings, concluded that "a rigid creed suited neither his kind of intellect, nor the problems floating in men's minds during his adolescence. His faith in that creed was foredoomed. Its rigidity was its weakness. A more elastic mould might have continued to hold the spiritual consciousness which, though not definitely associated with dogma and not susceptible of exact statement, was a feature in Gosse's character. But with things as they were the belief in the Second Coming was soon thrown aside, and with it went much else."[47] Charteris thought that although Gosse decisively repudiated the evangelical faith of the Plymouth Brethren, his immersion in the "very sanctuaries of sincerity and bigotry" gave him special insight into worlds of spiritual eccentricity that otherwise would have been closed to him. I am not so sure.

In Gosse's biographies of John Donne and Jeremy Taylor it is less their theology, piety, or holiness that engages his attention than it is their importance as writers of poetry and prose.[48] It is Taylor's syntax, imagery, metaphors, and ornamental style that intrigue him more than what he had to say about the Christian life in his great works *Rule and Exercises of Holy Living* (1650), *Twenty-Eight Sermons* (1651), and *Rule and Exercises of Holy Dying* (1652). His biography of Taylor is not without insight into the trials and tribulations of his life as a churchman living through the tempestuous middle decades of the seventeenth century, but only rarely does Gosse display vivid enthusiasm for the religious content of Taylor's works. On the whole Gosse was more engaged by the beauty of the language than the beauty of the holiness being described.[49] He writes as a wordsmith interested in a fellow wordsmith, not as a Christian believer seeking spiritual insight from an apostle of holy living.

After the death of his father it is difficult to get at Gosse's religious opinions, if there were any. Doubt, uncertainty, and fear of mortality were not his common bedfellows. His life was too full, too successful, and too interesting for him to be much preoccupied by the afterlife that so entranced his father. Although he criticized his father for his remorseless rationality and the lack of mysticism in his spirituality, there was also little of the mystic in Gosse the son. He seems not to have suffered the same kind of anguish experienced by George Eliot in her intellectually necessary, but emotionally draining, dissection of the life of Christ on her way to a reluctant infidelity. He distrusted her stern moralizing, and felt no compulsion to propagate any kind of moral or metaphysical creed. He was more at home among cultivated company in the library of the House of Lords than he was worshipping at any particular religious shrine apart from those that happened to be beautiful. One can understand why his group of friends thought him to be splendid company, quite without religious cant and rough edges, while others regarded him as egocentric, prickly, and a little smug. Virginia Woolf pulled no punches when she wrote of him that he could be "as touchy as a housemaid and as suspicious as a governess. He could smell out an offence where none was meant, and hoard a grievance for years. He could quarrel permanently because a lamp wick was snuffed out too vigorously at a table under his nose. Hostile reviews threw him into paroxysms of rage and despair. . . . It seems possible that one severe review by Churton Collins gave him more pain than he suffered from any public or private sorrow in the course of seventy-nine years."[50]

There is a famous Max Beerbohm caricature of Edmund Gosse being presented with a bust of himself in bronze at the house of Lord Balfour in 1920.[51] At the center of the cartoon are Gosse and Gosse's bust on a pedestal staring at one another with mutual admiration. Surrounding Gosse and his bust are a host of distinguished literary figures including G. K. Chesterton, George Moore, Rudyard Kipling, Arnold Bennett, and Thomas Hardy. With brilliant and largely affectionate satire, Beerbohm captured something of the essence of Gosse—his love of literary companions, his delight in being close to the center of power and influence, and his quirky narcissism. One can only imagine what Beerbohm, given the chance, would have drawn of Edmund's father preaching the certainties of the Second Advent to the rustic peasants of Marychurch in Devon. Between Lord Balfour's house in Carlton Gardens in London, and the Plymouth Brethren gathering in a square, empty room above a stable, there was more than just a generational gap. There was a cultural chasm of unbridgeable proportions between a quirky dissenting sect waiting for the return of Christ in the clouds, and a gathering of worthies in the capital city of a great world empire convened to celebrate the achievements of Edmund Gosse.

It is time to return to the epilogue of *Father and Son,* with which this chapter started. In these his last words on the relationship between the father and the son before the latter broke free from the tight reins of Puritanism, Edmund makes three points with great clarity. The first has to do with his relationship with his father, which he thought had been perverted by his father's peculiar version of evangelical religion. He writes, "what a charming companion, what a delightful parent, what a courteous and engaging friend my Father would have been, and would pre-eminently have been to me, if it had not been for this stringent piety which ruined it all."[52] Here could be no clearer statement of the son's belief that the father's religion, not the father, was the root of the evil he believed he suffered in their relationship. The second point, which he makes with equal clarity, is the idea that the father stood in direct succession from the great English divines of the seventeenth century in his insistence that faith was more important than love, charity, or ethics in his hierarchy of Christian virtues. The father relentlessly harried the son, not because he thought the son was living immorally, but because he thought he had become infected with the terminal disease of infidelity. Edmund, who had real expertise in early modern religion, believed, perhaps correctly in England at the turn of the century, that a sea change was overtaking Christianity, altering it from a religion of faith to one of love and charity. He writes, "This propaganda of beneficence, this constant attention to the moral and physical improvement of persons who have been neglected, is quite recent as a leading feature of religion, though indeed it seems to have formed part of the Saviour's original design. It was unknown to the great preachers of the seventeenth century, whether Catholic or Protestant, and it offered but a shadowy attraction to my Father, who was the last of their disciples."[53] Edmund approved of this change; the father most certainly did not.

Finally, in the many discussions between father and son over religion, it became ever more apparent to Edmund that what was most at stake was a distinctively Victorian clash over religious authority. For the father, the Bible was the key to all knowledge about everything—past, present, and future. For Edmund the Bible had no such authority. In fact, so often had he been driven through its pages in both Greek and English that he confessed to being bored by it. His father sent him the most expensive of bibles and urged him to read the most "reliable" of evangelical commentators, but nothing could deflect

Edmund from the opinion that other forms of literature were more interesting. In taking "a human being's privilege to fashion his inner life for himself," Edmund repudiated not only his father's authority, but also biblical authority and the weight of the English religious tradition, from Jeremy Taylor to John Henry Newman. In short, Edmund was a child of the twentieth century growing up in the nineteenth century. His portrait of his father is of a child of the seventeenth century who somehow survived into the late nineteenth century, a living human embodiment of the fossils Philip spent his life studying.

8 James Baldwin—Preacher and Prophet
Evangelicalism and Race

One is born in a white country, a white Protestant Puritan country, where one was once a slave, where all the standards and all the images . . . when you open your eyes on the world, everything you see: none of it applies to you. . . . I was born in the church, for example, and my father was a very rigid, righteous man. But we were in Harlem—you lived, you know, in a terrible house. . . . When I was a little older, that whole odor of home-made gin, pigs' feet, chitlin,' and poverty, and the basement: all this got terribly mixed in my mind with the Holy Roller, White God business. I really began to go a little out of my mind.
—James Baldwin in an interview with Studs Terkel (1961)

Shortly after James Baldwin died in self-imposed exile in southern France, his brother played Sara Jordan Powell's version of "Amazing Grace," perhaps the best loved hymn of both white and African American evangelicals. Yet the author of the hymn, John Newton, was once a slave trader, one of those exploitative servants of the imperial system that transported West Africans to the Caribbean Islands and America, where they were sold into plantation agriculture to grow cotton for the spinning mills of the north of England. The African victims of this dehumanizing triangular trade who fetched up in the

James Arthur Baldwin, by Mark Gerson. Modern bromide print from original negative, July 1971 (© Mark Gerson/National Portrait Gallery, London)

New World were periodically subjected to the religion of the whites who captured them, but unsurprisingly not many were won over to the religious faith of the established colonial denominations before the outbreak of the Revolutionary War. Over the next half century a remarkable change occurred, which has had incalculable consequences for African American culture and identity. Beginning with the Moravians, but speeded up by the Methodists and Baptists, African Americans converted by the thousands to a populist form of pietist evangelicalism that was minted among the displaced Protestant minorities of central Europe, then appropriated and disseminated by Arminian Methodists and evangelical Baptists.[1]

For reasons that scholars still find difficult fully to comprehend, the electrical charge between survivalist African tribal religiosity and an emotionally redolent form of popular Protestantism was sufficiently potent to sweep large numbers of black Africans into religious traditions forged largely by white Europeans. It was one of those unlikely junction boxes of history that carried unforeseeable consequences. Although the majority of African slaves in America did not convert to evangelical Protestantism, the majority of those who did convert to Christianity chose one of the evangelical populist faiths. Moreover, in both Methodist and Baptist traditions, African Americans were able to forge black-only traditions of surprising durability. Attracted by the rituals of conversion and baptism, emotionally drawn by themes of redemption and deliverance, equipped by their faith with moral dignity and communal support, and given sufficient space to construct culturally appealing forms of praise and worship, the black evangelical churches became the most articulate and distinctive form of African expression in North America. By the beginning of the twentieth century, as predominantly Methodist holiness traditions morphed into Pentecostalism, black evangelicalism threw up a dizzying number of new religious traditions in American cities. It was at one of these churches, the Mount Calvary Assembly Hall of the Pentecostal Faith Church for All Nations in Harlem, that James Baldwin had his early teenage conversion experience.[2]

Although Baldwin had been raised a Baptist, his relationship with his stepfather, who was a Baptist preacher, was enormously problematic. Describing him as "righteous in the pulpit, and a monster in the house," Baldwin stated that "Maybe he saved all kinds of souls, but he lost all his children, every single one of them. And it wasn't so much a matter of punishment with him: he was trying to kill us. I've hated a few people, but actually I've hated only one person, and that was my father."[3] Hence it was Baldwin's encounter with Mother Horn's Pentecostal church in Harlem, not with the preaching of his hated father, that led to one of the pivotal experiences of his life. Rosa Artimas Horn, who was the inspiration for Margaret, the lead character in Baldwin's first staged play, *The Amen Corner,* was born in South Carolina, worked as a dressmaker, became a Pentecostal preacher, and established a powerful ministry in eastern seaboard cities in the Depression years. Baldwin has left two accounts of his conversion experience, one the semiautobiographical account of John Grimes's conversion in his most famous novel, *Go Tell It on the Mountain,* and the other an account published in the *New Yorker* as "Letter from a Region in My Mind" (collected in *The Fire Next Time*) some twenty-four years after the event.

Baldwin's nonfictional account, filtered by memory and rationalized for sense, is both an insightful description of the life choices available to a poor fourteen-year-old African American boy in Harlem during the Depression and a brilliant evocation of the ambiguous role of evangelical religion in black culture. He writes, "I underwent, during the summer that I became fourteen, a prolonged religious crisis. I use the word 'religious' in the common, and arbitrary, sense that I then discovered God, His saints and angels, and His blazing Hell. And since I had been born in a Christian nation, I accepted this Deity as the only one. I supposed Him to exist only within the walls of a church—in fact of *our* church—and I also supposed that God and safety were synonymous."[4] Tormented by sexual feelings he could neither understand nor control, fearful of a surrounding culture of pimps, drunks, and criminals, and subjected to endless harassment by white policemen, Baldwin forsook the bright lights of the city for the "safety" of the theatrical rituals of the church. In Harlem, where "the wages of sin were visible everywhere," Baldwin writes that every Negro boy needed a "gimmick" to survive, and since he could not fight, dance, or sing, his gimmick was the church. His best friend at school, who had already "surrendered his life to the Lord," brought him to see the exotic Mother Horn. "There she sat, in her robes, smiling, an extremely proud and handsome woman, with Africa, Europe, and the America of the American Indians blended in her face." She asked Baldwin whose little boy he was, ironically the same question asked by Harlem's pimps, and Baldwin, surrendering to "a spiritual seduction long before I came to any carnal knowledge," replied at once, "why, yours." Baldwin was now on his way to what he regarded as the ultimate spiritual seduction of the conversion experience. His account is graphic.

> I became more guilty and more frightened, and kept all this bottled up inside me, and naturally, inescapably, one night, when this woman had finished preaching, everything came roaring, screaming, crying out, and I fell

to the ground before the altar. It was the strangest sensation I have ever had in my life—up to that time, or since. I had not known that it was going to happen, or that it could happen. One moment I was on my feet, singing and clapping and, at the same time working out in my head the plot of a play I was working on then; the next moment, with no transition, no sensation of falling, I was on my back, with the lights beating down into my face and all the vertical saints above me. I did not know what I was doing down so low, or how I had got there. And the anguish that filled me cannot be described. It moved in me like one of those floods that devastate counties, tearing everything down, tearing children from their parents and lovers from each other, and making everything an unrecognizable waste. All I really remember is the pain, the unspeakable pain; it was as though I were yelling up to Heaven and Heaven would not hear me. And if Heaven would not hear me, if love could not descend from Heaven—to wash me, to make me clean—then utter disaster would be my portion. Yes, it does indeed mean something—something unspeakable—to be born, in a white country, an Anglo-Teutonic, antisexual country, black. You very soon, without knowing it, give up all hope of communion. Black people, mainly, look down or look up but do not look at each other, not at you, and white people, mainly, look away. And the universe is simply a sounding drum; there is no way, no way whatever, so it seemed then and has sometimes seemed since, to get through a life, to love your wife and children, or your friends, or your mother and father, or to be loved. The universe, which is not merely the stars and the moon and the planets, flowers, grass, and trees, but *other people*, has evolved no terms for your existence, has made no room for you, and if love will not swing wide the gates, no other power will or can. And if one despairs—and who has not?—of human love, God's love alone is left. But God—and I felt this even then, so long ago on that tremendous floor, unwillingly—is white. And if His love was so great, and if He loved all His children, why were we, the blacks, cast down so far? Why? In spite of all I said thereafter, I found no answer on the floor—not *that* answer, anyway—and I was on the floor all night. Over me, to bring me "through," the saints sang and rejoiced and prayed. And in the morning, when they raised me, they told me that I was "saved."

Well, indeed I was, in a way, for I was utterly drained and exhausted and released, for the first time, from all my guilty torment.[5]

Although Baldwin's account is redacted by his subsequent inability to reconcile the promise of spiritual egalitarianism implicit in the evangelical message with the reality of the African American urban experience, there is at the core of his conversion narrative a psychologically compelling description of a vivid adolescent experience. His psyche, riven with guilt, was dismantled and partially rebuilt in the context of a communal ritual of extraordinary potency. The rhythms of the gospel meeting literally floored him and forced him to look up from a position of mental and spiritual prostration. Clutching for an image that would do justice to the experience, he settles on a flood of tsunami-like proportions that swept away everything in its path. Whatever relief he found from the torments of guilt and shame, Baldwin clearly associated the event with anguish, pain, and existential dissonance. Whatever else was deconstructed and reconstructed through his thunderbolt experience, Baldwin still regarded the god of African American Pentecostalism as white, disengaged from black suffering, and unworthy of worship. Or, to put it another way, black Pentecostalism, whatever its claims to the contrary, was according to Baldwin a mere collaborator in the structural racism of American society. When he looked back on his conversion experience later in life, Baldwin asked himself why human relief had to be achieved in a "fashion at once so pagan and so desperate," and concluded that both white and black evangelical churches were governed by similar principles of blindness, loneliness, and terror. "I would love to believe," he writes, "that the principles were Faith, Hope, and Charity, but this is clearly not so for most Christians, or for what we call the Christian world."

Baldwin's religious conversion ushered in a three-year phase of Pentecostal preaching in which he exploited his youthfulness to attract crowds and also to best his stepfather on his own ground. Baldwin admits that, once "saved," he wanted to become a preacher—there is an evangelical pattern here—as much to satisfy his ego as to reclaim the lost. There were other benefits as well. The weekly rhythms of sermon preparation and delivery opened up culturally sanctified space where he could retreat from his stepfather and wider social pressures without suffering recrimination. In this way Baldwin concludes that he immobilized his stepfather, but that only later did he realize that he immobilized himself.

Although Baldwin's adolescent flirtation with black Pentecostalism was relatively brief, his working out of its effects lasted a lifetime. The sheer vivaciousness and compelling theatricality of black Pentecostal praise and worship almost overwhelmed him and could not be repudiated by anger and resentment alone. Its power of expressing sensible experience and communal mutuality, whatever its faults and weaknesses, made a profound impression on Baldwin. He writes about it with such insight and panache that it is impossible to trump his own words or render them into prosaic summary. Hear him preach it.

> The church was very exciting. It took a long time for me to disengage myself from this excitement, and on the blindest, most visceral level, I never really have, and never will. There is no music like that music, no drama like the drama of the saints rejoicing, the sinners moaning, the tambourines racing, and all those voices coming together and crying holy unto the Lord. There is still, for me, no pathos quite like the pathos of those multicolored, worn, somehow triumphant and transfigured faces, speaking from the depths of visible, tangible, continuing despair of the goodness of the Lord. I have never seen anything to equal the fire and excitement that sometimes, without warning, fill a church, causing the church, as Leadbelly and so many others have testified, to "rock." Nothing that has happened to me since equals the power and the glory that I sometimes felt when, in the middle of a sermon, I knew that I was somehow, by some miracle, really carrying, as they said, "the Word"—when the church and I were one. Their pain and their joy were mine, and mine were theirs—they surrendered their pain and joy to me, I surrendered mine to them—and their cries of "Amen!" and "Hallelujah!" and "Yes, Lord!" and "Praise His name!" and "Preach it brother!" sustained and whipped on my solos until we all became equal, wringing wet, singing and dancing, in anguish and rejoicing, at the foot of the altar.[6]

It is hard to read these words and not understand the profound tension and ambiguity at the heart of Baldwin's being, or indeed at the heart of the whole black evangelical experience. To have experienced what Baldwin described is one thing, but once to have been the director of the drama, the conductor of the music, the choreographer of the dance, the creator of the words, the regulator of the emotional temperature, and the leader of the response is quite another. Once tasted, the sweet elixir of mutuality resonating through word, music, drama, and bodily experience could not easily be replaced. Many years later, when Baldwin was asked about his preaching style as a teenager in Harlem, he replied, "I would improvise from the texts like a jazz musician improvises from a theme. I never wrote a sermon—I studied the texts. I've never written a speech. I can't read a speech. It's kind of give and take. You have to sense the people you're talking to. You have to respond to what they hear."[7] It is characteristic of Baldwin that he chose a metaphor taken from black music to describe his method, and emphasized the mutuality of the black worship experience in the delivery of his message. These were the two aspects of the black church he admired the most. However much Baldwin later castigated African American religion for carrying on the devil's work of black self-loathing and racial inferiority, his fiction, plays, and essays are preoccupied by many of the religious themes he first encountered as a puny, ugly (his self-identification), and sexually confused black teenager in Harlem during the Great Depression.

Baldwin's teenage disenchantment with black Pentecostalism, or, as he described it, "the slow crumbling of my faith, the pulverization of my fortress," happened imperceptibly but inexorably. He encountered a secularizing battering ram composed of many materials. He started reading again outside the encircling wall of the Scriptures, beginning with Dostoevsky. He came to believe that the little evangelical tracts he brought to his Jewish friends in school were patently ridiculous. His Jewish friends, who were armed with standard arguments about the unreliability of the New Testament, helped undermine his confidence in the inspiration of the Bible, a process furthered by his growing awareness of the weak foundations of his own claim to inspiration as a preacher. He became aware that sections of Christendom believed that blacks were the accursed descendants of Ham, and behaved as if that were true. His stepfather's unredeemable anger, the petty corruptions of his fellow gospel ministers, the great human stain of the Holocaust, his own uncleansed heart still preoccupied by sexual fantasies, and much else besides persuaded him that Christianity rarely delivered on its own propaganda of making people better. Increasingly he saw church as a piece of human theater where everyone conspired to keep up an illusion of love and piety. Even the great payoff of eternal life in heaven he came to see was the mere wish fulfillment of those who essentially sanctified and projected their own values into eternal space. Far from seeing heaven as a place of perfect holiness, Baldwin considered it an invention of white Christian culture, sanctifying its own power and prejudice, and having the audacity to claim it for eternity. Although disenchantment was clearly gaining the upper hand, Baldwin's ambivalence about what he was leaving behind was painfully palpable. He admired the courage of his fellow church members in facing and surviving disaster, and he loved the easy conviviality of black fellowship, a kind of social expression of the freedoms of jazz and gospel music. But it was not enough to hold him.

Although Baldwin is separated by almost a century from some of the earlier figures in this book, his repeatedly expressed concern about the asymmetry between Christianity and moral excellence is almost Victorian in its moral earnestness, though of course his definition of morality is fundamentally different and more modern. So too is his clear-eyed determination to do without God if necessary. He writes, "whoever wishes to become a truly moral human being . . . must first divorce himself from all the prohibitions, crimes, and hypocrisies of the Christian church. If the concept of God has any validity, or any use, it can only be to make us larger, freer, and more loving. If God cannot do this, then it is time we got rid of Him."[8]

Baldwin did not as a teenager finally get rid of God, but he did rid himself of his career as a popular preacher of black Pentecostal Christianity. He left the ministry, as he later put it, "not to betray myself," but to try to become "an honest man."[9] In Baldwin's eyes there were at least two aspects to the dishonesty of ministry in the black church, the first having to do with the messengers, and the second with the message. He writes, "Being in the pulpit was like being in the theater; I was behind the scenes and knew how the illusion was worked. I knew the other ministers and knew the quality of their lives. And I don't mean to suggest by this the 'Elmer Gantry' sort of hypocrisy concerning sensuality; it was a deeper, deadlier, and more subtle hypocrisy than that, and a little honest sensuality, or a lot, would have been like water in an extremely bitter desert. I knew how to work on a congregation until the last dime was surrendered—it was not very hard to do—and I knew where the money for 'the Lord's work' went. I knew, though I did not wish to know it, that I had no respect for the people with whom I worked. I could not have said it then, but I also knew that if I continued I would have no respect for myself."[10] How much Baldwin actually saw of the petty corruptions of the ministerial profession, and how much is a commentary on his own self-consciousness in creating illusions from the pulpit, is hard to say, but either way it allowed Baldwin to escape from ministry, and from his central role in the black religious community, on the high moral ground.

If the messengers were less than noble, the message, rooted as it was in the history of a predominantly white Christendom, was yet more problematic for Baldwin. Twenty-seven years after he left the pulpit, Baldwin was offered another opportunity to preach, this time not in a black Pentecostal church in Harlem, but as a replacement speaker for the recently assassinated Martin Luther King Jr. at the 1968 meeting of the World Council of Churches. Baldwin did not mince his words. He addressed his audience as "one of God's creatures, whom the Christian Church has most betrayed." He spoke as the representative of a worldwide black humanity which had been enslaved, oppressed, and exploited by a white Christendom that claimed to follow the Jesus who once said, "Insofar as you have done it unto the least of these, you have done it all unto me."[11] Baldwin articulated the shameful paradox that lies at the heart of black Christianity.

In the church I grew up in we sang—and we knew what we meant when we sang it—"I've been rebuked and I've been scolded." We won our Christianity, our faith, at the point of a gun, not because of the example afforded by white Christians, but in spite of it. It was very difficult to become a Christian if you were a black man on a slave ship, and the slave ship was called "The Good ship Jesus." These crimes, for one must call them crimes, against the human being have brought the church and the entire Christian world to the dangerous place we find ourselves today. . . . And if that is so, then it may very well mean that the revolution which was begun two thousand years ago by a disreputable Hebrew criminal may now have to be begun again by people equally disreputable and equally improbable. It's got to be admitted that if you are born under the circumstances in which most black people in the West are born, that means really black people over the entire world, when you look around you, having attained something like adulthood, it is perfectly true that you see that the destruction of the Christian Church as it is presently constituted may not only be desirable but necessary.[12]

Baldwin stated that the terrifying pain at the heart of the black experience in Africa and America, encapsulated in song, dance, and speech, was entirely baffling to white Christians, who had no idea how to begin to relate to it, never mind repent of it or embrace it. That being so, a nervous white Christendom, unable to find a true moral plumb line from which to make judgments, condemned black leaders such as Stokely Carmichael, Malcolm X, and Martin Luther King Jr. as dangerous black fanatics in search of power, while winking at the cruel exercise of power by white institutions, including churches. White Christians were literally tone-deaf to the black experience, "unable to comprehend the force of such a woman as Mahalia Jackson, who does not sound like anyone in Canterbury Cathedral, unable to accept the depth of sorrow, out of which a Ray Charles comes, unable to get itself in touch with itself, with its selfless tonality."[13] With an almost prophetical anticipation of the issues that were about to consume Christianity in the public square, Baldwin stated that "the morality by which the Christian Church claims to live, I mean the public morality, that morality governing our sexual relations and the structure of the family is terribly inadequate for what the world, and the people in the world, must deal with now." What white Christians needed more than anything was to get in touch with human emotions of joy, spontaneity, and freedom, and to dare to "atone, to repent, to be born again"; otherwise a long and bloody bill would have to be paid by their children.

Baldwin's speech was made to the World Council of Churches in the immediate aftermath of the assassination of Martin Luther King Jr. during the rise of the black power movement in America and of protests against apartheid in South Africa, and in the midst of the Vietnam War. But his speech was more than just another '60s protest against the structures of power and influence; it was a prophetic command to white Christendom to repent and follow the example of the crucified Savior it claimed to, but in truth did not, follow. It was the last official sermon of the boy preacher struggling to become an honest man. It was also characteristic of Baldwin that what interested him about Christianity were not so much its doctrines and sacred texts, but its fidelity or otherwise to the principles of love that it preached but did not practice.

One way of getting at Baldwin's complicated views on religion is to look at his relationship with the man whose place he took at the gathering of the World Council of Churches. Martin Luther King Jr., who, like Baldwin, was the preacher son of a preacher, and who was the real and symbolic head of a distinctively Christian black consciousness, first met Baldwin in Atlanta in the late '50s. King was unlike any preacher Baldwin had ever met before; "For one thing, to state it baldly, I liked him. It is rare that one *likes* a world-famous man—by the time they become world-famous they rarely like themselves, which may account for this antipathy. Yet King is immediately and tremendously winning, there is no other word for it."[14] Although he found King to be emotionally restrained and self-contained, he also admired his integrity, which saved him from "the ghastly self-importance" that Baldwin thought was characteristic of black leaders. King impressed him as a "man solidly anchored in those spiritual realities concerning which he can be so eloquent. This divests him of the hideous piety which is so prevalent in his profession."[15]

Baldwin's admiration of King as a black leader who would never accept segregation and as a serious Christian who understood the reality of suffering and sacrifice was reinforced, not diminished, when he first heard him preach in his home church in Montgomery. What particularly impressed Baldwin about King was not his oratory or his presence, but the evident love and mutual respect between the preacher and the congregation. The secret of King's power as a speaker lay not in his demagogic flights of the imagination but in his intimate knowledge of the people he was addressing, "and in the forthrightness with which he speaks about those things which hurt and baffle them. He does not offer any easy comfort and this keeps his hearers absolutely tense. He allows them their self-respect—indeed, he insists on it."[16] There is no doubt that despite his regularly recurring bouts of cynicism about the capacity of American whites to address the nation's race problem, Baldwin was partly captivated by King's insistence that love was a more powerful force than bigotry and that something approaching liberation was possible. King, unlike Baldwin, had been nurtured by a father's and a wife's love, and Baldwin sensed the "striking mixture of steadiness and peace" in his temperament.

Baldwin was well aware that the path ahead of King would not be an easy one. White hatred, black jealousy, and generations of personal and structural evil were difficult foes to defeat. The next time Baldwin heard King preach was in the Ebenezer Baptist Church in Atlanta soon after the failure of the trumped-up case of financial fraud against the people of Montgomery that was brought against him. Baldwin detected a new note of anguish and torment in his voice, prompting Baldwin to some serious theological reflection on the nature of evil. "For evil is in the world: it may be in the world to stay. No creed and no dogma are proof against it, and indeed no person is; it is always the naked person, alone, who, over and over and over again, must wrest his salvation from these black jaws."[17] It is characteristic of Baldwin to look the problem straight in the face and to rely on the individual will, not a benevolent deity, to stare it down.

Over the course of the 1960s Baldwin became more irritated with the white liberal adulation of King, and at times gravitated more to the angrier black radicalism of Malcolm X and Stokely Carmichael than to King's strategy of nonviolent marching and petitioning. Although skeptical of what was achieved, Baldwin was moved by the great march on Washington and joined King on the march from Selma to Montgomery in 1965. Increasingly, however, Baldwin believed that King's approach was merely postponing "the hour of dreadful reckoning that was sure to come. Shortly before King's death the two men met again in Hollywood, where Baldwin was working on a screenplay about Malcolm X. Here is yet another example of Baldwin's interstitial persona. One can find any number of critical references to Malcolm and the Nation of Islam in his various collections of nonfiction, and yet he clearly empathized with Malcolm's diagnosis of Christianity as a cruel and oppressive religion in the history of black humanity. A tidy configuration of Baldwin as an uncritical supporter of Martin Luther King's "nonviolent integration" against Malcolm X's "violent nationalism" is as inappropriate for Baldwin as it is as a rigid template for the whole black experience in the Civil Rights era.[18] In his interview with Studs Terkel in 1961, for example, Baldwin explained how he thought the self-conscious sense of superiority of white people created a counterweight "which is simply to take the whole legend of Western history—and its entire theology, changing one or two pronouns, and transferring it from Jerusalem to Islam, just this small change—and turn it all against the white world. The white world can't do anything about this, can't call down the Muslim leaders, or anyone else on this, until they are willing to face their own history."[19]

When Baldwin met King in Hollywood, he picked up from King a sense of disapproval over his work on Malcolm X's screenplay, but he was also stirred by King's eloquent and humble speech on behalf of the Southern Christian Leadership Conference. "And yet," Baldwin writes, "how striking to compare his tone that night with what it had been not many years before." Five years after the great Washington summit, according to Baldwin, Martin was "five years wearier and five years sadder, and still petitioning. But the impetus was gone, because the people no longer believed in their petitions, no longer believed in their government."[20] All had collapsed into bloodshed and despair.

A century earlier Theodore Dwight Weld became disenchanted with the abolitionist movement and its Christian foundations because he believed it merely delayed the inevitable day of reckoning that came with the American Civil War. Baldwin increasingly saw King's civil rights campaign in the same way. Soon after Baldwin and King met in Hollywood they shared a platform in Carnegie Hall in New York. It was the last time the two men met before Baldwin received the shocking news that King had been killed. Baldwin attended the funeral service in Atlanta, describing it as "the most real church service I've ever sat through in my life, or ever hope to sit through." Characteristically, Baldwin's account of the service featured more on the music than the words, for it was the music of the black church he loved most about it. He was particularly moved by a woman soloist's rendition of "My Heavenly Father Watches Over Me." "The song rang out as it might have over dark fields, long ago; she was singing of a covenant a people had made, long ago, with life, and with that larger life which ends in revelation and which moves in love."[21]

Once the emotion settled, Baldwin was left with the sad reality that, since that "tremendous day in Atlanta, something has altered in me, something has gone away." What had gone away were the vestiges of Baldwin's belief in the redemptive suffering of American blacks and the last shreds of optimism about the possibility of American whites owning up to the truth of their lives. "The failure and the betrayal are in the record book forever," he wrote, "and sum up, and condemn, forever, those descendants of a barbarous Europe who arbitrarily and arrogantly reserve the right to call themselves Americans."[22] The moral of the whole sad story of King's life and death, according to Baldwin, was that the hope of the world lay not with God, or ideologies, or faith in human potential, but rather "in what one demands, not of others, but of oneself." Although it would be wrong to infer from this discussion that Baldwin and King were close friends or that they shared a similar strategy to ameliorate America's racial sores, it seems clear from Baldwin's writings that he admired King enormously, not least the spiritual foundations of his moral power and convictions. King's death, coming as it did in the wake of the violent deaths of many other black activists in the 1960s, persuaded Baldwin that America's ruling God was still the God of the whites and of their moral mendacity. King's death also removed from view the one avowedly Christian leader in American society that Baldwin unconditionally respected. In that sense, the bullet that killed King also shattered the redemptive influence that one black preacher's son had over another. It confirmed Baldwin's opinion that Christianity offered no solution to America's race problem; if anything, it exacerbated and sanctified it.

Whatever his disappointment and anger with the message and the messengers of a predominantly white Christendom, Baldwin's rejection of churchly Christianity, whether black or white, was no uncomplicated matter, for the music, theater, ritual, and symbols of black Christianity—that is, its entire communal experience—were etched deeply on his soul. According to his own notes, Baldwin, after completing and hawking his first and most famous novel, *Go Tell It on the Mountain*, began thinking of a second work about black Christianity, the black experience, and his own complicated family dynamics. At that time he did not trust himself to write another novel, which he feared might become a mere diminished version of *Go Tell It*, so he experimented with writing a play that he called *The Amen Corner*. Although written from his self-imposed exile in Paris in 1952–53, the play was not published until 1968 and has received surprisingly little attention from critics more interested in Baldwin's social commentary than in his religious struggles.[23] Yet possibly none of Baldwin's other writings, whether fiction or nonfiction, gets closer to the heart of his interpretation of the ambiguities and complexities of the black Christian tradition. Written partly as a psychological exploration of his relationship with his parents, and partly as an attempt to show that black Christianity is best approached through the medium of theater, *The Amen Corner*, though short and accessible, contains a complex message about the nature of African American Christianity and why Baldwin could never find a place in one of its temples. The play is situated in a Harlem tenement that holds the home and church of Sister Margaret Alexander. Margaret devoted herself to the ministry of the church after the death of her infant daughter (a victim of her mother's poverty and malnourishment) and the resulting collapse of her marriage with Luke, a jazz musician with a taste for whiskey. Margaret expiates her guilt and tries to rebuild her shattered psyche by embracing an all-consuming piety that left no room for her husband and little room for her son, David, who is subjected to the iron disciplines of the church as a way of keeping him from the sins of the flesh. David, who is a gifted pianist, is caught in a tug-of-war between the church and the saloon, between his mother's desire for his salvation and his father's instinct that he should follow his musical gift and live.

The play opens in the little Harlem church with its stock of Bibles, tambourines, and hymnbooks, its humble congregation singing gospel music. The bluesy rhythms of David's piano playing and Baldwin's carefully chosen words of the gospel songs act as a recurring refrain in the play. The chorus strikes the keynote for Margaret's sermon:

> *Let me tell you now*
> *Whilst I am in His care,*
> *I'm in my Saviour's care,*
> *Jesus got His arms wrapped around me,*
> *No evil thoughts can harm me*
> *'Cause I'm so glad I'm in His care.*[24]

Margaret's text is taken from Isaiah's instruction to King Hezekiah, "set thine house in order, for thou shalt die and not live," and her message is an uncompromising assertion that the "way of holiness is a hard way," leaving no room for drinking, smoking, moviegoing, cardplaying, reading the funny paper, or adultery. The hermeneutical slide that leads Margaret from Israel's ancient prophets to the sins of Harlem's black men is intuitive, not intellectual, and arises from her experience as a suffering woman. Indeed, one of Baldwin's more amusing subthemes in the play is the way in which Margaret's little congregation constantly uses scriptural texts and gospel songs as a means of sanctifying their own self-interest. It is in the dialectic between pious platitudes at the surface and what is "really" going on underneath that Baldwin locates the disease of the black evangelical churches, or indeed of all churches. *The Amen Corner* makes the point that Sister Margaret's little band of black believers are just as much preoccupied by money, power, status, hierarchy, jealousy, competition, control, and self-interest as those outside their fellowship, and Baldwin delights in juxtaposing their pious language and their impious thoughts and actions. Sister Moore, for example, begins the play by thanking God for keeping her humble, for saving her from the lusts of the flesh, and for keeping her pure, but we learn as her character is developed that she covets power, uneasily accepts her own singleness, and is a relentless behind-the-scenes schemer.

Throughout the play there is an ongoing disagreement between Margaret and the church elders, Brother and Sister Boxer, over Brother Boxer's willingness to take a job as a truck driver for a liquor company. "The Word" tells Margaret that no one can serve two masters, but later in the play, when she is willing to welcome musicians from a sister church to spice up the worship, Boxer's wife engages Margaret in some folk theologizing: "Sister Margaret, I ain't trying to dig up things what buried. But you told Joel and me he couldn't take that job driving that truck. And now you bringing down drums and trumpets from Philadelphia because you say the evil ain't in the thing, it's in what you do with the thing. Well ain't that truck a *thing?* And if it's all right to blow a trumpet in church, why ain't it all right for Joel to drive that truck, so he can contribute a little more to the house of God? This church is *poor,* Sister Margaret, we ain't got no cars to ride you around in, like them folks in Philadelphia. But do that mean we got to stay poor?"[25] Margaret supplies the conventional answer that there is a difference between playing praise music in a church and driving a liquor truck, but Baldwin uses this little dialogue to explore bigger issues about the relationship between the sacred and the profane, wealth and poverty, and power and control in black religious culture.

These issues surface in a more tragic way in the broken relationship between Margaret and her husband, Luke. The couple separated ten years before the action of the play begins, and Luke, a jazz trombonist, returns to see his wife and son before he dies. The decisive point in their past relationship came when Margaret bore a stillborn child, and she turned to religion while Luke turned to jazz and whiskey. Each resented the other's choice. Margaret found the Lord in her tragedy and believed that He calmed the waters, beat back the powers of darkness, and made her a new woman. Luke saw it differently. He lost the "funny, fast-talking, fiery little thing" he used to hold in his arms and was left with a religious automaton whose repressed guilt, anger, and blame birthed her career as a preacher. While Margaret interpreted the death of her child as God's judgment on her sinful life with Luke, Luke interpreted it as the grimly natural result of poverty and malnutrition. Margaret thought she had been cursed by God, Luke thought that poverty was the real curse. As Luke lies dying, Margaret's mission is to save his soul and to prevent him from corrupting their son David, who shares his father's musical talent, while Luke's mission is to rediscover the love he had for his wife and son. Luke dies in Margaret's embrace with Margaret not thanking God for being born again while her husband was not, but wistfully wishing that they could both start over again.

A superficial reading of *The Amen Corner* could lead to the conclusion that Baldwin saw nothing good in black evangelical Christianity. In their efforts to create a safe and secure fellowship untainted by the wickedness of their surrounding culture, Sister Margaret's Harlem disciples are scarcely an attractive bunch. They argue incessantly over money as Luke lies unvisited and dying in an adjoining room; they claim to know the Lord's will but mostly sanctify their selfish wills; and they undermine trust with constant gossip and backbiting. No wonder Luke concludes that people don't change much and dismisses Margaret's pious retort that only the Lord can change hearts with the comment "you ain't changed much, neither—you dress a little different."[26] On one level Baldwin seems to be saying that black churches, by refusing to deal honestly with matters of poverty, race, sexuality, and human nature, create little subcultures of pious evasion where safety is privileged over honesty. Thus, when David leaves the church and his mother's influence to reach out for a musical career, his reasons for leaving are to avoid telling any more lies, to become a man, to realize his artistic potential, and to engage the world in a serious way. These are close to Baldwin's own reasons for leaving the church.

While such a shallow reading of *The Amen Corner* could lead to these conclusions, Baldwin's treatment of black Christianity is not entirely negative. Throughout the play the quiet, wise, and honest voice of Odessa, Margaret's sister, is employed as a force for good amid the low-grade plotting of the Harlem congregation. Unlike Sister Moore, she refuses to use her singleness as a badge of God's favor, or her relationship to Margaret as an excuse for lording it over the others. Within her limitations she speaks with courage and humility. When baited by Sister Boxer for her singleness, she states, "I ain't got no regrets. No I ain't. I ain't claiming I'm pure, like Sister Moore here. I ain't claiming that the Lord had such special plans for me that I couldn't have nothing to do with men. Brothers and sisters, if you knew just a little bit about folks' lives, what folks go through, and the low, black places they finds their feet—you *would* have a meeting here this afternoon. Maybe I don't know the Lord like you do, but I know something else. I know how men and women can come together and change each other and make each other suffer, and make each other glad. If you putting my sister out of this church, you putting me out too."[27]

Odessa sticks with Margaret through the death of her husband, the departure of her only son, and the rebellion of her congregation. At last, bereft of almost everything, and educated by suffering, Margaret breaks down in her last sermon and, uncluttered by pious language and sermonic affectation, she speaks the honest truth, perhaps for the first time since the death of her baby daughter a decade before: "Children. I'm just now finding out what it means to love the Lord. It ain't all in the singing and the shouting. It ain't all in the reading of the Bible. (*She unclenches her fist a little.*) It ain't even—it ain't even—in running all over everybody trying to get to heaven. To love the Lord is to love all His children—all of them, everyone!—and suffer with them and rejoice with them and never count the cost."[28] Ironically, this moment of insight, when Margaret was at her strongest, was perceived by her congregation as her weakest moment. Sister Boxer thought the gift of God had left her, and Sister Moore was left to celebrate the victory of their shabby little coup d'état in sullied words of praise.

It is clear from his notes on the play that Baldwin did not want his readers and audiences to miss the significance of what he was saying, for sister Margaret is not only his own mother, but the representative of all black mothers in a remorselessly racist country. His notes are worth reproducing at length, because they come as close to anything in his whole corpus to a theory of race, religion, and culture in America.

It is because I know what Sister Margaret goes through, and what her male child is menaced by, that I become so unmanageable when people ask me to confirm their hope that there has been *progress*—what a word!—in white-black relations. There has certainly not been enough progress to solve Sister Margaret's dilemma: how to treat her husband and her son as men and at the same time to protect them from the bloody consequences of trying to be a man in this society. No one yet knows, or is in the least prepared to speculate on, how high a bill we will have to pay for what we have done to Negro men and women. She is in the church because her society has left her no other place to go. Her sense of reality is dictated by the society's assumption, which also becomes her own, of her inferiority. Her need for human affirmation, and also for vengeance, expresses itself in her merciless piety; and her love, which is real but which is also at the mercy of her genuine and absolutely justifiable terror, turns her into a tyrannical matriarch. In all of this, of course, she loses her old self—the fiery, fast-talking little black woman whom Luke loved. Her triumph, which is also, if I may say so, the historical triumph of the Negro people in this country, is that she sees this finally and accepts it, and, although she has lost everything, also gains the keys to the kingdom. The kingdom is love, and love is selfless, although only the self can lead one there. She gains herself.[29]

For Baldwin, the black evangelical churches, for all their vitality of music and worship, and for all their opportunities for fellowship, leadership, and significance, were essentially both the collaborators and the victims of racism and inequality. By trying to keep their men and young adults safe, they succeeded only in making them unmanly and dishonest; in attempting to keep their women pure, they succeeded only in making them prostitutes of piety.

Baldwin's ambivalence about Christianity, if ambivalence is in fact the right word for his view of a religious tradition that he thought stood relentlessly for the privileges of whites, property owners, and heterosexuals, was both deep and unresolved by the end of his life. As with many disenchanted evangelicals Baldwin had a sharp and cynical eye for the gaps between the apparent gospel emphases on love, sacrifice, and compassion for the weak and the poor, and the smug self-righteousness of a predominantly white Western Christendom. In the introduction to his collected nonfiction, written only a few years before he died, Baldwin wrote, "If I were still in the pulpit which some people (and they may be right) claim I never left, I would counsel my countrymen to the self-confrontation of prayer, the cleansing breaking of the heart which precedes atonement."[30] In place of these painful affairs of the heart and the soul Baldwin alleged that American Protestantism substituted mass conversions, which changed nothing, and a cheap emphasis on being born again, which he interpreted as a mere property contract. He denied that the "quite spectacularly repentant 'born again' of the present hour give up this world to follow Jesus. No, they take Jesus with them into the marketplace where He is used as proof of their acumen and as their Real Estate Broker, now, and, as it were, forever."[31] Later in the same introduction Baldwin stated that there could be no true fellowship between black and white Christians so long as the latter retained their claim to the Constantinian heritage of state power. Baldwin could never make his peace with a religious tradition that began with the teachings and sacrifices of an outcast preacher and ended with the authoritarian values of white property owners.

What, then, remained of the religion of the boy preacher? In recent years there has been a noticeable shift in the critical literature on Baldwin, away from the position that he largely abandoned the religious frameworks of his early life and toward a more nuanced approach suggesting that although Baldwin "rails passionately against the sins of professed Christians and the institutional church, his deep though troubled faith in God and in Christian ideals has gone all but unrecognized."[32] The evidence for such a view comes largely from a more sophisticated interpretation of Baldwin's earlier works, a more careful reading of Baldwin's often neglected later writings, and more attention to the transcripts of Baldwin's recorded interviews when he is often put on the spot by direct questions and is therefore forced to clarify evasive answers.[33]

The most revealing of these interviews was a seven-and-a-half-hour marathon with the distinguished anthropologist Margaret Mead.[34] Mead was questioning him about the nature of his American identity in the light of his self-imposed exile in France. Baldwin opined that he had to leave his country in order to realize he was a part of it and it was a part of him, and then he stated, "The whole question of religion, for example has always obsessed me. I was raised in the church and I left it when I was seventeen and never joined anything else again, not even a riding academy. Nothing. But I never understood white Christians. I still don't." What Baldwin could not understand is how followers of a religion founded on sacrificial love could endorse racism, segregation, violence, and cruelty. The two examples he gave were the school integration crisis in the South when white women in New Orleans standing with babies in their arms spat on black women also standing with babies in their arms, and the Holocaust. Baldwin confessed that he was haunted by a Second World War photograph of a beautiful young boy surrounded by the Gestapo that would subsequently kill him because he was a Jew, "and this in the name of Christianity!" Mead refused to accept that the Holocaust was caused directly by Christianity and the conversation moved on to Baldwin's foundation for making moral judgments such as the ones he had just made. Under pressure from Mead, Baldwin stated that his moral sense came not from the Bible, nor from church, but from his Christian mother, who somehow made her children believe that it was "more important to love each other and love other people than anything else." Mead tried to persuade him that an emphasis on the supremacy of love for fellow humans was both Christianity's essence and its greatest gift to civilization. Mead's point to Baldwin was why, apart from the appeal of antiestablishment rhetoric, he preferred to see the essence of Christianity in acts of hypocrisy and cruelty rather than in his mother's love. Baldwin responded, "what Christians seem not to do is identify themselves with the man they call their Savior, who, after all, was a very disreputable person. . . . So, in my case in order to become a moral human being, whatever that may be, I have to hang out with publicans and sinners, whores and junkies, and stay out of the temple where they told us nothing but lies." To Mead's retort that that was precisely what Jesus did, Baldwin replied that "it is only in that sense that I can be called a Christian." Mead had not intended to push Baldwin to a personal confession; she had merely tried to get him to acknowledge that Christianity had contributed something good to civilization. Baldwin's response that unless Christianity is interiorized it is meaningless, and that it is a terrible crime to profess one thing and do another, has been a mantra of the pietist and holiness traditions since the early eighteenth century, and shows the extent to which Baldwin repudiated churchly Christianity with surprisingly evangelical language.

Similar points could be made about some of his other interview "confessions." In an interview recorded by the BBC in 1965, Colin MacInnes asked Baldwin if he was a religious writer and if he was in any sense a believer. Baldwin replied, "I'm not a believer in any sense which would make sense to any church, and any church would obviously throw me out. I believe—what do I believe? I believe in . . . I believe in love—that sounds very corny." MacInnes interjected that he did not consider love to be corny and Baldwin followed up by stating that he thought human beings had an obligation to save one another and that his belief in the power of love was not trite or passive. "I mean something active, something more like a fire, like the wind, something which can change you. I mean energy. I mean a passionate belief, a passionate knowledge of what a human being can do, and become, what a human being can do to change the world in which he finds himself." Albeit without an appeal to a personal and empowering God, these are the words of an evangelical preacher.[35] Five years later, in an interview with John Hall, Baldwin, reflecting on his sense of responsibility as the most famous black writer of his generation, stated that passion was more important than talent and that what was important about his work, "which I realized when I was a little boy, partly from the Church perhaps, and whatever happened to my mind all those years I was growing up in the shadow of the Holy Ghost, is that nothing belongs to you."[36] It is comments like these that have persuaded one recent critic of Baldwin's corpus that he had a strong personal theology comprising three complementary avenues toward salvation: "saving oneself through developing the ability to survive and to love, saving another through preferential or erotic love, and saving others through selfless action based on accepting responsibility for all people," including their suffering. Of course all of these could be combined with casting a cold eye on the manifold hypocrisies of the adherents of white institutional Christianity and the God they worshipped.

It is tempting to conclude from a careful selection of Baldwin's writings and statements, as some interpreters have, that he was merely an artistic counterpart to the black liberation theologians of the 1960s and '70s, and that he remained a primitivist Christian who happened to be at war with almost every aspect of Christian establishments both black and white. But in truth the evidence does not support such a tidy conclusion. Baldwin knew himself and his culture well enough to know that populist evangelical Christianity of a holiness Pentecostal variety had helped shape his thought, his language, and his identity, but he also knew he had to keep his moral distance from a faith and a tradition that he believed was responsible for subjugating his race and distorting genuinely humanitarian aspirations. Baldwin's ambivalence about Christianity is at the heart of what he thought about Christianity and was never resolved before his death.

Part of Baldwin's ambivalence about Christianity had to do with his attitude to human love and sexuality and its customary place in the Christian tradition. Any tradition that celebrated a virgin birth, sanctified celibacy, marginalized sexual desire, and condemned homosexuality was unacceptable to Baldwin. His novels and plays are full of earthy and sweaty sexuality, portrayed not as mere titillation, but as complex encounters of love, life, alienation, and revelation. A tradition literally birthed in virginity was inherently problematic for Baldwin. In his second major play, *Blues for Mister Charlie*, Juanita, the lover of her murdered childhood sweetheart, bitterly laments his death and hopes that she is pregnant. Comparing her own embrace of physicality, sexuality, and fertility with her mother's faith in God and respectability, Juanita states, "I suppose God does for Mama what Richard did for me. Juanita! I don't care! I don't care! Yes, I want a lover made of flesh and blood, of flesh and blood, like me, I don't want to be God's mother! He can *have* His icy, snow-white heaven!"[37] Safety, iciness, and whiteness are good descriptions for Baldwin's view of the repressed sexual ethics of traditional Christianity. Juanita's soliloquy in praise of love, life, and sexuality over the constraints imposed by the sexual taboos of black religion is not atypical of Baldwin's treatment of black women in his plays and fiction. Trudier Harris has shown how Baldwin creates many women characters who "move out from under the shadow of their own guilt and doubt about their humanity to singing praises to life and living." Nevertheless, whatever degree of liberation his women achieve from church and respectable values, Baldwin's women largely occupy the niches created for them by men.[38]

Although he did not speak often about the subject, to the disappointment of some who wanted a bolder "outing," Baldwin's views about homosexuality are also part of a much broader critique of Christianity's influence on human sexuality. In one of his early essays, "Preservation of Innocence," Baldwin argued that it was profoundly illogical to describe something as unnatural that was so clearly found in nature. What made homosexuality unnatural was not its sterility, for that is also the fate of the unmarried, the poor, and the weak, but the human invention of God, which marked the death of innocence and set up the duality of good and evil, sin and redemption. According to Baldwin, "it is not in the sight of nature that the homosexual is condemned, but in the sight of God. This argues a profound and dangerous failure of concept, since an incalculable number of the world's humans are condemned to something less than life; and we may not, of course, do this without limiting ourselves."[39] In the same essay Baldwin characteristically widened the scope of the subject to take into account conventional constructions of gender relations in American literature and society that he found so lamentable. In order to evade the unavoidable complexity of the issues, and thus to avoid growing up into maturity (a favorite Baldwin theme), Baldwin stated that Americans created yet more dangerous stereotypes. "In the truly awesome attempt of the American to at once preserve his innocence and arrive at a man's estate," he writes, "that mindless monster, the tough guy, has been created and perfected; whose masculinity is found in the most infantile and elementary externals and whose attitude towards women is the wedding of the most abysmal romanticism and the most implacable distrust."[40] Hence homosexuals were portrayed in the literature of the time as violent, feckless, and unreliable, all convenient stereotypes for a society reared on the values of white Christendom and *The Rover Boys*.

The chief reason why Baldwin was so keen to avoid being labeled as a gay man or writer was his profound belief that labels were themselves the enemies of human fellow feeling and empathy. Without a passionate understanding of how all things involving human beings interlock, "we may all smother to death, locked in those airless, labeled cells, which isolate us from each other and separate us from ourselves."[41] This is as close as one is likely to get to Baldwin's mission as a writer and black intellectual, and shows how impossible it was for him to accept the dogmatic certainties of his early embrace of black evangelical Christianity. But it is the argument of an increasing number of writers on Baldwin that even in his exploration of the complex themes of human sexuality Baldwin retains something of the flavor of the evangelical preacher in his celebration of human love and his dark warnings that there would be a future judgment on the sexual alienation and crude stereotyping of blacks and whites in America.[42] In his approach to sexuality, both personally and as a writer, Baldwin could neither embrace conventional Christian understandings nor entirely escape from their influence.

As Baldwin approached death from cancer he spoke with his friend and biographer David Leeming about church and religion. Leeming writes, "He realized that the church's role in his life had been significant, especially with respect to what he called his 'inner vocabulary.' As for the larger questions, he did not 'believe' in God, but he felt—especially when he was alone—that there was something out there."[43] Another biographer concludes that Baldwin was not in any obvious sense a Christian believer but that "his life was based on faith that can only be called religious, just as his thought was infused with religious belief. His Scripture was the old black gospel music:

Just above my head
I hear music in the air
And I really do believe
There's a God somewhere.[44]

In a similar vein Clarence Hardy concludes that Baldwin was partly the creation of a black evangelicalism he later repudiated but never quite escaped.[45] At various times in his life Baldwin was angry with his stepfather, with God, with white liberals (for whom he reserved some of his most pungent prose),[46] with black authors, with the black sense of victimhood, and with the structures of economic and political power. He was an unsettled, argumentative, interstitial figure who did not fit into any available category. In his attempts to become "an honest man" Baldwin first left his family, then his church, and then his country, but he never fully escaped the ties that bind. He was one of the last black American writers to focus his major works on black Christianity, and one of the first to "distance himself from the lone enduring black institution, the black church." Baldwin's view of that church was appropriately ambivalent. In an interview for *The Black Collegian* in 1979 Baldwin was asked by Kalamu ya Salaam if he saw the church as a redemptive institution for black humanity. Baldwin replied that one of the results of Christianity was the enslavement of black people, "who were given the bible and the cross under the shadow of the loaded gun, and who did something with it absolutely unprecedented which astounds Black people to this day. Finally, everything in Black history comes out of the church." Characteristically Baldwin tried to put some distance between the religion of white European Christendom and that of American blacks; "When Black people talk about true religion, they're 'speaking in tongues' practically. It would not be understood in Rome."[47] Baldwin clearly asserted that black Christianity was instrumental in forging the identity of American blacks, and that he did not know how a new unchurched generation would find an alternative with anything like the same power.

In his deeply personal afterword to his book on *James Baldwin's God,* Clarence Hardy confesses how much of Baldwin's ambivalence about the black evangelical experience is true of himself and of countless others who were raised in black holiness culture. In Baldwin's case "he was willing to leave God's house for the art, drink, and risks of a life fully lived, but he retained notions of redemptive suffering even after Martin King's death. Baldwin throughout his career would both employ and disdain the language of judgment that animates evangelicalism and evangelicalism itself."[48] In short, Baldwin was both fortunate enough, and unfortunate enough, to have his most powerful teenage experiences associated with a tradition that originated in the white pietism of Old Europe and that built one of its most enduring cultures within the slave populations of the New World. The ambivalence he had about all aspects of the tradition—its joyous music, churchly theater, religious ecstasy, half-absorbed sexual Puritanism, and almost totally repressed human worth—was there from the start and is at the heart of the black religious experience in North America. No one felt it more acutely, or wrote about it with such searing honesty and insight, as James Baldwin did.

9 Conclusion
Enchantment and Disenchantment

Theron spread some old manuscript sermons before him on the desk, and took down his scribbling-book as well. But there his application failed, and he surrendered himself instead, chin on hand, to staring out at the rhododendron in the yard. . . . The spirit of that wonderful music [Chopin] came back to him, enfolded him in its wings. It seemed to raise itself up—a palpable barrier between him and all that he had known and felt and done before. That was his new birth—that marvelous night with the piano. The conceit pleased him— not the less because there flashed along with it the thought that it was a poet that had been born. Yes; the former country lout, the narrow zealot, the untutored slave groping about in the dark after silly superstitions . . . was dead. There was an end of him, and good riddance. In his place there had been born a Poet— he spelled out the word now unabashed—a child of light, a lover of beauty and sweet sounds, a recognizable brother to Renan and Chopin—and Celia!
—Harold Frederic, *The Damnation of Theron Ware* (1896)

In Harold Frederic's fin-de-siècle novel *The Damnation of Theron Ware,* the novelist creates a character who sets out as a serious young Methodist preacher and ends as a disillusioned minister ready to swap the world of camp meetings and revivals for a job in real estate and an imagined career as a political orator.[1] Theron Ware's disenchantment with the narrow Methodism of his life and preaching station in the Mohawk Valley is the result of many influences. In the imaginary town of Octavius, which is drawn largely from Frederic's hometown of Utica, New York, Ware encounters a range of people and influences that, depending on one's point of view, contribute to his "illumination" and/or "degeneration." In his pilgrim's regress he meets a Darwinian doctor, a liberal Catholic priest, and in Celia a bohemian beauty who tantalizes him with Chopin, Greek sculpture, and smart talk. He reads Renan's disavowal of faith in his *Recollections of My Youth* and dabbles in some new Germanic ideas about religion in preparation for his book on the biblical character Abraham, a project for which he is singularly ill-equipped. He starts off wanting to write a pious character study that will earn him career kudos within the Methodist fold, but in his ignorance he is unaware of new trends in Hebrew Bible interpretation, and he woefully underestimates the sheer complexity of the task ahead of him.

From this brief description one might assume that Theron Ware was the religious victim of the new intellectual forces disturbing orthodox Christianity at the end of the nineteenth century, and that is partly the case; but although Frederic worked very hard to both understand and communicate those forces, that is not his primary angle of approach. While not underestimating the effect of these new challenges on Theron Ware's ill-prepared mind, which extended little beyond the parameters of a basic Methodist seminary education, Frederic is at pains to show that the roots of Ware's disenchantment were located deep within his own aspirations and limitations. Theron, like many other evangelical preachers in life and in fiction, liked the sound of his own voice and had aspirations to be a great figure within his own religious tradition. He also liked all the things that money could buy. The financial privations under which he had to operate as a poor Methodist preacher in a niggardly preaching station versus the easy luxury and elegance of his newfound acquaintances is one of the novel's main themes. Frederic is particularly successful in showing how Theron's new association with the social and intellectual elite of Octavius leads him to disparage the penny-pinching narrowness of the town's primitive Methodists and, more seriously, the humble piety of his adoring Methodist wife. The more appealing the lives of his new friends become, the less appealing are his own circumstances. He becomes infatuated with the town's wealthy beauty and makes a fool of himself chasing a woman who once saw him as a new fresh-faced "acquisition" to Octavian life but later repudiated him, not without foundation, as a gauche, gossipy, social-climbing "bore." Theron's utterly unrealistic aspirations of sailing the world with his wealthy bohemian queen are rudely shattered and he is partly put back together by Mrs. Soulsby, a worldly wise Dickensian character who had been around a few dark corners before pragmatically settling on a career as a church fundraiser. At the end of the novel Theron seems to accept Sister Soulsby's manipulative pragmatism as a surer path through life's vicissitudes than either the old-style fervent religion of his first vocation or its liberal, modernist successor. He quits the Methodist ministry, reconciles with his wife, and, in the time-honored traditions of Victorian literature, "heads west" to begin a new life in Seattle.

The reason for describing Frederic's novel at some length is not only to highlight what a fine treatment it is of religion in a late nineteenth-century American community and also of evangelical disenchantment, but also to illustrate that novelists have at once an easier and a more difficult task than historians in dealing with the main theme of this book. Their task is more difficult in the sense that they have to invent their characters, situate them within convincing intellectual and social contexts, and then present them to the reader in a credible and entertaining way. But their task is also easier in that they are in complete control of the inner and outer lives of the characters they create, and, more importantly, they can control how character is altered by both relationships and a wider social setting. In contrast, historians have a more difficult task dealing with religious disenchantment, because in this deeply personal area of human experience they can reach only as far as the surviving evidence will permit. As Frederic shrewdly observed through his character Theron Ware, religious disenchantment is a complex phenomenon caused by the interaction of external influences on deeply personal circumstances. The problem for the historian is that the former are easier to get at than the latter.

What this book has shown is that deeply embedded issues of sexual identity, personal aspiration, social status, gender and racial consciousness, and temperamental characteristics often collectively help to determine the spiritual journeys of its subjects. Relational dynamics, disappointed idealism, and life-cycle changes add further complexity to the mix. In addition, the historian has to work mostly from printed sources, which often send mixed messages. In the realm of religious disenchantment the ways people explain and defend their positions, though always deeply revealing, are often not very reliable, even in points of verifiable detail. For those smitten by evangelical idealism at some stage of their lives, there is generally a tendency to cast their subsequent disenchantment in the best possible light. If there is to be an exit from the tradition, it had better be on the high moral ground, even if circumstances and motives are generally more mixed than that. No person, and certainly no biographer, however honest the self-evaluation or however thorough and professional the biographical method, can state for sure what produces religious enchantment or disenchantment, faith or infidelity.

That said, a number of common themes and shared characteristics are identifiable in the lives represented in these pages. These themes not only reveal a good deal about the nature of the evangelical tradition—from an admittedly unusual direction—but also illuminate some of the common causes and consequences of disenchantment. Perhaps the most obvious point to emphasize is that, with the possible exception of Edmund Gosse, who was indoctrinated into evangelicalism and who was therefore not given the liberty of choice, the others at one point in their lives found something appealing in the evangelical tradition. Most were enchanted, and some remained enchanted, with the person of Jesus Christ and with his emphasis on love, forgiveness, and sacrifice. Most were led to this position through the influence of a mentor or a friend not only who pointed them to Jesus and the Bible, but also who exhibited qualities they admired. As evangelicalism moved beyond its first and second generations, it is not surprising that many of its adherents fetched up in positions that enabled them to influence and inspire the young. School masters and mistresses, clergymen and preachers, editors of periodicals and organizers of voluntary associations, leaders of classes and teachers of Sunday schools, all show up in the conversion narratives of young evangelicals. It is a tribute to the quality of those exemplary lives that earnest young people like George Eliot and Francis Newman were inspired to follow their example. Of course, there are any number of hypocrites and egotists in the evangelical tradition, in both life and fiction, but they were more often at the margins than at the center of the tradition.

The scholarship on evangelical conversion narratives shows that most conversions took place early, often in teenage or early adult years, and were often associated with some form of personal crisis.[2] In most cases conversion was accompanied by a strong commitment to the person of Jesus Christ and an idealistic determination to make a difference in the world. Not only did the story of Jesus represent a compelling example of sacrificial love, but also Christianity offered a model of empowerment, a way of escaping from the drab humdrum of families, localities, and social conventions. Disenchantment, on the other hand, often followed from the growing realization that evangelical Christianity not only was about following a heroic savior into a needy world, but also carried with it an inheritance of doctrines and dogmas, precepts and propositions. Among the more serious converts, such as most of those represented in this book, conversion was followed by serious Bible reading and self-examination. This is where a degree of cognitive dissonance opened up, for they discovered that the Bible not only is a book of love and forgiveness, but also contains violence, judgment, and notions of eternal punishment. Some scholars have shown how Bible reading could be a secularizing dynamic in the lives of Christians who were unable to square the love that attracted them to faith with the hard sayings of the biblical narratives.[3] Among some thoughtful evangelicals, moral repudiation of biblical ethics preceded, and was often more important than, difficulties presented by biblical criticism and Darwinian evolution. These intellectual challenges did not so much cause doubt and infidelity as they did inform, rationalize, and justify both.

Hard sayings and hard doctrines were often more difficult to accept for creative and intuitive personalities who chafed against theological systems. The more unappealing the doctrines, the more difficulties they presented. Some were challenged because of their perceived intellectual implausibility, and these included the doctrine of the Trinity, biblical inerrancy, and miracles. Some were challenged because of their perceived ethical mendacity, and these included substitutionary atonement, predestination, eternal punishment, and selective salvation for evangelical Protestants alone. Still others were challenged because they seemed to limit the sphere of human action in this world, and these included the various millennial schemes that treated life on earth as a mere warm-up act for the life to come. Nothing dimmed the ardor of young evangelical idealists more than the proposition that the earth was a failed experiment headed for divine elimination. The more all these ideas were insisted upon and the narrower and more exclusive they became, the more unacceptable they were.

If the realization that fidelity to evangelicalism carried with it a necessary embrace of an unwelcome dogmatic system was perhaps the most troubling issue faced by the disenchanted, the unhappy relationship between evangelicalism and structures of power followed close behind. For those who became evangelicals partly out of an idealistic desire to reform "social evils" the unpleasant reality that evangelicals were as likely to be on the side of the demons as the angels was hard to bear. Whether the issue was slavery, racial or gender equality, or simple ethical probity in relation to sex or money, it seemed to many of the disenchanted that evangelicalism could act more as a brake than as an engine of social reform. Nothing eroded the confidence of evangelical idealists more than the sober reality that many of their co-religionists were regrettably on the other side of what for them were nonnegotiable issues. The fact that their opponents defended their positions on slavery, race, gender, and sexual identity by an appeal to the Bible merely added insult to injury. One of the most consistent factors in disenchantment is the alignment of evangelical leaders of seminaries, churches, and voluntary organizations with what were regarded as reactionary forces.

Most of the people represented in this book were idealists. From Newman's desire to redeem Islam for Christ, to Theodore Dwight Weld's campaign to end slavery in the United States; from Vincent van Gogh's desire to express sacrificial love to the burdened Belgian miners, to James Baldwin's urge to preach the gospel to the Harlem poor; and from Sarah Grimké's repudiation of the fecklessness of Southern society to Frances Willard's desire to rid the world of alcohol, evangelicals were those who wanted to make a difference. That these aspirations are typical, not atypical of the tradition, can be deduced from many important books on evangelical social activism throughout its long history.[4] For most evangelicals such activism was not easily thwarted by disappointments or setbacks. Nowhere is this more evident than in the evangelical missionary enterprise that has thrived for centuries despite high levels of casualties and despite apparently low levels of success, at least in some locations. Indeed, opposition, properly understood and sanctified by piety, not only is to be expected, but also paradoxically corroborates the desirability of the objective. But for some other evangelicals, missionary zeal and social activism introduced the same kind of cognitive dissonance as that produced by Bible reading. What happens when the desired goal is either perceived to be unobtainable, or is made more, not less, unachievable by evangelical means? That is the position Weld reached over slavery, Stanton over female liberation, and Baldwin over black liberation. Disappointment and frustrated idealism were the midwives of evangelical disenchantment. So too were bad experiences with fellow evangelicals. Eliot emptied her spleen on the hapless Dr. Cumming, Weld was outraged by the sexual scandals of some of the evangelicals he knew, Newman fell out with Darby and was disappointed in him, van Gogh ridiculed the directors of his Belgian evangelical mission, and Baldwin was less than enamored with some of the black preachers (including himself and his stepfather) in his acquaintance. Nothing bred disenchantment faster than profound disillusionment with the lives, characters, behaviors, and opinions of fellow evangelicals. It is no accident that, in the treatment of evangelicals in the history of English fiction and drama, one of the most repeated tropes is the idea that evangelicals are hypocrites, people whose pious claims are not matched by the quality of their lives.[5] In that gap between proclamation and performance lies space for the germination of seeds of disenchantment.

Given the artistic sensibilities and intellectual distinction of many of the figures in this book, it is not surprising to discover that the closer evangelicalism sailed to dogmatism and exclusivity, the less acceptable it became to them. The evangelical tradition has always contained a diverse spectrum of adherents and opinions. Scholars have found it difficult to map and describe that spectrum without using anachronistic or inappropriate terms. Perhaps it is better to think not of a single spectrum but rather of a set of overlapping spectrums—or a kaleidoscope—some of which have to do with social class, style, and culture, while others relate to doctrines, denominations, and scriptural hermeneutics. Moreover, these spectrums are not fixed but rather shift in response to cultural changes. Generally speaking, the more evangelical traditions feel under pressure from the surrounding culture, the more likely they are to adopt conservative and defensive positions, whether in theology, politics, or social behavior. In that sense evangelicalism has displayed fundamentalist proclivities long before, and long after, the term itself was used in the second decade of the twentieth century to describe those reacting against modernist theology and the implications of biblical criticism.[6] In the lives of many disenchanted evangelicals there is no doubt that the narrower, more dogmatic, more sectarian, and more exclusive evangelicalism became, the less it appealed to those on the creative edges of the tradition. Eliot chose a protofundamentalist to focus her attack on the baleful effects of evangelical teaching. Weld lost interest in, and eventually refused to cooperate with, the attempts of his friend Charles Stuart to check and control Weld's evangelical orthodoxy, point by point, doctrine by doctrine, proposition by proposition in wearying and inquisitorial lists of what he called "evangelical essentials." Gosse was horrified at the way his otherwise kindly Plymouth Brethren father could assuredly declare that the inhabitants of an entire country would go to Hell because they were Roman Catholics. Newman came to see that Christian exclusivity, however it was dressed up, was a midwife of religious and sectarian conflict at home and abroad, and made the world an unhappier place. Van Gogh grew to hate the formalized religious rhetoric of professors of theology and evangelical bureaucrats, which seemed to him spectacularly to miss the point of what the gospel message was about. In short, those who embraced evangelicalism because of the openness of its message of love and forgiveness were just as likely to repudiate it for its emphasis on dogma and the letter of the law.

What the preceding paragraphs have attempted to show is that, although the faith journeys of my chosen subjects are unique, as are the complex factors resulting in disenchantment—case by case—there are nevertheless some shared commonalities. The same is true of the impact of evangelicalism on their lives. Some of the determining characteristics of evangelicalism include moral earnestness, a desire to witness and preach, a commitment to social activism on behalf of disadvantaged people, and a concern for the truth.[7] These are also the qualities that were nurtured in the lives of these individuals, and they survived in modified forms even after their disenchantment with the evangelical tradition. It is impossible to read Eliot's fiction, for example, and not conclude that she holds her characters accountable to a stern moral standard and that their choices, whether made out of self-interest or altruism, define the kinds of people they are. Similarly, many literary critics make the point that Baldwin never gave up being a preacher; he simply changed the content of his message, the genre in which it was expressed, and the audience to whom he spoke. Weld and Newman devoted much of their lives to noble causes, at least some of which had their origins in the moral crusades of their earlier evangelicalism. It is also important to emphasize that this book does not subscribe to a simple moral typology emphasizing either the superiority or inferiority of the lives of its subjects before and after their disenchantment with evangelicalism. For example, it is as possible to suggest that Weld's evangelical phase was the most dynamic and productive period of his life as it is to state that Eliot's evangelical disenchantment led to a broader range of human sympathies that mark her greatest novels. Similarly, although Gosse's more liberal views on some issues are clearly more palatable to a modern audience than is some of his father's narrow fundamentalism, the father, for all his Victorian sternness, has some noble qualities that are lacking in his narcissistic son. Van Gogh may have exhibited a disturbing religious extremism in his evangelical phase, but his repudiation of evangelicalism did not make him any less prone to bouts of unstable behavior, even though the quality of his art improved. There is therefore a complex, not a unilinear, relationship between religious beliefs on the one hand and human psychology and temperament on the other. For example, one of the more intriguing aspects of the subjects in this book is how many of them (especially Newman and Baldwin) retained a love for some of the hymns and sacred songs of the evangelical tradition long after they abandoned its propositional truth claims. Poetry, cadence, and music left lingering echoes of old emotions in the hearts of disenchanted evangelicals even as their heads moved in different directions.[8]

Although the sample of religious biographies contained within this book is too small to act as a solid foundation for more generic comments about evangelicalism and society in the last two centuries, they do offer some suggestive hints about the way lives are shaped by wider cultural changes. For example, there are some grounds for suggesting that evangelical disenchantment worked rather differently in Europe than it did in the United States. In England the existence of an established church with formal articles of faith that had to be signed to gain access to the two great English universities, and where the religious traditions of families were an important part of public respectability, private faith transactions had important public consequences. For those like Newman who were bound for Oxbridge and/or Holy Orders in the Church of England, an inability to sign the Thirty-Nine Articles, for whatever reason, was a serious matter. Equally, for a middle-class respectable woman like Eliot to abandon churchgoing or, more seriously, to live with a man out of wedlock, carried significant social implications. The British *Dictionary of National Biography* has scores of entries of eminent Victorians whose crises of faith, whether produced by infidelity or conversion to Roman Catholicism (another large cohort), were matters that required a public defense or occasioned public comment.[9] For many, a change of religious orientation presaged a change of career or involved a decline of public acceptability. Religious infidelity or changes of denominational affiliation were matters of interest in the public square and were not confined to private conscience.

Although such consequences were not completely absent in the United States, the relative absence of religious establishments and the existence of a far greater degree of religious pluralism enabled individuals to slide in and out of faith traditions with greater flexibility and less public obloquy. With less at stake there is also less of a public record, and less need, publicly, to defend private transitions of faith. There is therefore no exact equivalent in America of the great Victorian apologias of faith or lack of faith. Over the course of his life Weld moved through various faith transitions, which sometimes irritated his friends and disappointed his supporters, but interpreters of his life have to search hard for them, whereas Newman published his doubt for all to see and recognized that as a non-Anglican some avenues of public service were now closed to him. It is not that individuals experienced less intense personal experiences in their navigation of faith and doubt in America than in Europe, it is simply that ecclesiastical structures and the wider culture allowed for easier and less punitive transitions.

Another implicit argument in this book is that, although my particular focus is on evangelical disenchantment, many of the factors producing that disenchantment were not unique to evangelicalism, but were also operative in a more general secularization of intellectual life in the nineteenth and twentieth centuries.[10] The challenges facing orthodox Christianity were formidable. German higher criticism of the Bible, along with new developments in philosophical theology, posed new threats to the whole credibility of ancient texts and their supernatural assumptions. Scientific advances, including persuasive evidence for a long earth history and Darwin's theory of the evolution of species by natural selection, not only cast doubt on traditional readings of Genesis, but also raised difficult questions about Christian emphases on the uniqueness of humans, and the Fall as an explanation for death and imperfections in the natural order. Although the rise of Protestant missions and the growth of information about cultures and religions in other parts of the world supplied the faithful with heartwarming stories of the dissemination of Christianity, commerce, and civilization, they also raised uncomfortable questions in the areas of cultural anthropology and comparative religion. What exactly was unique about Christianity, and to what extent were its emphases on creation myths, sacrificial rituals, and cultic practices mere parallels with other religions? For some, these questions alone were sufficient to promote skepticism, for others they supplied an intellectual rationale for preexisting ethical disquiet about the biblical narratives and the speckled record of the Christian church throughout history. To these more purely intellectual foundations of skepticism were added the more insidious secularizing dynamics of new traditions of realist literature and new experiments in artistic representation. In one sense evangelicals who were intellectuals and creative artists suffered no more from these questions than did other orthodox Christians, but in another sense they did. A tradition that built so much on the inspiration and authority of Scripture and on the vital importance of supernatural events such as the Virgin Birth and the physical resurrection of Jesus Christ was especially vulnerable to the new climate of thought. What made these problems more difficult to solve for the figures represented in this book is that evangelical Christianity, under the pressure of new and threatening questions, was particularly prone to fundamentalist answers, thereby further undermining its appeal to its more thoughtful adherents.[11] For these people the plausibility structure of evangelical Christianity declined in proportion to the increase in its fundamentalist assertions.

More also needs to be said about the style of discourse in evangelical disenchantment narratives. There is a powerful asymmetry, for example, between the entrance to, and exit from, the evangelical tradition. The former often involves the acceptance of a new believer into the welcoming arms of a believing community. Communal rituals of baptism and reception into church membership mark and celebrate the arrival of a new addition to the community of faith. Moreover, conversion narratives have a different pathology from expressions of disenchantment.[12] Though not without pain and angst—as sin and guilt are confronted—they generally end in joy, release, and acceptance. Disenchantment is a different matter, however. Here there are no pre-scribed forms, no celebratory rituals, no welcoming community (mostly), and no idealistic excitement about a new life. Hence disenchantment often can be a painful and lonely experience, with no ecstatic release at the end. Some-times, as with Eliot and van Gogh, disenchantment is accompanied by a sense of release from the constraints of dogmatism, but even that is not a uni-formly happy experience. It is also true, as Timothy Larsen has pointed out, that militant secularists have sometimes constructed replacement communi-ties of infidelity, ironically with some of the same egotistical jockeying for power that characterized the churches from which they escaped.[13]

Disenchantment was nevertheless not normally a happy experience. It is not surprising, therefore, that the disenchantment narratives in this book are not lighthearted or joyful affairs. To be sure there are many historical ex-amples of humorist secularists who delighted in entertaining audiences with illustrations of the absurdities of religious traditions and their sacred texts. Robert Ingersoll, the late nineteenth-century orator and humorist, carved out a niche as one of the most popular lecturers in American history by brilliantly exploiting that genre.[14] In more recent times Billy Connolly, the Scottish co-median, has done the same thing, only in an incomparably more bawdy and irreverent style. Indeed, comparing the styles of humor with which religion is attacked is itself revealing of changes in social mores. Ingersoll, whose antire-ligious satire was informed by self-confessed debts to Voltaire and the Scot-tish poet Robert Burns, was careful always not to attack living religious figures or to sail too close to blasphemy; Connolly couldn't care less.

The people in this book were not in that tradition, however. With the possible exception of Gosse, who like Ingersoll repudiated the religion of a religious father without hating him, and who likewise delighted in telling stories about the absurdities of fundamentalism, this book's cast of characters were, at times, tortured souls. Both Eliot and Gosse were capable of subject-ing evangelical religion to withering satire, but the stakes were too high for either of them to embrace a discourse of mere lampoonery. Unlike today, the almost painfully earnest tone of disenchantment narratives was perhaps more characteristic of the nineteenth century and the first half of the twentieth century, when religion supplied more of the moral ballast of culture. Differ-ent eras bring different genres. For example, there are now any number of blogs and Web sites constructed by ex-evangelicals, recovering evangelicals, escaped fundamentalists, and so on. Indeed, it could be argued that cyber-space offers a kind of global community for the religiously disenchanted in a way that was not possible in an earlier period. In the past, periodicals, books, and lectures offered some of the same opportunity for discursive interaction, and for explaining new ideas and positions, but they rarely offered a sense of community. Hence, the sheer loneliness of the journey from evangelical faith to something else cannot be underestimated, and it is no surprise that many of the subjects of this study either were, or thought of themselves as, interstitial characters—pilgrims with no fixed abode.

It is not part of the intention of this book to deny that disenchantment from evangelicalism has been, and remains, the path of a minority, or that there are not manifold counterexamples of re-enchantment after periods of disillusionment; though often the re-enchanted faith is not the same as the first version.[15] Indeed, it is possible to argue that many of the most enthusiastic participants in the emerging church movement in the United States are evangelicals disenchanted with the trajectory of some of the more conservative traditions of American evangelicalism in the last quarter of a century. Hence, my aim has not been to present a master narrative to be yoked together with secularization theory, or with the rise of modernity and postmodernity, or anything of the kind. My subjects are self-evidently too unrepresentative to make such grand claims. Nevertheless, I do think that many of the issues raised in this book about how evangelicalism relates to fundamentalism, Islamic civilization, feminism, race, art and creativity, political reform, social justice, and new knowledge about religion and/or science are more often the cause of reflection and soul-searching among ordinary evangelicals than many of the noisier representatives of the tradition either acknowledge or care to address.[16]

My intention therefore has been to present the little-known stories of important figures from the past who once embraced a version of evangelical Protestantism and who subsequently repudiated that tradition for something else. Both how they entered the evangelical tradition and why, how, and with what consequences they left it are deeply revealing of the strengths and weaknesses of what is now one of the largest and fastest-growing faith traditions in the world. These stories are part of that tradition—not shameful aberrations from it—and they deserve to be told.

Notes

Chapter 1. Introduction

1. Edward T. Babinski, *Leaving the Fold: Testimonies of Former Fundamentalists* (Amherst, NY: Prometheus Books, 1995).

2. For a parallel treatment of how some Victorian secularists reconverted to ortho-dox Christianity see Timothy Larsen, *Crisis of Doubt: Honest Faith in Nineteenth-Century England* (New York: Oxford University Press, 2006). Larsen's aim is to attack the view of nineteenth-century England as a growing secular culture by showing that a "crisis of doubt" makes at least as much sense for the period as a "crisis of faith." His angle of attack is to look at the plebeian leaders of nineteenth-century secularism who reconverted to Christianity after having made their mark as popular leaders of the Secular Movement. His book consists of seven biographical portraits topped and tailed by a helpful introduction and conclusion. His chosen figures are William Hone, Frederic Rowland Young, Thomas Cooper, John Henry Gordon, Joseph Barker, John Bagnall Bebbington, and George Sexton. They were all important leaders of Victorian secularism, and they all eventually reconverted to a more-or-less orthodox brand of Christianity, though most of them retained their radical political convictions.

3. For a more conservative estimate of numbers see George M. Marsden, *Understanding Fundamentalism and Evangelicalism* (Grand Rapids, MI: Eerdmans, 1991), 5. For more expansive estimates see Douglas A. Sweeney, *The American Evangelical Story: A History of the Movement* (Grand Rapids, MI: Baker, 2005), 9, and Philip Jenkins, *The Next Christendom: The Coming of Global Christianity* (New York: Oxford University Press, 2002). For up-to-date comment on definitions and numbers of evangelicals worldwide, see the Web site of the Institute for the Study of American Evangelicalism at Wheaton College, Illinois, www.wheaton.edu/isae.

4. See David Hempton, *Methodism: Empire of the Spirit* (New Haven: Yale University Press, 2005).

5. David W. Bebbington, *Evangelicalism in Modern Britain: A History from the 1730s to the 1980s* (London: Unwin Hyman, 1989). It is not often pointed out that Bebbington's definition is flexible enough to take into account how evangelicalism is continuously affected and changed by its surrounding culture. One scholar who did recognize how flexibly Bebbington's definition could be used over time was the Canadian

historian George Rawlyk. See his introduction to *Amazing Grace: Evangelicalism in Australia, Britain, Canada, and the United States* (Montreal: McGill-Queen's University Press, 1994), 17–18.

6. W. R. Ward, *Early Evangelicalism: A Global Intellectual History, 1670–1789* (Cambridge: Cambridge University Press, 2006), 4.

7. Marsden, *Understanding Fundamentalism*, 1. For some helpful survey histories of evangelicalism see Mark A. Noll, *The Rise of Evangelicalism: The Age of Edwards, Whitefield and the Wesleys* (Downers Grove, IL: InterVarsity, 2004); David W. Bebbington, *The Dominance of Evangelicalism: The Age of Spurgeon and Moody* (Downers Grove, IL: InterVarsity, 2005).

8. For some excellent recent biographies of evangelical leaders see Henry D. Rack, *Reasonable Enthusiast: John Wesley and the Rise of Methodism* (London: Epworth, 2002); D. Bruce Hindmarsh, *John Newton and the English Evangelical Tradition* (Oxford: Clarendon, 1996); Anne Stott, *Hannah More: The First Victorian* (Oxford: Oxford University Press, 2003); George M. Marsden, *Jonathan Edwards: A Life* (New Haven: Yale University Press, 2003); and Kevin Bradley Kee, *Revivalists: Marketing the Gospel in English Canada 1884–1957* (Montreal: McGill-Queen's University Press, 2006).

9. See for example Valentine Cunningham, *Everywhere Spoken Against: Dissent in the Victorian Novel* (London: Oxford University Press, 1975).

10. Some have abandoned the tradition altogether, but others respectfully have criticized the tradition from within. See Mark A. Noll, *The Scandal of the Evangelical Mind* (Grand Rapids, MI: Eerdmans, 1994); Randall Balmer, *Thy Kingdom Come: How the Religious Right Distorts the Faith and Threatens America: An Evangelical's Lament* (New York: Perseus, 2006); and Charles Marsh, *Wayward Christian Soldiers: Freeing the Gospel from Political Captivity* (New York: Oxford University Press, 2007).

11. For a more extensive treatment of Charles Wesley's poems and hymns of suffering, including those composed around the time of Samuel's conversion to Roman Catholicism, see Joanna Cruickshank, "Charles Wesley and the Construction of Suffering in Early English Methodism," Ph.D. diss., University of Melbourne, 2006, 21, 49.

12. Ford K. Brown, *Fathers of the Victorians: The Age of Wilberforce* (Cambridge: Cambridge University Press, 1961), 517.

13. Brown, *Fathers*, 518.

14. Ibid., 518–19.

15. For an excellent short summary of Ruskin's life see the entry by Robert Hewison in the Oxford *Dictionary of National Biography* (New York: Oxford University Press, 2004). See also the *DNB* entry on Sir Leslie Stephen, who was the first editor of the *DNB*. Stephen was the heir of the evangelical tradition of the Stephen and Venn (on his mother's side) families, but abandoned his religious faith soon after Ruskin's disenchantment with evangelicalism, supposedly under the influence of Comte, Darwin, Spencer, and *Essays and Reviews*.

16. This version of what happened to Ruskin in Turin is taken from "The Grande Chartreuse" chapter of *Praeterita* (1888). See E. T. Cook and Alexander Wedderburn, eds., *The Works of John Ruskin,* library ed., 39 vols. (London: G. Allen, 1903–12), vol. 35, 495–96. For other versions of Ruskin's account of this life-changing event, along with an insightful interpretation of the reasons for the disparities in Ruskin's recollections of the event, see Michael Wheeler, *Ruskin's God* (Cambridge: Cambridge University Press, 1999), 125–52.

17. Wheeler, *Ruskin's God,* 143.

18. See Paul A. Carter, *The Spiritual Crisis of the Gilded Age* (De Kalb, IL: Northern Illinois University Press, 1971); James Turner, *Without God, Without Creed: The Origins of Unbelief in America* (Baltimore: Johns Hopkins University Press, 1985); and Evelyn A. Kirkley, *Rational Mothers and Infidel Gentlemen: Gender and American Atheism, 1865–1915* (New York: Syracuse University Press, 2000).

19. Kirkley, *Rational Mothers,* 88. Samuel Putnam is also the author of a standard text on the American free thought tradition titled *400 Years of Freethought* (New York: Truth Seeker, 1894).

20. James H. Jones, *Alfred C. Kinsey: A Public and Private Life* (New York: W. W. Norton, 1997), 154.

21. One of the products of the Internet age is the emergence of ex-evangelical blog sites in which people, generally from fundamentalist backgrounds, share their experiences of liberation. In the absence of a genuine community to welcome the disenchanted, as there is for those experiencing a religious conversion, the Internet partly supplies an alternative kind of community.

22. Herbert Asbury, *Up from Methodism* (New York: Alfred A. Knopf, 1930), 111.

23. Sinclair Lewis, *Elmer Gantry,* with an afterword by Mark Schorer (New York: New American Library, 1980).

24. See David N. Livingstone, D. G. Hart, and Mark A. Noll, eds., *Evangelicals and Science in Historical Perspective* (New York: Oxford University Press, 1999).

25. For an excellent discussion of evangelical attitudes to the theater, novel-reading, the fine arts, and other aspects of culture see Doreen M. Rosman, *Evangelicals and Culture* (London: Croom Helm, 1984).

26. Ibid., 3–4.

27. I am referring here to the portrait of Dinah Morris in George Eliot's *Adam Bede* (London: Blackwood, 1858).

28. See Nancy A. Hardesty, *Women Called to Witness: Evangelical Feminism in the Nineteenth Century* (Knoxville: University of Tennessee Press, 1999), and Carol Lasser and Marlene Deahl Merrill, eds., *Friends and Sisters: Letters Between Lucy Stone and Antoinette Brown Blackwell, 1846–93* (Chicago: University of Illinois Press, 1987).

29. See Kathi Kern, *Mrs. Stanton's Bible* (Ithaca: Cornell University Press, 2001).

30. Christine Rosen, *My Fundamentalist Education: A Memoir of a Divine Girlhood* (New York: Public Affairs, 2005), 221–29.

31. Kirkley, *Rational Mothers,* 134–47.

Chapter 2. George Eliot

1. George Eliot, "Evangelical Teaching: Dr Cumming," *Westminster Review* 64 (October 1855). Although published anonymously, this essay appeared subsequently in George Eliot, *Essays and Leaves from a Note-Book* (Edinburgh and London: William Blackwood and Sons, 1884), 145–99. For a reliable context for George Eliot's life and writing see Gordon S. Haight, *George Eliot: A Biography* (London: Oxford University Press, 1968), and also his edition of the Eliot letters.

2. George Eliot, *Adam Bede* (first published in two volumes, London: Blackwood, 1858), ch. 2, "The Preaching."

3. R. Buick Knox, "Dr John Cumming and Crown Court Church, London," *Records of the Scottish Church History Society* 22, no. 1 (1984): 57–84.

4. Eliot, *Essays*, 151–22.

5. Ibid., 159.

6. Ibid., 182–85.

7. Ibid., 188–97. In a subsequent review of W. E. H. Lecky's *History of the Rise and Influence of Rationalism in Europe*, Eliot linked Calvinism, selective salvation, and belief in eternal punishment with a host of cruelties from torturing witches to religious persecution. She noted that "the only two leaders of the Reformation who advocated tolerance were Zuinglius and Socinus, both of them disbelievers in exclusive salvation." *Essays*, 222. Eliot's interpretation of the Reformation and the rise of religious toleration is of course far from uncontentious.

8. Eliot, *Essays*, 189.

9. See John Cumming, *Voices of the Night* (London: John Farquhar Shaw, 1851).

10. John Cumming, *The Sounding of the Last Trumpet or The Last Woe* (London: James Nisbet, 1867), 1–2. Eliot, *Essays*, 154–55.

11. Cumming, *The Last Woe*, 394–413.

12. Ibid., 97.

13. Knox, "Dr John Cumming," 83.

14. Haight, *George Eliot*, 8. Eliot was also influenced by Francis Franklin, an evangelical General Baptist pastor at Cow Lane Chapel in Nuneaton. Nuneaton was also within the Anglican diocese of Lichfield and Coventry, where, under the influence of Henry Ryder (the first evangelical to be made bishop), an ardent evangelical curate, John Edmund Jones, stirred up the religious temperature of the town between 1828 and 1831. Jones was a formative influence on Maria Lewis.

15. Gordon S. Haight, ed., *The George Eliot Letters* (New Haven: Yale University Press, 1954–78), vol. 1: 45, 63.

16. Ford K. Brown, *Fathers of the Victorians* (Cambridge: Cambridge University Press, 1961), 520. See also David Newsome, *The Parting of Friends* (London: Murray, 1966) and Timothy C. F. Stunt, "John Henry Newman and the Evangelicals," *Journal of Ecclesiastical History* 21 (1970): 65–74.

17. David Hempton, "Evangelicalism and Eschatology," *Journal of Ecclesiastical History* 31, no. 2 (April 1980): 179–84. The most cogent and reliable account of evangeli-

calism in this period is supplied by David W. Bebbington, *Evangelicalism* (London: Unwin Hyman, 1988).

18. Eliot, *Letters*, 1: 11–12.

19. Francis Newman, *Phases of Faith* (London: 1850), 136.

20. Hugh Evan Hopkins, *Charles Simeon of Cambridge* (London: Hodder and Stoughton, 1977), 177.

21. Eliot, *Letters*, 1: 120–22.

22. Ibid., 124–26.

23. Ibid., 128.

24. Ibid., 143–44.

25. Ibid., 162.

26. For differing opinions see Basil Willey, *Nineteenth Century Studies* (London: Chatto and Windus, 1950), and Haight, *George Eliot*. Willey states that Eliot's outlook changed "instantaneously" and "decisively" upon reading Charles Hennell's *Inquiry*, which "descended like a bomb into her lap." Haight, from his experience of editing Eliot's letters, argues for a lengthier and more concealed departure from evangelical orthodoxy.

27. Susan Budd, *Varieties of Unbelief: Atheists and Agnostics in English Society 1850–1960* (London: Heinemann, 1977), 106.

28. Eliot, *Letters*, 1: 206. See Howard R. Murphy, "The Ethical Revolt against Christian Orthodoxy in Early Victorian England," *American Historical Review* 60 (1955): 800–17.

29. Margaret Harris and Judith Johnston, eds., *The Journals of George Eliot* (Cambridge: Cambridge University Press, 1998), 54–58.

30. Eliot, *Letters*, 5: 358.

31. George Eliot, "O May I Join the Choir Invisible," in *Complete Poems* (New York: Doubleday, Page and Co., 1901).

32. George Eliot, *Scenes of Clerical Life: Janet's Repentance* (New York: Oxford University Press, 1985), ch. 10.

33. Ibid., 213, 255. It has been suggested that this emphasis on the concrete moral praxis of evangelicalism with its material dimension is taken directly from Eliot's reading of Feuerbach. See Derek and Sybil Oldfield, "'Scenes of Clerical Life': the Diagram and the Picture," in *Critical Essays on George Eliot*, ed. Barbara Hardy (London: Routledge and Kegan Paul, 1979), 2–7. I am grateful to Klaus Yoder for these suggestions.

34. George Eliot, *Middlemarch: A Study of Provincial Life* (London: William Blackwood and Sons, 1871–72; rpt. London: Penguin, 1965), 881.

35. Ibid., 807.

36. Eliot, *Letters*, 3: 230–31.

37. Eliot, *Middlemarch*, 427.

38. Ibid., 537–38.

39. J. Radford Thomson, "George Eliot's Life as Illustrative of the Religious Ideas of Our Time," *British and Foreign Evangelical Review* 34 (1885): 517–43. See also,

W. G. Blaikie, "George Eliot's Surrender of the Faith," *British and Foreign Evangelical Review* 35 (1886): 38–65. I am grateful to Dr. Andrew Holmes for bringing these references to my attention.

Chapter 3. Francis W. Newman

1. Francis Newman, although recognized as an important figure in the nineteenth century, has received much less attention than his brother John Henry Newman in more recent scholarship. For an insightful comparison of the two brothers see William Robbins, *The Newman Brothers: An Essay in Comparative Intellectual Biography* (Cambridge, MA: Harvard University Press, 1966). The most thorough recent treatment of Francis Newman's life, alas, remains unpublished. See Ann Margaret Schellenberg, "Prize the Doubt: The Life and Work of Francis William Newman," Ph.D. diss., University of Durham, 1994. Schellenberg quotes extensively from unpublished manuscripts in diverse locations, and supplies a complete bibliography of Newman's many publications and reviews. Still the best short introduction to Francis Newman's life is Basil Willey, *More Nineteenth Century Studies: A Group of Honest Doubters* (New York: Columbia University Press, 1956), 11–52. Turning to his older brother, the best treatment of John Henry Newman's evangelicalism and the impact it made on his later life is by Sheridan Gilley, *Newman and His Age* (London: Darton, Longman and Todd, 1990). For a more controversial biography of John Henry Newman that emphasizes both his early evangelicalism and his often fraught relationships with his brothers see Frank M. Turner, *John Henry Newman: The Challenge to Evangelical Religion* (New Haven: Yale University Press, 2002). For a well-edited collection of J. H. Newman's writings see Ian Ker, *The Genius of John Henry Newman: Selections from His Writings* (Oxford: Clarendon Press, 1989).
2. As an old man Francis Newman published a poorly received account of his brother's life, which was certainly not characterized by fraternal bonhomie. See Francis W. Newman, *Contributions Chiefly to the Early History of the Late Cardinal Newman* (London: Kegan Paul, 1891).
3. Francis William Newman, *Phases of Faith; Or, Passages from the History of My Creed* (first published in 1850). Quotations are taken from the sixth edition, which contained changes made by Newman and which was republished with an introduction by U. C. Knoepflmacher (New York: Humanities Press, 1970). Knoepflmacher makes the point that although *Phases of Faith* underwent at least ten editions or reprints by 1881, it was not reissued after 1907 until his own edition appeared.
4. Knoepflmacher, Introduction to *Phases of Faith,* 15.
5. Robbins, *The Newman Brothers,* 27.
6. See, for example, Ernest Robert Sandeen, *The Roots of Fundamentalism: British and American Millenarianism 1800–1930* (Chicago: University of Chicago Press, 1970). The essential elements of early Plymouth Brethren theology were "The oneness of the Church of God, involving a fellowship large enough to embrace all saints, and narrow enough to exclude the world. The completeness and sufficiency of the written Word in all matters of faith, and pre-eminently in things affecting our Church

life and walk—the speedy pre-millennial advent of the Lord Jesus." I. Giberne Sieveking, *Memoir and Letters of Francis W. Newman* (London: Kegan Paul, 1909), 29. She quotes from the *Memoir of Lord Congleton*. For more information on the early history of the Plymouth Brethren see Harold Hamlyn Rowdon, *The Origins of the Brethren, 1825–1850* (London, Pickering and Inglis, 1967); F. Roy Coad, *A History of the Brethren Movement* (London: Paternoster, 1968); Jonathan Burnham, *A Story of Conflict: The Controversial Relationship Between Benjamin Wills Newton and John Nelson Darby* (Carlisle, U.K.: Paternoster, 2004); and Neil T. R. Dickson and Tim Grass, eds., *The Growth of the Brethren Movement* (Milton Keynes, U.K.: Paternoster, 2006).

7. Brompton Oratory, Francis William Newman to John Henry Newman, October 8, 1827, quoted in Schellenberg, "Prize the Doubt," 25.

8. Francis William Newman to Charles Pourthales Golightly, October 25, 1827, in Schellenberg, "Prize the Doubt," 27.

9. See Robert Bernard Dann, *Father of Faith Missions: The Life and Times of Anthony Norris Groves* (Waynesboro, GA: Authentic Media, 2004), 65–75.

10. Ibid., 184.

11. Newman, *Phases of Faith*, 27.

12. Newman was accompanied on the mission to Baghdad by John Vesey Parnell, Dr. Edward Cronin, Mr. Hamilton, Cronin's mother, his sister Nancy (who was engaged to Parnell), and his infant daughter. Cronin's wife had died in childbirth.

13. Newman, *Phases of Faith*, 32–33.

14. Ibid., 33.

15. Francis W. Newman, *Personal Narratives in Letters Principally from Turkey in the Years 1830–3* (London: Holyoake, 1856), 32–33 and 38.

16. Robbins, *The Newman Brothers*, 44–45; Newman, *Personal Narratives*, 36.

17. Newman, *Personal Narratives*, 82.

18. For more information on Francis Newman's missionary journey to Baghdad see his *Personal Narratives* and Sieveking, *Memoir and Letters*, 26–55. See also Dann, *Father of Faith Missions*, 194–201, and Sentinel Kulp, ed., *Memoir of the Late Anthony Norris Groves* (London: James Nisbet, 2002). The latter edition also contains Groves's influential pamphlet on *Christian Devotedness*.

19. Newman, *Personal Narratives*, Preface.

20. Robbins, *The Newman Brothers*, 46.

21. Newman, *Personal Narratives*, 116.

22. Robbins, *The Newman Brothers*, 47.

23. Newman, *Phases of Faith*, 36–37.

24. John Nelson Darby and Francis William Newman, *The Irrationalism of Infidelity: Being a Reply to "Phases of Faith"* (London: Groombridge and Sons, 1853). I am grateful to Max Mueller for sharing his interpretation of the conflict between Newman and Darby.

25. Newman, *Phases of Faith*, 43–45.

26. Ibid., 87.

27. Ibid., 125.

28. Knoepflmacher, Introduction to *Phases of Faith*, 11.

29. For example, Robert Bernard Dann, who gives an impeccably fair-minded account of *Phases of Faith* in his biography of Anthony Norris Groves, writes, "To this point, we can probably feel a degree of sympathy for a man from whom we have reluctantly parted company. But the darkest of Newman's ever-darkening 'phases' lies yet ahead . . . he finally grasps the ghastly nettle and asserts his considered opinion that the character of Jesus was marred by 'vain conceit . . . blundering self-sufficiency . . . error and arrogance.'" *Father of Faith Missions*, 299.

30. Anonymous, "F. W. Newman and His Evangelical Critics," *Westminster Review* (October 1858): 376–425.

31. Newman, *Phases of Faith*, 133–34.

32. Sieveking, *Memoir and Letters*, xii.

33. Francis William Newman, *The Soul, Her Sorrows and Her Aspirations: An Essay Towards the Natural History of the Soul as the True Basis of Theology* (London: John Chapman, 1849).

34. Ibid., 65–66.

35. Ibid., 103.

36. Ibid., 131.

37. Ibid., 123.

38. Ibid., 207.

39. Ibid., 216–17.

40. Ibid., 221.

41. For the mixed reception of *The Soul* see Schellenberg, "Prize the Doubt," 118–19.

42. Maisie Ward, *Young Mr. Newman* (London: Sheed and Ward, 1848).

43. Gordon S. Haight, ed., *The George Eliot Letters* (New Haven: Yale University Press, 1954–78), vol. 6: 34. Willey, *More Nineteenth Century Studies*, 46.

44. Francis W. Newman, *Miscellanies*, 6 vols. (London: Kegan Paul, 1891).

45. Schellenberg, "Prize the Doubt," 183.

46. Francis W. Newman, *Life After Death? Palinodia* (London: Turner, 1886), 50. For an amplification of this idea see Howard R. Murphy, "The Ethical Revolt Against Christian Orthodoxy in Early Victorian England," *The American Historical Review* 60, no. 4: 800–817.

47. Schellenberg, "Prize the Doubt," 173.

48. Brompton Oratory, Francis William Newman to John Henry Newman, January 14, 1865, quoted in Schellenberg, "Prize the Doubt," 167.

49. Francis W. Newman, "Reply to a Letter from an Evangelical Lay Preacher" (1869), in *Miscellanies*, vol. II: *Essays, Tracts or Addresses Moral and Religious* (London: Kegan Paul, 1887), 172–76. On the important theme of morality see also in the same volume, "The New Testament Inadequate as a Standard of Morals" and "Moral Theism."

50. N. Annau, *Leslie Stephen: The Godless Victorian* (Chicago: The University of Chicago Press, 1984), 149.

51. See Schellenberg, "Prize the Doubt," 44–47, where the evidence is presented. Newman's nephew, John Rickards Mozley, identified Newman's "persecution" by the Brethren as the most significant crisis in his life, and this is corroborated by a letter written by Newman to the American Unitarian clergyman Joseph Henry Allen in 1889. The letter is located at Harvard University. Schellenberg persuasively speculates that the instigator of much of the venom against Newman was Mr. Hamilton, a Plymouth Brother who accompanied Newman on his trip to Baghdad, returned early, and spread rumors about Newman's heretical views on the Trinity. Newman's references to Hamilton in his *Personal Narratives* are consistently unflattering. Hamilton disdained Ottoman culture, refused to learn Arabic, and made little contribution to the team.

52. Newman certainly expressed great respect for Groves when they met in Baghdad, and Groves and his wife visited Newman and his wife early in 1836 at a time when Newman was virtually excommunicated from the fellowship of the Brethren. Unfortunately, I can find no record of Groves's subsequent opinions about Newman, especially after the publication of *Phases of Faith* in 1850. Groves died soon after, in 1853.

53. Francis William Newman to Frances Power Cobbe, August 16, 1876, quoted in Schellenberg, "Prize the Doubt," 192.

54. Willey, *More Nineteenth Century Studies,* 51–52; Francis W. Newman, *Hebrew Theism: The Common Basis of Judaism, Christianity and Mohammedanism* (London: Trubner, 1874), 171; and Sieveking, *Memoir and Letters,* 381.

55. Schellenberg, "Prize the Doubt," 231. For Newman's ideas on immortality see his *Life After Death? Palinodia.* He sums up his argument in these words: "They [his previous pages] assert that the doctrine of Heaven and Hell has its source, not in Christianity, much less in Judaism, but in a shallow and monstrous Oriental Theosophy. They plead that this doctrine is not only unproved, but unprovable; that the idea of Hell or fiery Purgatory is wholly [sic] pernicious, and that of Heaven (variously and on the whole) far from harmless."

Chapter 4. Theodore Dwight Weld

1. Weld's life can best be followed through two modern biographies, Benjamin P. Thomas, *Theodore Weld, Crusader for Freedom* (New Brunswick, NJ: Rutgers University Press, 1950), and Robert H. Abzug, *Passionate Liberator, Theodore Dwight Weld and the Dilemma of Reform* (New York: Oxford University Press, 1980). The latter is the more penetrating and authoritative. There is also an excellent edition of some of Weld's correspondence, particularly letters relating to Weld's antislavery activities, by Gilbert H. Barnes and Dwight L. Dumond, eds., *Letters of Theodore Dwight Weld, Angelina Grimké and Sarah Grimké* (New York: D. Appleton-Century Company, 1934) (hereinafter *Weld-Grimké Letters*). A more extensive collection of Weld's correspondence is available for consultation at the William L. Clements Library in the University of Michigan. For brief accounts of Weld's career, along with those with whom he interacted, see Daniel G. Reid, Robert D. Linder, Bruce L. Shelley,

and Harry S. Stout, eds., *Dictionary of Christianity in America* (Downers Grove, IL: InterVarsity, 1990).

2. See Elizabeth Weld to Weld, [Apulia, NY], February 26, 1826, and Fabius [NY], April 25, 1826, in *Weld-Grimké Letters*, I: 7–9.

3. See, for example, Charles Stuart to Weld, New York, November 16, 1825; January 10, 1826; Apulia [NY] May 19, 1828, and July 8, 1828, in *Weld-Grimké Letters*, I: 6–7, 19–22.

4. Weld to Charles Grandison Finney, Fabius [NY], April 22, 1828, in *Weld-Grimké Letters*, I: 15.

5. Weld to Henry B. Stanton, Mifflin Township, Ohio, February 15, 1832, in *Weld-Grimké Letters*, I: 60–65.

6. For Stuart's influence see Charles Stuart to Weld, London, England, March 26, 1831, in *Weld-Grimké Letters*, I: 42–43.

7. Weld to William Lloyd Garrison, Hartford, CT, January 2, 1833, in *Weld-Grimké Letters*, I: 98.

8. See Weld to Rev. John J. Shipherd, Cincinnati, Ohio, June 21, 1834, in *Weld-Grimké Letters*, I: 153.

9. Weld to James Hall, editor of the *Western Monthly Magazine*, Cincinnati, OH, c. May 20, 1834, in *Weld-Grimké Letters*, I: 146.

10. Weld to Lewis Tappan [Rochester, NY, March 9, 1836] in *Weld-Grimké Letters*, I: 132–35 and 273. Weld made the point that although he was a wholehearted advocate of African American rights he would not openly walk arm in arm with a black woman lest it invite reprisals from the African American community in Cincinnati.

11. Abzug, *Passionate Liberator*, 144–49. See also Weld to Lewis Tappan, Rochester, NY, April 5, 1836, in *Weld-Grimké Letters*, I: 286–87, in which he declined to speak at an anniversary meeting because of its "stateliness and Pomp and Circumstance," and warned against antislavery agents getting in the "habit of *gadding*, attending anniversaries, sailing round in Cleopatra's barge," and generally avoiding "boneing down" to work and more work.

12. Weld to Lewis Tappan, Oberlin, OH, November 17, 1835, in *Weld-Grimké Letters*, I: 242–45.

13. Charles Grandison Finney to Weld, Oberlin, OH, July 21, 1836, in *Weld-Grimké Letters*, I: 318–20. See William T. Allan, Sereno W. Streeter, J. W. Alvord, and James A. Thome to Weld, Oberlin, OH, August 9, 1836, in *Weld-Grimké Letters*, I: 323–29.

14. For more information on the Grimké sisters see Gerda Lerner, ed., *The Feminist Thought of Sarah Grimké* (Oxford: Oxford University Press, 1998); Gerda Lerner, *The Grimké Sisters of South Carolina: Pioneers for Women's Rights and Abolition* (New York: Schocken Books, 1967); Catherine H. Birney, *Sarah and Angelina Grimké: The First American Women Advocates of Abolition and Woman's Rights* (n.p.: Lee and Shepard, 1885; rpt. Westport, CT: Greenwood Press, 1969); and David A. McCants, "Evangelicalism and the Nineteenth-Century Woman's Rights: A Case Study of Angelina E. Grimké," *Perspectives in Religious Studies* 14, no. 1 (Spring 1987): 39–57. I am grateful to Bethany Murphy for this reference.

15. Sarah Grimké and Angelina and Theodore Weld to Gerrit and Anne Smith, Belleville, NJ, June 18, 1840, in *Weld-Grimké Letters,* II: 843.

16. Weld to James Gillespie Birney, Washington DC, January 22, 1842, in Dwight L. Dumond, ed., *Letters of James Gillespie Birney 1831–1857,* II: 663.

17. Weld to James Gillespie Birney, Belleville [NJ], May 23, 1842, in ibid., 693–94.

18. Weld to Angelina G. Weld and Sarah Grimké, Washington [DC], January 9, 1842, in *Weld-Grimké Letters,* II: 889; Abzug, *Passionate Liberator,* 228–29.

19. Weld to Lewis Tappan, Washington [DC], January 23, 1843, in *Weld-Grimké Letters,* II: 966–67; and Weld to Angelina G. Weld, Washington [DC], February 1, 1843, in ibid., 971–73.

20. Weld to Prof. George Whipple, Belleville [NJ], December [17], 1843, in ibid., 985–88.

21. Weld to Lewis Tappan, Belleville, [NJ], December, 29, 1943, in ibid., 988–89.

22. Weld to Lewis Tappan, Belleville [NJ], February 6, 1944, in ibid., 994–95.

23. Lewis Tappan to Weld, New York, March 8, 1844, in ibid., 1001.

24. Abzug, *Passionate Liberator,* 246.

25. Weld to Lewis Tappan, Belleville [NJ], February 6, 1844, in *Weld-Grimké Letters,* II: 995.

26. Abzug, *Passionate, Liberator,* 248.

27. See Charles Stuart to James Gillespie Birney, Grey County, Canada West, March 6, 1855, in *Birney Letters,* II: 1170.

28. Weld to James Gillespie Birney, Belleville, NJ, December 16, 1848, in ibid., 1120.

29. Angelina to Theodore Weld [n.d., but probably 1849] in the Weld-Grimké papers in the Clements library.

30. Quoted by Abzug, *Passionate Liberator,* 276.

31. Ibid., 280.

32. Ibid., 288–89. Francis Grimké became a notable black Presbyterian pastor who, even as a staunch critic of American racism, remained quite evangelical over the course of a long life.

33. Abzug, *Passionate Liberator,* 292.

34. *Norfolk County Gazette,* June 14, 1879, "Resignation of Rev. Mr. Williams," by W.S.E.

35. *Norfolk County Gazette,* June 21, 1879, Theodore Dwight Weld to Dr. W. S. Everett.

36. *Norfolk County Gazette,* June 10, 1876. Please note that the quotation is not from Weld, but from the author's report of Weld's lecture.

37. Abzug, *Passionate Liberator,* 296–300.

38. *Weld-Grimké Letters,* II: 1005.

39. See especially Charles Stuart to Theodore Dwight Weld, Lora, August 1859, in the Weld-Grimké Papers, William Clement Library, University of Michigan. Stuart supplies the testimony of his own life and asks Weld eleven questions to establish his evangelical orthodoxy. The questions are a good summary of evangelical theological emphases in the mid nineteenth century. See also Charles Stuart to

Theodore Dwight Weld, Lora, July 20, 1856, and January 14, 1860. There is no evidence to suggest that Stuart's ardent entreaties and hectoring tone had any effect on Weld or the Grimké sisters, who had long since abandoned evangelical Christianity.

40. The full title is *The Bible Against Slavery: Or an Inquiry into the Genius of the Mosaic System, and the Teachings of the Old Testament on the Subject of Human Rights.* It was first published in the *Anti-Slavery Quarterly Magazine* in 1837 and went through four editions before it was reissued by the Board of Publication of the United Presbyterian Church in 1864. Also, *American Slavery As It Is: Testimony of a Thousand Witnesses* (New York: The American Anti-Slavery Society, 1839).

41. Weld to a Member of His Family, June 1833, in *Weld Grimké Letters,* I: 109–12.

42. Weld to Sarah and Angelina Grimké, New York, December 15, 1837, in ibid., 496. See also, Sarah and Angelina Grimké to Weld, Brookline, MA, December, 17, 1837, in ibid., 497–500. Confirming Theodore's disenchantment with churches, Sarah wrote, "I have given up going to any place of worship. I have tried all and they are all alike to me places of spiritual famine. My experience is the same in colored, as in white congregations." See also, Boston Public Library Ms. A. 1. 1 v. 3, p. 10, William Lloyd Garrison to Helen E. Garrison, Philadelphia, May 1838; and Weld to Angelina Grimké, New York, March 1, 1838, in *Weld-Grimké Letters,* II: 603.

43. Weld to Angelina Grimké, New York, March 12, 1838, in ibid., 575–84.

Chapter 5. Sarah Grimké, Elizabeth Cady Stanton, and Frances Willard

1. I am grateful to Bethany Murphy for helping to stimulate my interest in this topic and for allowing me to read her dissertation. Bethany Wade Murphy, "Evangelical and Feminist? An Evaluation of Nancy Hardesty's Assessment of the Relationship Between Evangelicalism and the Woman's Rights Movement in America," Master of Christian Studies Thesis, Regent College, 2005. See Nancy A. Hardesty, *Your Daughters Shall Prophesy: Revivalism and Feminism in the Age of Finney* (New York: Carlson, 1991), and *Women Called to Witness: Evangelical Feminism in the Nineteenth Century,* 2nd ed. (Knoxville: University of Tennessee Press, 1990). For a more recent interpretation see Mark David Hall, "Beyond Self Interest: The Political Theory and Practice of Evangelical Women in Antebellum America," *Journal of Church and State* 44, no. 3 (Summer 2002): 477–99.

2. See Nancy F. Cott, *The Bonds of Womanhood: Woman's Sphere in New England, 1780–1835* (New Haven: Yale University Press, 1977); Nancy Isenberg, *Sex and Citizenship in Antebellum America* (Chapel Hill: University of North Carolina Press, 1998). Some scholars do not afford religion a significant place in the emergence of American feminism. See, for example, Ellen Carol Dubois, *Woman Suffrage and Women's Rights* (New York: New York University Press, 1998), and Sylvia D. Hoffert, *When Hens Crow: The Woman's Rights Movement in Antebellum America* (Indianapolis: Indiana University Press, 1995).

3. One possible candidate is Catharine Beecher, but her relationship with her father, Lyman Beecher, was so psychologically convoluted (especially over her inability or

unwillingness to undergo a conventional evangelical conversion experience), and her withdrawal from her father's evangelicalism, though obvious, is not well recorded by her. See the insightful biography of Beecher by Kathryn Kish Sklar, *Catharine Beecher: A Study in American Domesticity* (New York: Norton, 1976).

4. Catherine H. Birney, *Sarah and Angelina Grimké: The First American Women Advocates of Abolition and Woman's Rights* (Boston: Lee and Shepard, 1885; rpt. Westport, CT: Greenwood, 1969). See also, Gerda Lerner, *The Feminist Thought of Sarah Grimké* (New York: Oxford University Press, 1998) and Gerda Lerner, *The Grimké Sisters from South Carolina: Pioneers for Women's Rights and Abolition* (Chapel Hill: University of North Carolina Press, 2004).

5. Sarah Grimké in her diary, "Account of Religious Development," June 3, 1827, quoted in Pamela R. Durso, *The Power of Woman: The Life and Writings of Sarah Moore Grimké* (Macon, GA: Mercer University Press, 2003), 26.

6. Sarah Grimké, "The Education of Women," in *Sarah Grimké, Letters on the Equality of the Sexes and Other Essays,* ed. Elizabeth Ann Bartlett (New Haven: Yale University Press, 1988), 115.

7. Larry Ceplair, ed., *The Public Years of Sarah and Angelina Grimké: Selected Writings 1835–1839* (New York: Columbia University Press, 1989), 136.

8. Sarah Grimké, *An Epistle to the Clergy of the Southern States* (New York: American Anti-Slavery Society, 1836), which is reproduced in Ceplair, ed., *The Public Years,* 103.

9. Grimké, *An Epistle,* in Ceplair, ed., *The Public Years,* 101.

10. *New England Spectator,* July 12, 1837, "Pastoral Letter; The General Association of Massachusetts to the Churches Under Their Care." See Ceplair, ed., *The Public Years,* 211.

11. Sarah M. Grimké, "Letters on the Equality of the Sexes and the Condition of Woman, Addressed to Mary S. Parker, President of the Boston Female Anti-Slavery Society." The series commenced in the *New England Spectator* on July 19, 1837, and was reproduced in *The Liberator* in 1838. See also, Ceplair, ed., *The Public,* Letter XIV, "Ministry of Women," 246.

12. Robert H. Abzug, *Cosmos Crumbling: American Reform and the Religious Imagination* (New York: Oxford University Press, 1994).

13. Grimké, Letter VII, "On the Condition of Women in the United States," in Ceplair, ed., *The Public,* 220.

14. Anna M. Speicher, *The Religious World of Antislavery Women: Spirituality in the Lives of Five Abolitionist Lecturers* (New York: Syracuse University Press, 2000), 62–63.

15. Ibid., 85.

16. For an excellent account of the intersection between women's rights and Spiritualism see Ann Braude, *Radical Spirits: Spiritualism and Women's Rights in Nineteenth-Century America,* 2d ed. (Indianapolis: Indiana University Press, 2001).

17. Speicher, *The Religious World of Antislavery Women,* 137.

18. For a more extensive treatment of this phase of Sarah Grimké's life, with a strong emphasis on the enduring role of her religious convictions, see ibid., 123–40.

19. For an insightful biography of Stanton see Elisabeth Griffith, *In Her Own Right: The Life of Elizabeth Cady Stanton* (Oxford: Oxford University Press, 1984). See also Mary D. Pellauer, *Toward a Tradition of Feminist Theology: The Religious Social Thought of Elizabeth Cady Stanton, Susan B. Anthony, and Anna Howard Shaw* (Brooklyn, NY: Carlson, 1991).

20. Elizabeth Cady Stanton, *Eighty Years and More: Reminiscences 1815–1897,* with an introduction by Gail Parker (New York: Schocken Books, 1971), 20–24.

21. Ibid., 25.

22. Ibid., 42–43.

23. Ibid., 44.

24. Kathi Kern, *Mrs. Stanton's Bible* (Ithaca, NY: Cornell University Press, 2001), 44.

25. Elizabeth Cady Stanton (*Boston Investigator,* 1875), quoted in Evelyn A. Kirkley, *Rational Mothers and Infidel Gentlemen: Gender and American Atheism, 1865–1915* (New York: Syracuse University Press, 2000), 126.

26. This aspect of Stanton's life is well treated in Kern, *Mrs. Stanton's Bible,* 50–91.

27. Elizabeth Cady Stanton, *The Woman's Bible,* with a foreword by Maureen Fitzgerald (Boston: Northeastern University Press, 1993), 213.

28. Carolyn De Swarte Gifford, ed., *Writing Out My Heart: Selections from the Journal of Frances E. Willard, 1855–96* (Chicago: University of Illinois Press, 1995), 8.

29. Ibid., 37–44.

30. Frances E. Willard, *Glimpses of Fifty Years, the Autobiography of an American Woman* (Chicago: H. J. Smith, 1889), 622–23.

31. Willard writes on December 14, 1859, that it was a sermon preached by the eminent Methodist divine, Bishop Matthew Simpson, which persuaded her that public sinning required a public, not just private, repentance. She clearly found the public side of open confession the most difficult part of the Christian faith to practice. See Willard, *Writing Out My Heart,* 53–54.

32. Ibid., 57.

33. Ibid., 58.

34. For a reliable and well-organized account of Frances Willard's public career and religious convictions see Ruth Bordin, *Frances Willard: A Biography* (Chapel Hill: University of North Carolina Press, 1986).

35. Willard, *Writing Out My Heart,* 134.

36. Jean H. Baker, *Sisters: The Lives of America's Suffragists* (New York: Hill and Wang, 2005), 148.

37. Willard departed for a grand tour of Europe in 1868 accompanied by her friend Kate Jackson. While staying in Berlin she met a young American woman, Julie Briggs, about whom Willard writes with the same kind of intensity as she did about her relationship with Mary Bannister. Jackson's jealousy was hard for Willard to manage. See Willard, *Writing Out My Heart,* 282–85.

38. Ibid., 222–23.

39. Willard, *Glimpses of Fifty Years,* 361; see Willard's letter to Moody's wife explain-

ing her actions in ibid., 359–60, and also the interpretation of this episode offered by Bordin, *Frances Willard*, 87–90.

40. Ibid., 158; and Willard, *Writing Out My Heart*, 388–89.

41. Unusually for Protestant women, especially those from Methodist backgrounds, Willard was quite willing to build connections with Roman Catholic temperance advocates. In the later years of her life she also took up the cause of the Armenian refugees from Turkish persecution and wrote movingly about an Armenian service she attended in Marseilles. She wrote in her journal on September 27, 1896: "We went to Armenian Church services in the impromptu Chapel at the refuge. It was memorable & [. . .] pathos too deep for tears. In his gold-embroidered robes here stood the gentle old priest at the altar above which was a large painting of the Ascension of Christ—a scene full of inspiration for these dear people who believe that a hundred thousand of their country folk who have been slaughtered have made a similar ascent." Ibid., 417.

42. Willard, *Glimpses of Fifty Years*, 627–28.

43. Willard, *Writing Out My Heart*, 363.

44. Bordin, *Frances Willard*, 160.

45. Frances E. Willard, *Woman in the Pulpit* (Chicago: Woman's Temperance Publication Association, 1889), 25–26. Reproduced with a helpful introduction by Carolyn De Swarte Gifford in Gifford, ed., *The Defense of Women's Rights to Ordination in the Methodist Episcopal Church* (New York: Garland, 1987).

46. Willard, *Woman in the Pulpit*, 39.

47. Stanton, *The Woman's Bible*, appendix, 200–201.

48. Abzug, *Cosmos Crumbling*, 228.

Chapter 6. Vincent Van Gogh

1. The secondary literature on Vincent van Gogh is voluminous. Useful biographies include Marc Tralbaut, *Vincent van Gogh* (New York: Viking, 1969); Alfred J. Lubin, *Stranger on the Earth: A Psychological Biography of Vincent Van Gogh* (New York: Da Capo, 1996); and Abraham Marie Hammacher, *Van Gogh: A Documentary Biography* (New York: Macmillan, 1982). The various hypotheses about the root cause(s) of van Gogh's mental instability are outlined in Wilfred Niels Arnold: *Chemicals, Crises, and Creativity* (Boston: Birkhäuser, 1992). This chapter makes no claims to add anything new about either the material details of van Gogh's life or his art. Rather, it seeks to treat more seriously than previous work has done his engagement with, and his disenchantment with, evangelical religion. Those particularly interested in the religious dimension of van Gogh's life will find some help, as I have, in the works listed in the following notes. As always, the best place to start is with van Gogh's letters.

2. The sermon (and Bible reading and hymn), with superb accompanying images, is also reproduced in Martin Bailey, *Van Gogh: Portrait of the Artist as a Young Man in England* (London: Barbican Art Gallery, 1992), 116–17. Also in this edition is an insightful essay on van Gogh's evangelical populism and its roots in John Bunyan's

Pilgrim's Progress; see Debora Silverman, "*Pilgrim's Progress* and Vincent van Gogh's Métier," 95–115.

3. Martin Bailey presents compelling, but not conclusive evidence, for the identification of this painting as George Boughton's *God Speed!;* Bailey, *Van Gogh,* 96–99.

4. A sermon preached by van Gogh in the autumn of 1876 in a Wesleyan Methodist church in Richmond, England. For the full text see *The Complete Letters of Vincent Van Gogh* (Greenwich, CT: New York Graphic Society, 1959), 1, 87–91. For Vincent's own reflections on his sermon see his letter to his brother Theo in *Letters,* 1: 172–73. He wrote, "It is a delightful thought that in the future wherever I go, I shall preach the Gospel; to do that well, one must have the Gospel in one's heart. May the Lord give it to me. You know enough of life, Theo, to understand that a *poor* preacher stands rather alone in the world, but the Lord can increasingly rouse in us the consciousness and belief in, . . . 'yet I am not alone, because the Father is with me.'"

5. Lubin, *Stranger on the Earth,* 20.

6. Vincent to his youngest sister, Wilhelmien J. Van Gogh, Paris, summer or autumn 1887. *Letters,* 3: 425–28.

7. The debate is carefully and sensitively examined by Cliff Edwards, *Van Gogh and God: A Creative Spiritual Quest* (Chicago: Loyola University Press, 1989), 15–37. See also, Jan Hulsker, *The Complete Van Gogh* (New York: Henry N. Adams, 1980). The "Memoir of Vincent Van Gogh" by his sister-in-law is reproduced in *Letters,* 1: xv–lxvii. For the various clues about the state of Van Gogh's religious sensibilities in the crucial years 1874–75 see *Letters,* nos. 21, 25, 26, 31, and 33.

8. There has been some confusion about the first name of van Gogh's first great love. It now seems clear that her name was Eugenie Loyer, and that it was her mother who was called Ursula. For a discussion of how the error crept into the literature see Martin Bailey, *Young Vincent: The Story of Van Gogh's Years in England* (London: W. H. Allen, 1990).

9. Van Gogh's desire for a loving relationship with a woman can hardly be exaggerated. Lubin recounts that when the artist visited the Rijksmuseum in Amsterdam, "he told his pupil Kerssemakers that he would give ten years of his life if he could go on gazing at Rembrandt's *The Jewish Bride,* a portrait of a man embracing a young woman." *Stranger on the Earth,* 7.

10. See also the essays on van Gogh's religion by J. Frits Wagener, Judy Sund, Tsukasa Ködera, and Clifford Walter Edwards, in Joseph D. Mascheck, *Van Gogh 100* (Westport, CT: Greenwood, 1996), 193–260.

11. *Letters,* 26, 33, 34, 37, 41 and 42. Van Gogh frequently uses the Pauline phrase "sorrowful yet always rejoicing" in his correspondence with Theo. See *Letters,* 112 and 115.

12. See Bailey, *Young Vincent,* 85, and Bailey, *Van Gogh,* 64. Van Gogh made reference to *Felix Holt* several times in relation to the inspiration it gave him for some of his paintings, including *The Soup Kitchen* and *Bedroom in the Yellow House.* Van Gogh also read C. H. Spurgeon, *Spurgeon's Gems, Being Brilliant Passages from the Discourses of the Rev. C. H. Spurgeon* (New York: Sheldon, Blakeman, 1858).

13. Silverman, "*Pilgrim's Progress* and Vincent van Gogh's Métier," 97.

14. Other important characteristics of his sojourn in England are his remarkable capacity for very long walks (including one of a hundred miles to visit his sister), and the deep reaction he had to the death and funeral of Harry Gladwell's sister; yet more isolation and death.

15. See "Vincent van Gogh as Bookseller's Clerk," in *Letters*, 1: 107–14. "In theory Vincent had the show goods, and now and then the delivery goods, under his care . . . but whenever anyone looked at what he was doing, it was found that instead of working, he was translating the Bible into French, German and English, in four columns, with the Dutch text in addition."

16. *Letters*, 1: 88 and 89.

17. Ibid., 1: 111. The encounter with Gladwell is described in letter 109. See also ibid., 1: 96–108.

18. Ibid., 1: 103 and 113.

19. Ibid., 1: 115.

20. Ibid., 1: 119. See also, Dr. M. B. Mendes da Costa, "Personal Memories of Vincent Van Gogh During His Stay at Amsterdam," originally published in *Het Algemeen Handelsblad*, December 2, 1910, and reproduced in *Letters*, 1: 169–71.

21. Hulsker, *Vincent and Theo*, 61–62.

22. For some of the weaknesses of theological education in the nineteenth century see K. D. Brown, *A Social History of the Nonconformist Ministry in England and Wales 1800–1930* (Oxford: Oxford University Press, 1988).

23. While in Amsterdam van Gogh continued to express the influence of English religion in his life by attending the English Reformed Church in the Begijnhof. He also taught Sunday school at Zion Chapel run by the British Society for the Propagation of the Gospel Among the Jews. Bailey, *Young Vincent*, 111.

24. Mendes da Costa, "Personal Memories," 170.

25. *Letters*, 1: 123.

26. Ibid.

27. Ibid., 1: 123–26.

28. Ibid., 1:126. See also, "Vincent van Gogh and Master Bokma," in Ibid., 1: 180–82. Master Bokma was van Gogh's director at the Training School for Evangelists in Brussels.

29. Reproduced in Bailey, *Van Gogh*, 104–5.

30. *Letters*, 1: 126–31.

31. Hulsker, *Vincent and Theo*, 79–80.

32. *Letters*, 1: 109. Quoted in Bailey, *Young Vincent*, 114.

33. See, for example, the comments of the city missionaries in Glasgow reproduced by S. J. Brown, *Thomas Chalmers and the Godly Commonwealth* (Oxford: Oxford University Press, 1982). A similar pattern emerges in many of the reports of city missionaries in British cities during the industrial revolution.

34. *Letters*, 1: 133.

35. Hulsker, *Vincent and Theo*, 107–8.

36. *Letters,* 1: 133.

37. Hulsker, *Vincent and Theo,* 87.

38. Debora Silverman, *Van Gogh and Gauguin: The Search for Sacred Art* (New York: Farrar, Straus, and Giroux, 2000). See also Alfred Nemeczek, *Van Gogh in Arles* (Munich: Prestel, 1995).

39. *Letters,* 3: 496. Quoted in Silverman, *Van Gogh and Gauguin,* 175.

40. Ibid., 82. See also Van Gogh's painting *The Potato Eaters* (1885), which portrays a group of rough peasants eating a simple meal under the glow of lamplight. His aim was "to emphasise that those people, eating their potatoes in the lamplight, have dug the earth with those very hands they put in the dish, and so it speaks of manual labour, and how they have honestly earned their food."

41. *Van Gogh/Gauguin: The Studio of the South* (Amsterdam: Van Gogh Museum, 2002). The most reliable guide to van Gogh's early paintings is Louis van Tilborgh and Marije Vellekoop, *Vincent Van Gogh Paintings,* vol.1, *Dutch Period 1881–1885* (Van Gogh Museum, Amsterdam, 1999). Much of the following discussion relies on this comprehensive guide to Van Gogh's forty-four paintings from this period in the Van Gogh Museum in Amsterdam.

42. For useful biographical summaries see Melissa McQuillan, *Van Gogh* (London: Thames and Hudson, 1989), 19–87, and A. M. Hammacher, *Vincent Van Gogh* (London: Spring Books, 1961).

43. Tilborgh and Vellekoop, *Van Gogh,* 156–57.

44. See W. R. Ward, *Christianity Under the Ancien Regime, 1648–1789* (Cambridge: Cambridge University Press, 1999).

45. For an excellent historical treatment of these themes see Hugh McLeod, *Secularisation in Western Europe, 1848–1914* (New York: St. Martin's, 2000). For a fresh and more controversial treatment of secularization that puts more emphasis on the role of women and the importance of the events of the 1960s see Callum G. Brown, *The Death of Christian Britain* (London: Routledge, 2001).

46. Vincent Van Gogh to Wilhelmien, Summer/Autumn 1887. *Letters,* 3: 425–28.

47. That interpretation is persuasively argued by Edwards, *Van Gogh and God,* 45–51.

48. Vincent van Gogh to Theo, late October 1885. *Letters,* 2: 429.

49. See Hugh McLeod, *Secularisation in Western Europe.* The triptych typology presented here does not appear in McLeod's book, but was presented in a conference paper on secularization, ironically at the University of Amsterdam. I am grateful to him for sharing this insight.

50. *Letters,* 3: 542 and B21.

51. For a sensitive and very helpful account of van Gogh's approach to religion in the 1880s see Edwards, *Van Gogh and God,* 85–153.

52. Silverman, *Van Gogh and Gauguin,* 421–23; Martin Bailey states that van Gogh did paint two other original religious pictures, both of the Garden of Gethsemane in 1888, but he destroyed them. *Young Vincent,* 88.

53. Bailey, *Young Vincent,* 154.

Chapter 7. Edmund Gosse

1. Edmund Gosse, *Father and Son, a Study of Two Temperaments* (London: Penguin, 1983), 248. *Father and Son* was first published by William Heinemann in 1907. All quotations refer to the Penguin English Library edition.

2. Short and helpful biographical portraits of Edmund Gosse, Philip Gosse, and Emily Gosse, with suggestions for further reading, can be found in *Oxford Dictionary of National Biography* (New York: Oxford University Press, 2004).

3. Ann Thwaite, *Edmund Gosse, a Literary Landscape, 1849–1928* (Chicago: University of Chicago Press, 1984), 436.

4. Although published posthumously in 1903, Samuel Butler's *The Way of All Flesh* was written largely in the 1880s. Butler's novel, which was partly autobiographical, and his letters reveal a less loving relationship between father and son than in Gosse's book. The tone is also more self-consciously irreverential and iconoclastic. For an insightful comparison of the two authors see David Grylls, *Guardians and Angels: Parents and Children in Nineteenth-Century Literature* (London: Faber and Faber, 1978), 153–90.

   In Orwell's case I am thinking more of his documentary-style works published in the 1930s, *Down and Out in Paris and London* (1933), *The Road to Wigan Pier* (1937), and *Homage to Catalonia* (1938), than his more famous works published in the 1940s, namely *Animal Farm* (1945) and *Nineteen Eighty-Four* (1949).

5. Gosse, *Father and Son,* 35.

6. See, for example, George P. Landow, ed., *Approaches to Victorian Autobiography* (Athens, Ohio: Ohio University Press, 1979).

7. For an engaging survey of biographical writing from an avowedly secularist viewpoint see Harold Nicolson, *The Development of English Biography* (New York: Harcourt, Brace, 1928).

8. Gosse, *Father and Son,* 251.

9. See Howard Helsinger, "Credence and Credibility: The Concern for Honesty in Victorian Autobiography," in Landow, ed., *Approaches to Victorian Autobiography,* 56–63. See also Linda H. Peterson, *Victorian Autobiography: The Tradition of Self-Interpretation* (New Haven: Yale University Press, 1986), 28.

10. For an insightful discussion of the genre of *Father and Son* and its relation to the tradition of Western autobiography, see the introduction to the Penguin English Library edition by Peter Abbs.

11. Gosse, *Father and Son,* 185. For a wider discussion of the authorial tone in *Father and Son,* see Grylls, *Guardians and Angels,* 172–90.

12. This theology has a particular emphasis on the second coming of Christ and employs a particular eschatological scheme, based on dispensations of rule by Christ and Antichrist. For an account of the importance of the dispensational theology of John Nelson Darby on the origins of fundamentalism see Ernest Robert Sandeen, *The Roots of Fundamentalism: British and American Millenarianism, 1800–1930* (Chicago: University of Chicago Press, 1970). For more information on the Ply-

mouth Brethren see Harold Hamlyn Rowdon, *The Origins of the Brethren, 1825–1850* (London: Pickering and Inglis, 1967).

13. Henry James to Edmund Gosse, Rye, England, November 10, 1907, in Rayburn S. Moore, ed., *Selected Letters of Henry James to Edmund Gosse, 1882–1915, a Literary Friendship* (Baton Rouge: Louisiana State University Press, 1988).

14. Thwaite, *Edmund Gosse,* 23.

15. The story of the painful and protracted conflict between Gosse and John Churton Collins is well told by Thwaite, *Edmund Gosse,* 277–97.

16. Thwaite, *Edmund Gosse,* 71–72.

17. Virginia Woolf, *Collected Essays,* vol. 4 (New York: Harcourt, Brace and World, 1925), 82.

18. See, for example, Callum G. Brown, *The Death of Christian Britain: Understanding Secularisation, 1800–2000* (London and New York: Routledge, 2001). Brown suggests that the breakdown of female piety and maternal transmission, particularly in the 1960s, was one of the chief reasons for the rapid secularization of modern Britain.

19. Gosse, *Father and Son,* 79–80.

20. Ibid., 81.

21. Ibid., 94.

22. Ibid., 95.

23. Philip Henry Gosse, *Creation (Omphalos): An Attempt to Untie the Geological Knot* (London: J. Van Voorst, 1857).

24. Gosse, *Father and Son,* 104–6.

25. Ibid., 123.

26. This is the argument of David Morgan, *Protestants and Pictures: Religion and Visual Culture, in the Age of American Mass Production* (New York: Oxford University Press, 1999).

27. Gosse, *Father and Son,* 156–61.

28. Ibid., 174.

29. Ibid., 189.

30. Ibid., 231.

31. Ibid., 231–32.

32. Ibid., 143–44.

33. Ibid., 171.

34. Ibid., 88.

35. Thwaite, *Edmund Gosse,* 28. See Philip H. Gosse, *The Aquarium: An Unveiling of the Wonders of the Deep Sea* (London: J. Van Voorst, 1856), and *The Romance of Natural History* (Boston: Gould and Lincoln, 1861).

36. For this idea I am indebted to Dana Logan, whose unpublished paper titled "Edmund and Philip H. Gosse: Negotiations Between Fantasy and Reality" explores this subversive theme in a stimulating and more comprehensive way.

37. Gosse, *Father and Son,* 234–35.

38. Thwaite, *Edmund Gosse,* 315.

39. Evan Charteris, *The Life and Letters of Sir Edmund Gosse* (New York and London: Harper, 1931), 43–44.

40. Charteris, *Life of Gosse,* 45.

41. Edmund Gosse to his father, Tottenham, March 4, 1873, in Charteris, *Life of Gosse,* 45–56.

42. Charteris, *Life of Gosse,* 54.

43. Ibid., 60.

44. This is partly based on observations gleaned from over twenty years of teaching *Father and Son* on both sides of the Atlantic; but it is also true to say that some readers, especially those with strong religious convictions, regard Edmund's account of his father as unconscionably disloyal to a loving parent.

45. Gosse, *Father and Son,* 115. The best account of English rural religion in the nineteenth century is by James Obelkevich, *Religion and Rural Society: South Lindsey 1825–1875* (Oxford: Clarendon Press, 1976). For an extended discussion of literature and popular religion in the nineteenth century see my *Religion of the People: Methodism and Popular Religion c. 1750–1900* (London: Routledge, 1996), 49–72.

46. Edmund Gosse to Hamo Thornycroft, Torcross, Nr. Kingsbridge, July 10, 1879, in Charteris, *Life of Gosse,* 117.

47. Charteris, *Life of Gosse,* 218–19.

48. Edmund Gosse, *The Life and Letters of John Donne* (London: William Heinemann, 1899).

49. Edmund Gosse, *Jeremy Taylor* (New York and London: Macmillan, 1904).

50. Virginia Woolf, *Collected Essays,* vol. 4, 81–82.

51. There is a nice illustration of Max Beerbohm's caricature in Charteris, *Life of Gosse,* 440.

52. Gosse, *Father and Son,* 248.

53. Ibid., 239–40.

Chapter 8. James Baldwin

1. For helpful attempts to explain the attraction of evangelical Christianity to transplanted African slaves see Sylvia R. Frey and Betty Wood, *Come Shouting to Zion: African American Protestantism in the American South and the British Caribbean to 1830* (Chapel Hill: University of North Carolina Press, 1998), and Michael A. Gomez, *Exchanging Our Country Marks: The Transformation of African Identities in the Colonial and Antebellum South* (Chapel Hill: University of North Carolina Press, 1998).

2. James Baldwin has left an extensive corpus of fiction, plays, essays, interviews, and speeches, many of which have a close bearing on his lifelong, complex, and ambiguous relationship with Afro-Protestantism. The most important works for the themes dealt with in this chapter are *Go Tell It on the Mountain* (New York: Knopf, 1953), *Notes of a Native Son* (Boston: Beacon, 1955), *Giovanni's Room* (New York: Dial, 1956), *Another Country* (New York: Dial, 1962), *The Fire Next Time* (New York: Dial, 1963), *Blues for Mister Charlie* (New York: Dial, 1964),

and *The Amen Corner* (New York: Dial, 1968). See also his *The Price of the Ticket: Collected Nonfiction 1948–1985* (New York: St. Martin's, 1985); *Collected Essays* (New York: Library of America, 1998); Fred L. Standley and Louis H. Pratt, *Conversations with James Baldwin* (Jackson: University of Mississippi Press, 1989); and Nikki Giovanni and James Baldwin, *James Baldwin and Nikki Giovanni: A Dialogue* (Philadelphia: J. P. Lippincourt, 1973). For helpful biographies of Baldwin see James Campbell, *Talking at the Gates: A Life of James Baldwin* (New York: Viking, 1991), and David Leeming, *James Baldwin* (New York: Knopf, 1994). There is also a rich literature of literary criticism bearing on the theme of Baldwin and Afro-Protestantism. Some of the most useful books and collections of essays on Baldwin are: Carolyn Wedin Sylvander, *James Baldwin* (New York: Frederick Ungar, 1980); Therman B. O'Daniel, ed., *James Baldwin: A Critical Evaluation* (Washington, D.C.: Howard University Press, 1977); Quincy Troupe, ed., *James Baldwin: The Legacy* (New York: Simon and Schuster, 1989); Trudier Harris, ed., *New Essays on Go Tell It on the Mountain* (New York: Cambridge University Press, 1996); and D. Quentin Miller, ed., *Re-Viewing James Baldwin* (Philadelphia: Temple University Press, 2000). I wish to record my particular debt to a fine book on Baldwin's complex religious sensibilities, Clarence E. Hardy III, *James Baldwin's God: Sex, Hope, and Crisis in Black Holiness Culture* (Knoxville: University of Tennessee Press, 2003). For those who wish to read more about the whole context of James Baldwin's religion from a more expert interpreter, that is the best place to start.

3. James Baldwin, "Disturber of the Peace: James Baldwin—An Interview," carried out in 1969 by Eve Auchinloss and Nancy Lynch, in Standley and Pratt, *Conversations*, 78. On another occasion he described his father as one of the most bitter men he ever met, but that buried deep within him was "a rather crushing charm." James Baldwin, "Notes of a Native Son," in *Collected Essays* (New York: Library of America, 1998), 64.

4. James Baldwin, "Letters from a Region in My Mind," collected in *The Fire Next Time* and reproduced in *The Price of the Ticket: Collected Nonfiction 1948–1985* (New York: St. Martin's, 1985), 337.

5. Baldwin, *The Price of the Ticket*, 343–44.

6. Ibid., 345–46.

7. An interview of Baldwin conducted by Jordan Elgabry and George Plimpton, first published as "The Art of Fiction LXXVIII: James Baldwin," *The Paris Review* 26 (Spring 1984): 49–82. Republished in Standley and Pratt, *Conversations*, 234–35.

8. Baldwin, *The Price of the Ticket*, 352.

9. Ibid., xvi, and James Baldwin interview with Studs Terkel in Standley and Pratt, *Conversations*, 23.

10. Baldwin, *The Price of the Ticket*, 347–48.

11 James Baldwin, "White Racism or World Community," an address to the World Council of Churches, originally published in the *Ecumenical Review* (October 1968). Reprinted in Baldwin, *The Price of the Ticket*, 435–42.

12. Ibid., 436–37.

13. Ibid., 440.

14. James Baldwin, "The Dangerous Road Before Martin Luther King," in *The Price of the Ticket,* 245.

15. Ibid., 246.

16. Ibid., 250.

17. Ibid., 256–57.

18. I am grateful to Matthew James Cressler for allowing me to read his unpublished essay "From Mountains to Fires: James Baldwin's Disenchantment (s) with the Christian Church," in which Baldwin's attitudes to Martin Luther King and Malcolm X are treated in more depth.

19. "An Interview with James Baldwin," by Studs Terkel in 1961, in *Conversations,* 13–14.

20. Baldwin, "No Name in the Street," in *The Price of the Ticket,* 519–23.

21. Ibid., 531. For excellent treatments of the importance of music in Baldwin's conception of black religion see Saadi A. Simwe, "What Is in a Sound? The Metaphysics and Politics of Music in *The Amen Corner*," in *Re-Viewing James Baldwin,* ed. D. Quentin Miller (Philadelphia: Temple University Press, 2000), 12–32, and Hardy, *James Baldwin's God,* 54–58.

22. Baldwin, "No Name on the Street," 453–54; Hardy, *James Baldwin's God,* 51–54.

23. Baldwin, *The Amen Corner.* For a critic who has taken seriously the religious themes of Baldwin's play see Michael F. Lynch, "Staying Out of the Temple: Baldwin, the African American Church and *The Amen Corner*," in Miller, *Re-Viewing James Baldwin,* 33–71.

24. Baldwin, *The Amen Corner,* 7.

25. Ibid., 54.

26. Ibid., 28.

27. Ibid., 75.

28. Ibid., 88.

29. Ibid., xvi.

30. James Baldwin, Introduction to *The Price of the Ticket,* xviii.

31. Ibid., xviii.

32. Michael F. Lynch, "Just Above My Head: James Baldwin's Quest for Belief," *Literature and Theology* 11, no. 3 (1997): 284–98.

33. For a helpful commentary on Baldwin's later fiction, see Lynn Orilla Scott, *James Baldwin's Later Fiction* (East Lansing: Michigan State University Press, 2002).

34. The interview was recorded on August 26, 1970, and a transcript was published as Margaret Mead and James Baldwin, *A Rap on Race* (Philadelphia and New York: J. B. Lippincott, 1971), 86–96.

35. James Mossman, "Race, Hate, Sex, and Colour: A Conversation with James Baldwin and Colin MacInnes," in Standley and Pratt, *Conversations,* 46–58.

36. John Hall, "James Baldwin Interviewed," in Standley and Pratt, *Conversations,* 106.

37. James Baldwin, *Blues for Mister Charlie* (New York: Dial, 1964), 94. See also Scott, *Baldwin's Later Fiction*, 94–97.

38. Trudier Harris, *Black Women in the Fiction of James Baldwin* (Knoxville: University of Tennessee Press, 1985), 11.

39. James Baldwin, "Preservation of Innocence" (1949), in *Collected Essays* (New York: The Library of America, 1998), 596.

40. Ibid., 597.

41. Ibid., 600.

42. Hardy, *James Baldwin's God*, 59–76.

43. David Leeming, *James Baldwin* (New York: Knopf, 1994), 384.

44. James Campbell, *Talking at the Gates: A Life of James Baldwin* (New York: Viking Penguin, 1991), 281.

45. Hardy, *James Baldwin's God*, 106–8.

46. See, for example, Baldwin's essay "White Man's Guilt," in *The Price of the Ticket*, in which he states that this guilt "is heard nowhere more plainly than in those stammering, terrified dialogues which white Americans sometimes entertain with the black conscience, the black man in America. The nature of this stammering can be reduced to a plea. Do not blame me. I was not there. I did not do it. . . . But on the same day, in another gathering and in the most private chamber of his heart always, the white American remains proud of that history for which he does not wish to pay, and from which, materially, he has profited so much."

47. Sondra A. O'Neale, "Fathers, Gods, and Religion: Perceptions of Christianity and Ethnic Faith in James Baldwin," in *Critical Essays on James Baldwin*, ed. Fred L. Standley and Nancy V. Burt (Boston: G. K. Hall, 1988), 140; Standley and Pratt, *Conversations*, 182.

48. Hardy, *James Baldwin's God*, 111.

Chapter 9. Conclusion

1. Harold Frederic, *The Damnation of Theron Ware*, with an introduction by Scott Donaldson (New York: Penguin Books, 1986).

2. D. Bruce Hindmarsh, *The Evangelical Conversion Narrative: Spiritual Autobiography in Early Modern England* (Oxford: Oxford University Press, 2005).

3. Susan Budd, *Varieties of Unbelief: Atheists and Agnostics in English Society, 1850–1960* (London: Heinemann, 1977).

4. See, for example, Kathleen Heasman, *Evangelicals in Action: An Appraisal of Their Social Work* (London: Geoffrey Bles, 1962); and John Wolffe, *The Expansion of Evangelicalism: The Age of Wilberforce, More, Chalmers and Finney* (Downers Grove, IL: Intervarsity, 2007).

5. See David Hempton, *The Religion of the People* (London: Routledge, 1996), 49–72.

6. For insightful attempts to define and understand fundamentalism that go beyond mere disapproval see Martin E. Marty and R. Scott Appleby, *Fundamentalisms Comprehended* (Chicago: University of Chicago Press, 1995), and George Marsden, *Understanding Fundamentalism and Evangelicalism* (Grand Rapids, MI: Eerdmans,

1991); and his *Fundamentalism in American Culture* (New York: Oxford University Press, 2006).

7. For a good discussion of these values see Ian Bradley, *The Call to Seriousness: The Evangelical Impact on the Victorians* (London: Jonathan Cape, 1976).

8. For an attempt to explain the importance of hymnody in the evangelical tradition see my *Methodism: Empire of the Spirit* (New Haven: Yale University Press, 2005), 68–74.

9. For a fine analysis of why some evangelicals became Roman Catholics see David Newsome, *The Parting of Friends: A Study of the Wilberforces and Henry Manning* (London: Murray, 1966).

10. Owen Chadwick, *The Secularization of the European Mind in the Nineteenth Century* (Cambridge: Cambridge University Press, 1990). For an account of European secularization grounded more in social and cultural history see Hugh McLeod, *Secularization in Western Europe, 1848–1914* (New York: St. Martin's, 2000). For a recent interpretation from a more philosophical viewpoint, albeit informed by sociological analysis, see Charles Taylor, *A Secular Age* (Cambridge, MA: Harvard University Press, 2007).

11. See, for example, Mark Noll, *The Scandal of the Evangelical Mind* (Grand Rapids, MI: Eerdmans, 1994), and Charles Marsh, *Wayward Christian Soldiers: Freeing the Gospel from Political Captivity* (New York: Oxford University Press, 2007).

12. D. Bruce Hindmarsh, *The Evangelical Conversion Narrative: Spiritual Autobiography in Early Modern England* (Oxford: Oxford University Press, 2005), 32.

13. Timothy Larsen, *Crisis of Doubt: Honest Faith in Nineteenth-Century England* (New York: Oxford University Press, 2006).

14. Mark A. Plummer, *Robert G. Ingersoll: Peoria's Pagan Politician* (Macomb, IL: Western Illinois University, 1984). I am grateful to Kip Richardson for introducing me to Robert Ingersoll's life and humor.

15. Larsen, *Crisis of Doubt*, skillfully narrates a number of these stories from the ranks of nineteenth-century Secularist leaders. For more recent examples of this pattern see Frank Schaeffer, *Crazy for God: How I Grew Up as One of the Elect, Founded the Religious Right, and Lived to Take All (Or Almost All) of It Back* (New York: Carroll and Graf, 2007). Similar stories also repeatedly show up in newspapers, periodicals, and talk shows. See, for example, the personal narrative of Les Payne, the Pulitzer prize–winning journalist, "My Dance with Faith," *AARP Magazine* (March–April 2008): 84–86.

16. Although not specifically about evangelicalism see the data collected by the Barna Group and presented by David Kinnamon and Gabe Lyons, *Unchristian: What a New Generation Really Thinks About Christianity—and Why It Matters* (Grand Rapids, MI: Baker, 2007).

Index

Abzug, Robert, 83, 113
Adam Bede (Eliot), 19–23, 35, 37, 119
African Americans: and evangelicalism, 16–17, 164–70, 175–80, 185–86; experience of, in white America, 166–75, 179–81, 222n46; Weld and, 75–76. *See also* slavery
The Age of Reason (Paine), 33
Alford, Henry "Dean," 110
Allen, Joseph Henry, 207n51
"Amazing Grace" (Newton), 163
The Amen Corner (Baldwin), 165, 175–80
American and Foreign Anti-Slavery Society, 78, 81
American Anti-Slavery Society, 76, 78, 94, 95
American Slavery As It Is (Weld), 78, 89
American Tract Society, 73
L'Amour (Michelet), 119
Anglican Church. *See* Church of England
Anglo-Catholicism, 8, 30
Anthony, Susan B., 96
Apologia pro Vita Sua (Newman), 66
apostolic succession of Anglican bishops, 43
The Aquarium (P. H. Gosse), 147, 153
Armenian Church, 50, 51, 109, 213n41
Arnold, Matthew, 58, 157
art, 12, 194, 196. *See also* van Gogh, Vincent
Asbury, Francis, 10
Asbury, Herbert, 10–11
Athanasian Creed, 52

Babinski, Edward T., *Leaving the Fold*, 2
Baghdad, 45–51
Baker, Jean, 107

Baldwin, James, 16–17, 163–86; *The Amen Corner*, 165, 175–80; *Blues for Mister Charlie*, 183; disenchantment of, 169–70, 192; evangelicalism of, 164–71, 182, 194; *Go Tell It on the Mountain*, 165, 175; idealism of, 192; and King, 172–75; "Letter from a Region in My Mind," 165; and morality, 17, 169–70, 181; religious views of, 170–86; sexual identity of, 165, 183–84
Balfour, Arthur James, Lord, 160
Bannister, Mary, 107
baptism, 149–50
Baptists, 164
Barker, Dan, 2
Barker, Joseph, 199n2
Barnardo, Thomas John, 154
The Bearers of the Burden (van Gogh), 126
Bebbington, David, 5, 199n5
Bebbington, John Bagnall, 199n2
Beecher, Catharine, 210n3
Beecher, Lyman, 73, 76, 210n3
Beerbohm, Max, 160
Bennett, Arnold, 160
Bernard, Emile, 136–38
Bertrand, Emile, 130–31
Bible: Baldwin and, 169; conflicting messages in, 191; criticism of, 54–55 (*see also* German higher criticism); feminism and, 15, 97, 101, 104, 109, 110–13; van Gogh and, 117, 120, 121, 123, 125, 134–35, 137–38, 215n15; Gosse and, 156, 161–62; Newman and, 54–55; and slavery, 89; Stanton and, 15, 101, 104, 111–12; Willard and, 110–12. *See also* Scriptural interpretation

Nicolson, Harold, 154
Norfolk County Gazette (newspaper), 87
North British Review (journal), 56

Oberlin College, 76, 77, 81, 85
Oberlin Evangelist (newspaper), 81
Observer (newspaper), 81
Ohio Liberty Party, 81
The Old Church Tower at Nuenen (van Gogh), 132
Omphalos (P. H. Gosse), 147
Oneida Academy, 72–73, 79
On the Road (Kerouac), 140
The Origin of Species (Darwin), 147
Orwell, George, 140
Ottoman Empire, 47–51, 67

Paine, Thomas: *The Age of Reason*, 33; *The Rights of Man*, 33
Palmer, Phoebe, 108
Palmer, Walter, 108
Parker, Mary S., 96–97
Parnell, John Vesey, 205n12
Pattison, Mark, 12
Paul, Saint, 43, 97, 120
Peel, Robert, 8
Pentecostalism, 4, 16, 164–70, 183
perfectionism: Newman and, 61; Weld and, 88
Personal Narratives (Newman), 50
Phases of Faith (Newman), 42–43, 53, 56, 58, 61, 64, 204n3
The Philosophy of Necessity (Bray), 31
pietism, 61
Pilgrim's Progress (Bunyan), 121, 125
Plymouth Brethren: and baptism, 149–50; Darby and, 44; and dispensationalism, 17–18, 44, 143, 147; essential elements of, 157–58, 204n6, 217n12; and fundamentalism, 17–18, 143; Gosse family and, 16, 143, 147, 149–50, 154–55, 157–59, 193; Newman and, 67, 207n51; and priesthood of all believers, 157; and primitive Christianity, 145, 157; and second coming of Christ, 154–55; soteriology of, 151–52, 193
Popery, 43
The Potato Eaters (van Gogh), 216n40
Powell, Sara Jordan, 163
power, and disenchantment, 191

Presbyterianism, 110
The Presentation of the Queen of Sheba to Solomon (Veronese), 8–9
priesthood of all believers, 157
primitive Christianity: Newman and, 44, 46–48, 66; Plymouth Brethren and, 145, 157
prophecy: Cumming and, 25, 27–28; Eliot on, 25, 31; evangelical controversy over, 30–31; failed, 28, 30; Plymouth Brethren and, 147; rationalism and, 149. *See also* second coming of Christ
propositions of faith: Eliot on, 24; in evangelical tradition, 12
Protestant Reformation, 202n7
providence, 117
Pusey, Emily, 8
Putnam, Samuel Porter, 9–10, 201n19

Quakerism, 95, 98, 100

Rabelais, François, 134
Raritan Bay Union, 84
rationality: futility of justifying Christianity by, 47–48, 62–64, 99; Newman's, 41–43, 53–54, 60; prophecy and, 149; Stanton and, 103–4
reconversion, 3, 199n2
Reformation, 202n7
Religious Right, 18
Rembrandt van Rijn, 138
Renan, Ernest, *The Life of Jesus*, 119
revivalism, 10–11, 72–73, 92, 102–3
The Rights of Man (Paine), 33
Rochefort, Henri, 134
Rogers, Henry, 56, 57
Roman Catholicism: anti-Catholic sentiment, 6, 23, 24, 27, 28, 147, 151; in Baghdad, 50; characteristics of, 4; conversion to, 7, 8, 30; Gauguin and, 130; van Gogh and, 138; Ireland and, 30, 45; and Popery, 43; in Victorian England, 23; Willard and, 109, 213n41
Romanticism, 30
Rosen, Christine, *My Fundamentalist Education*, 18
The Rover Boys books, 184
Ruskin, John, 8–9
Ryder, Henry, 202n14

Uncle Tom's Cabin (Stowe), 78, 127
Union of Protestant Churches, Belgium, 127
Unitarianism: anti-Unitarian sentiment, 86–87, 151; Eliot and, 32; in Victorian England, 30; Weld and, 86–87
United States, evangelicalism in, 5, 195

van Gogh, Theo. *See* Gogh, Theo van
van Gogh, Vincent. *See* Gogh, Vincent van
van Gogh, Wilhelmien (Wil). *See* Gogh, Wilhelmien (Wil) van
van Gogh-Bonger, Johanna. *See* Gogh-Bonger, Johanna van
Veronese, Paolo, *The Presentation of the Queen of Sheba to Solomon*, 8–9
The Vicarage at Nuenen (van Gogh), 133
Victorian age: disenchantment in, 8, 29–30; evangelicalism in, 29–30; *Father and Son* and, 140; Methodism in, 21–22; secularism in, 3, 199n2
Virgil, 152
Voltaire, 104, 134, 197
Vos, Cornelia (Kee), 119, 128

Walther, David, 56
Ward, Maisie, 64
Ward, W. R., 5
Watts, Francis, 32
The Way of All Flesh (Butler), 140, 217n4
WCTU. *See* Woman's Christian Temperance Union
Weld, Ludovicus, 71
Weld, Theodore Dwight, 14, 70–91, 94, 95; and abolition of slavery, 74–79, 85, 88–89, 174; and African Americans, 75–76; *American Slavery As It Is*, 78, 89; *The Bible Against Slavery*, 89; career of, 71; disenchantment of, 79–83, 88–90, 174, 193; and education, 84, 89; evangelicalism of, 70–76, 88, 90–91, 194; idealism of, 192; later religion

of, 83–84, 86–91, 195; and morality, 72–73, 81–82; and reform causes, 86, 88; and retirement from public causes, 83–84, 89
Weld Institute, 84
Das Wesen Christenhums (Feuerbach), 34
Wesley, Charles, 7, 59–60, 146
Wesley, John, 16, 21, 87, 146
Wesley, Samuel, 7
Western Monthly Magazine, 75
Westminster Review (journal), 1–2, 19, 23, 34, 35, 57
Weston, Nancy, 86
Whig Party, 78
White, William Hale, 1
white America, black experience in, 166–75, 179–81, 222n46
Wilberforce, William, 8, 29, 30
Willard, Emma, 102–3
Willard, Frances, 14–15, 92; evangelicalism of, 105–8, 212n31; and feminism, 110–12; idealism of, 192; religious views of, 106–10, 213n41; sexual identity of, 107–8, 212n37; and temperance, 105, 108; *Woman in the Pulpit*, 110; and women's rights, 104–5
Willard, Oliver, 107
Willey, Basil, 64–65, 68, 203n26
Williams, John, 30
Woman in the Pulpit (Willard), 110
The Woman's Bible (Stanton), 15, 101, 104, 111–12
Woman's Christian Temperance Union (WCTU), 105, 108, 110, 111
women's rights: Stanton and, 101; Weld and, 78, 81. *See also* feminism
Woolf, Virginia, 144, 160
Wordsworth, William, 152
World Council of Churches, 170, 172
Wright, Martha Coffin, 85

Young, Frederic Rowland, 199n2

Zola, Emile, *La Joie de vivre*, 134–35